Preface Books

A series of scholarly and critical studies of major writers intended for those needing modern and authoritative guidance through the characteristic difficulties of their work to reach an intelligent understanding and enjoyment of it.

General Editor: MAURICE HUSSEY

A Preface to Wordsworth (*Revised ed.*)   JOHN PURKIS
A Preface to Donne (*Revised ed.*)   JAMES WINNY
A Preface to Jane Austen (*Revised ed.*)   CHRISTOPHER GILLIE
A Preface to Pope   I. R. F. GORDON
A Preface to Hardy   MERRYN WILLIAMS
A Preface to James Joyce   SYDNEY BOLT
A Preface to Hopkins   GRAHAM STOREY
A Preface to Conrad   CEDRIC WATTS
A Preface to Lawrence   GAMINI SALGADO
A Preface to Forster   CHRISTOPHER GILLIE
A Preface to Auden   ALLAN RODWAY
A Preface to Dickens   ALLAN GRANT
A Preface to Shelley   PATRICIA HODGART
A Preface to Keats   CEDRIC WATTS
A Preface to George Eliot   JOHN PURKIS
A Preface to Orwell   DAVID WYKES
A Preface to Henry James   S. GORLEY PUTT
A Preface to Milton (*Revised ed.*)   LOIS POTTER

Young Harry as a teenager.

A Preface to Henry James

S. Gorley Putt

Longman, London and New York

LONGMAN GROUP UK LIMITED
Longman House
Burnt Mill, Harlow, Essex, CM20 2JE, England
and Associated Companies throughout the world

Published in the United States of America
by Longman Inc. New York
© Longman Group UK Limited 1986

First published 1986

ISBN 0 582 35185 5

Set in 10/11pt Baskerville. Linotron 202.

Produced by Longman Group (F. E.) Limited
Printed in Hong Kong

British Library Cataloguing in Publication Data

Putt, S. Gorley
    A Preface to Henry James. — (Preface books)
    1. James, Henry, *1843–1916* — Criticism
and interpretation
    I. Title
    813'.4   PS2124

Library of Congress Cataloging in Publication Data

Putt, S. Gorley (Samuel Gorley)
    A Preface to Henry James.
    (Preface books)
    Includes index.
    Summary: A biography of Henry James with a discussion
of his major works.
    1. James, Henry, 1843–1916. 2. Authors, American —
19th Century — Biography. [1. James, Henry, 1843–1916.
2. Authors, American] I. Title.
PS2123.P78   813'.4 [B] [92]   86–68
ISBN 0-582-35185-5

Contents

List of illustrations

To Arthur Mizener

who launched me on the James ocean fifty years ago, at Pierson College, Yale.

In Heaven there'll be no algebra,
No learning dates or names,
But only playing golden harps,
And reading Henry James.

(Origin undetermined)

Foreword

Fiction so puzzling in its moral and psychological analysis and its verbal coruscation as that of Henry James was a novelty to Victorian and Edwardian readers on either side of the Atlantic, and that 'unremitting literacy' still extends a stiff challenge to modern readers of intelligence and literary taste and experience. Among the many reasons for his complexity may have been that as a tireless cultural pilgrim he mixed some of the characteristics of European traditions with those from his American upbringing and was not therefore exactly a part of any English-speaking tradition alone. Where others were moulded he was original and he grew. He became, in the years of his residence in England, an original in the social sense, an eccentric, but English readers seem always to have cherished artistic eccentricity and expected to find it.

In this most skilfully observed and written addition to the series Gorley Putt has not been entirely moulded by the format of his predecessors. While he has provided a wealth of fact, especially in Part Three, he is essentially interested in guiding our responses to the fact of the book under discussion. He has therefore minimized the materialistic elements in his survey of James's work. Historical and public issues seem to have played a decreasing part in James's intellectual nature: here was a writer committed to the private world, the arts of leisure and precisely to what we term 'the quality of life'. He was perhaps typical of his generation in one outstanding way; he left the United States for Europe and experienced a kind of colonization in reverse, a discovery of an older world, a west-to-east culture shock.

Mr Putt examines the novels in a prose of great elegance and subtlety pointing exactly to the crucial passage for discussion, the whole of it the fruit of long and devoted study of his subject. Taken altogether this book is a lesson of the master revealing the range of the novels and helping the reader to deepen his sympathies towards the plutocratic Americans visiting the art galleries and fingering their Baedeker guides, not simply the exploiters of Europe, and the aristocratic Europeans, but the true appreciators of their own civilization. We are invited to meet so many of these characters and assess them—all of them, the appreciators and the exploiters alike, sounding remarkably like James himself in their involved dialogue—and to understand them in a context of *salon*, drawing room or palazzo, and not always, as Mr Putt shows, on the *piano nobile*.

MAURICE HUSSEY
General Editor

Acknowledgements

We are indebted to the following for permission to adapt and reproduce copyright material by the author:

Penguin Books Ltd for adapted extracts from the introductions to *Roderick Hudson, The Aspern Papers and Other Stories* and *An International Episode and Other Stories*; Thames and Hudson Ltd for an adapted version of Chapter V from *A Reader's Guide to Henry James*.

I am grateful, as always, for the facilities provided by Christ's College, Cambridge, and especially for the services of the Fellows' Secretary, Mrs Sylvia Sylvester.

S. G. P.

We are grateful to the following for permission to reproduce photographs:
BBC Hulton Picture Library, pages 7 and 107; Heinemann Group, *Italian Hours*, 1909, page 192; Houghton Library, Harvard University, pages 15 (by permission of Eva Reichmann) and 21; National Portrait Gallery, page 127; National Trust, Lamb House, Rye, pages 143 and 173; Providence Public Library, Rhode Island Collection, page 70; William Royall Tyler Collection, page 184 (photo R.W.B. Lewis); Uffizi Gallery, Florence, page 118 (photo Alinari); Yale University, *Yale Wit and Humor*, 1894, page 31. Photograph on page 135 by Longman Photographic Unit (by permission of The Reverend C. E. Leighton Thomson).

The painting *An Interior in Venice*, 1897, by John Singer Sargent, is reproduced on the cover by permission of the Royal Academy of Arts.

GORLEY PUTT is a Fellow of Christ's College, Cambridge, where he was Senior Tutor for the decade 1968–78. His O.B.E. was awarded in 1966 'for services to Anglo–American relations' during his work for the Harkness Fellowships of The Commonwealth Fund of New York. His most recent publication was *The Golden Age of English Drama: Enjoyment of Elizabethan/Jacobean Plays* (D. S. Brewer, 1981).

Chronological table

This chronological table provides only a skeletal reference guide to Henry James's literary and other activities. All his twenty-two novels and one hundred and twelve tales are recorded, the former in italics and the latter in inverted commas. Dates of novels are of publication (e.g. *The Ambassadors*, 1903, was actually written before *The Wings of the Dove*, 1902). Tales are dated by their first appearance, usually in magazines, though some first saw print in one or other of his volumes of collected stories. Sometimes these collections bore a general title (e.g. *Terminations* or *The Soft Side*), in which case the title is recorded within brackets, the constituent stories having already been recorded. A selection of James's non-fictional volumes, such as critical essays (e.g. *French Poets and Novelists*), autobiography (e.g. *A Small Boy and Others*) and travel sketches (e.g. *Italian Hours*) has also been recorded within brackets, to distinguish them from the fiction.

The right-hand column records only the major geographical locations of the author on his wanderings; shorter trips from his various major bases at New York, the Boston area, London, Paris, Florence and so on, have been omitted. Similarly, in the life of so socially active an author who was devoted to so many friends and members of his kindred, only a few significant meetings and visits are recorded.

Thanks to the devoted labours of Professor Leon Edel, this skeleton chronology may be fleshed by reference to his five-volume biography of Henry James (1953–72), revised and reissued in two paperback volumes (1977); to his *Bibliography of Henry James* (with Dan H. Lawrence, second revised edition 1961); to his twelve-volume *Complete Tales of Henry James* (1962–4); and to his four-volume selection from the *Letters* (1974–84).

PUBLICATIONS	JAMES'S LIFE
	1842 William James, elder brother, born.
	1843 HJ born, 15 April, New York. Taken to England by family.
	1844 With family in Paris and New York.

1

1845 Brother Garth Wilkinson born. Family moves to Albany, N.Y.

1846 Brother Robertson born, Albany.

1847 Family returns to New York. Sister Alice born.

1855 With family in Paris, Switzerland, London.

1856 London, Paris.

1857 Paris, Boulogne.

1858 Boulogne, Newport (Rhode Island).

1859 Newport, New York, Geneva.

1860 Geneva, Germany, Newport.

1861 Newport (start of American Civil War). HJ suffers an obscure physical injury.

1862 Harvard Law School.

1863 Harvard and Boston.

1864 'A Tragedy of Error' (first printed story)

1864 Boston and Northampton (Mass.).

1865 'The Story of a Year' (first signed story)

1865 Summer visits to cousin Minny Temple.

1866 'A Landscape Painter' 'A Day of Days'

1866 Cambridge (Mass.).

1867 'My Friend Bingham' 'Poor Richard'

1867 HJ sees Charles Dickens in Boston.

1868 'The Story of a Masterpiece' 'The Romance of Certain Old Clothes' 'A Most Extraordinary Case' 'A Problem' 'DeGray: A Romance' 'Osborne's Revenge'	1868 Declines editorship of *North American Review*.
1869 'A Light Man' 'Gabrielle de Bergerac'	1869 HJ (without family) on tour of England, France, Switzerland, Italy.
1870 'Travelling Companions'	1870 London, Malvern, return to Cambridge (Mass.) Death of Minny Temple.
1871 'A Passionate Pilgrim' 'At Isella' 'Master Eustace' (*Watch and Ward*, first novel, printed as magazine serial)	1871 Cambridge (Mass.). Canadian trip.
1872 'Guest's Confession'	1872 HJ with sister Alice and aunt Kate tours Switzerland, north Italy, Germany, Paris. HJ remains in Paris.
1873 'The Madonna of the Future' 'The Sweetheart of M. Brisieux'	1873 Rome, Florence, with brother William, Switzerland, Bad Homberg.
1874 'The Last of the Valerii' 'Madame de Mauves' 'Adina' 'Professor Fargo' 'Eugene Pickering'	1874 Florence, Baden-Baden, Holland, return to Cambridge (Mass.).
1875 (*A Passionate Pilgrim*, and other tales) (*Transatlantic Sketches*) *Roderick Hudson* 'Benvolio'	1875 New York and Cambridge (Mass.). Returns to Paris. Meets Turgenev, Flaubert, other French writers.

1876 'Crawford's Consistency'
'The Ghostly Rental'

1876 Paris. HJ correspondent for N.Y. *Tribune.* Normandy and French provinces.

1877 *The American*
'Four Meetings'

1877 London. English country visits.

1878 (*French Poets and Novelists*)
Watch and Ward
The Europeans
'Daisy Miller'
'Rose-Agathe
'Longstaff's Marriage'
'An International Episode'

1878 London. English country visits. Brother William married.

1879 *Confidence*
(*Hawthorne*)
'The Pension Beaurepas'
'The Diary of a Man of Fifty'
'A Bundle of Letters'

1879 London, etc., Paris.

1880 *Washington Square*

1880 London, Florence, London.

1881 *The Portrait of a Lady*

1881 Venice, Rome, Italian trips, Switzerland, London, return to Boston and Cambridge (Mass.).

1882 'The Point of View'

1882 New York, Washington, Cambridge (Mass.) and Boston, London, tour of France, Boston. Death of HJ's mother and father and brother Garth Wilkinson.

1883 (First collected edition of novels and stories, 14 volumes)
(*Portraits of Places*)
'The Siege of London'
'The Impressions of a Cousin'

1883 Boston, New York, return to London.

1884 (*A Little Tour of France*) 'Lady Barberina' 'The Author of "Beltraffio" ' 'Pandora' 'Georgina's Reasons' 'A New England Winter' 'The Path of Duty'	1884 London, Paris visit; sister Alice comes to live in England.
1885 (*Stories Revived*: three-volume collection of fourteen stories)	1885 London, etc., Paris visit.
1886 *The Bostonians* *The Princess Casamassima*	1886 London.
1887 'Mrs. Temperly'	1887 Florence, Venice, London.
1888 *The Reverberator* (*Partial Portraits*) 'The Aspern Papers' 'Louisa Pallant' 'The Liar' 'The Modern Warning' 'A London Life' 'The Lesson of the Master' 'The Patagonia'	1888 London, Geneva.
1889 'The Solution'	1889 London, Paris.
1890 *The Tragic Muse*	1890 London. HJ begins to write for the theatre. Brief Italian trip.
1891 'The Pupil' 'Brooksmith' 'The Marriages' 'The Chaperon' 'Sir Edmund Orme'	1891 HJ's dramatization of *The American* produced in English provinces and London. Brief Irish trip.
1892 'Nona Vincent' 'The Private Life' 'The Real Thing' 'Lord Beaupré' 'The Visits' 'Sir Dominick Ferrand'	1892 London. Death of sister Alice. Siena, Venice, Switzerland.

'Collaboration'
'Greville Fane'
'The Wheel of Time'
'Owen Wingrave'

1893	'The Middle Years'	1893	London. HJ still writing for the theatre.
1894	'The Death of the Lion' 'The Coxon Fund'	1894	London; visits to Venice, Rome, etc. Death of HJ's friend Constance Fenimore Woolson.
1895	(*Terminations*: four recent stories) 'The Next Time' 'The Altar of the Dead'	1895	London. Failure of HJ's play 'Guy Domville'. Visits to Ireland, Torquay.
1896	(*Embarrassments*: four recent stories) *The Other House* 'The Figure in the Carpet' 'Glasses' 'The Way It Came'	1896	Sussex, London.
1897	*The Spoils of Poynton* *What Maisie Knew* 'John Delavoy'	1897	London; visits to Bournemouth, Suffolk. HJ purchases Lamb House, Rye.
1898	'The Turn of the Screw' 'Covering End' 'In the Cage' 'The Given Case'	1898	Visited at Rye by brother William's son Henry, Jonathan Sturges and others. Neighbourhood acquaintances include H. G. Wells and Stephen Crane.
1899	*The Awkward Age* 'The Great Condition' 'Europe' 'Paste' 'The Real Right Thing'	1899	Rye. Paris, French Riviera, Venice, Rome. Visited at Rye by Hendrik Andersen and by brother William and family.

*Henry James before shaving off his beard for the new century (compare
portrait on p. 173).*

1900 (*The Soft Side*: twelve
recent stories)
'The Great Good Place'
'The Tree of Knowledge'
'The Abasement of the
Northmores'
'The Third Person'
'Maud-Evelyn'
'Miss Gunton of
Poughkeepsie'
'Broken Wings'
'The Two Faces'
'The Tone of Time'
'The Special Type'

1900 Rye. HJ abandons
unfinished novel *The Sense
of the Past*. HJ shaves off
his beard—a new face
for the new century.
Acquires London base at
Reform Club.

1901 *The Sacred Fount*
'Mrs. Medwin'
'The Beldonald Holbein'

1901 Rye. HJ dictates his
work to typist–secretary.
Visit from William and
family.

1902 *The Wings of the Dove*
'Flickerbridge'
'The Story in It'

1902 Rye, London.

1903 *The Ambassadors*
(*The Better Sort*: eleven
recent stories)
'The Beast in the Jungle'
'The Birthplace'
'The Papers'
(*William Wetmore Story and
His Friends*)

1903 Rye, London. HJ meets
Jocelyn Persse and Edith
Wharton.

1904 *The Golden Bowl*
'Fordham Castle'

1904 Rye. Return visit to
U.S.A. New York, New
England.

1905 (*English Hours*)

1905 Philadelphia,
Washington, Southern
States.
St Louis, Chicago,
California and the West,
New York. HJ elected to
American Academy of
Arts and Letters. Return
to Rye.

1906 Rye.

1907 (*The American Scene*)
      (New York Edition of the
      Novels and Tales, 24
      volumes, 1907–9)

1907 Rye. Motor tour of
      France with Edith
      Wharton. Rome, Venice.
      Theodora Bosanquet
      becomes HJ's
      amanuensis.

1908 'Julia Bride'
      'The Jolly Corner'

1908 Rye, London, Paris.
      Visits from William and
      family. Stage production
      of 'The High Bid'.

1909 'The Velvet Glove'
      'Mora Montravers'
      'Crapy Cornelia'
      (*Italian Hours*)

1909 Rye, London. Visits
      Rupert Brooke and
      others at Cambridge.
      Meets Hugh Walpole.
      Destroys private papers.

1910 (*The Finer Grain*: five
      recent stories)
      'A Round of Visits'
      'The Bench of
      Desolation'

1910 HJ ill after nervous
      collapse. Death of
      brother Robertson.
      William and family with
      HJ at Rye and in
      Switzerland.
      Returns to America with
      William
      Death of William.

1911 *The Outcry*

1911 Cambridge (Mass.) and
      New York.
      Return to London and
      Rye.

1912 Rye and London.
      Poor health.

1913 (*A Small Boy and Others*)

1913 London (new home in
      Chelsea), Rye.

1914 (*Notes of a Son and Brother*)
      (*Notes on Novelists*)

1914 London, Rye. Outbreak
      of the Great War.

1915 (*Uniform Tales*: 14
      volumes, 1915–20)

1915 HJ naturalized as British
      subject.
      Bedridden after suffering
      stroke.

1916 HJ awarded the O.M.
Died 28 February.

1917 *The Ivory Tower*
The Sense of the Past
(*The Middle Years*)

1 Introduction

Can it be—it must be—that you are that embodiment of the incorporeal, that elusive yet ineluctable being to whom through generations novelists have so unavailingly made invocation; in short, the *Gentle Reader?*

(Henry James to Ada Leverson, as retold in
Sir Osbert Sitwell's *Noble Essences*)

It is a fair guess that a reader of this 'Preface' series who may already have gained some acquaintance with the reputation of Henry James will quite probably call up the figure of a plump expounder of balloon-like paragraphs on the social habits of rich Anglo-Americans, rather than the man who, writing in his sixties to a younger novelist, blurts out: 'We must know, as much as possible, in our beautiful art, yours and mine, what we are talking about—and the only way to know is to have *lived and loved and cursed and floundered and enjoyed and suffered*' (my italics).

Henry James's lifelong devotion to his art (his first collection of stories was published in 1875, but his first novel had been serialized in 1871, in his twenty-eighth year; on his death in 1916, he left behind two unfinished novels), and his development of a wholly personal style of writing, combine to render quite inappropriate, in his case, the customary hunting for literary 'influences' or, for the most part, the customary attempts to describe in detail the external events of his biography. As he himself wrote, 'The artist was what he *did*—he was nothing else.' So it comes about that in the present introduction to Henry James I am more likely to follow an instinct to relate the 'late' James to the 'early' James, rather than compare either of them to any other writer. In the history of the novel, he is a leader rather than a follower. As one of his characters in a little sketch (reprinted in his *Picture and Text*, 1893) puts it: 'He leads us into his own mind, his own vision of things: that's the only place into which the poet *can* lead us.'

As for the external events of his life, he was a lifelong traveller and his best-known works have 'international' themes—as became a man who was born in New York, lived much on the Continent of Europe, and died in London as a British subject. The 'Chronological table' lists his major comings and goings, and there are obviously some occasions when references to other writers—American or French or English—will be noted. But in general it has been my effort to display Henry James as a consciously dedicated creative writer whose aim in writing would have been much the same, wherever he had happened to find himself or whatever he had happened to read of other people's works. That he was, in fact, a brilliant observer of various national cultures, and also a scholarly and sensitive literary critic in at least three languages—these are happy by-products of the development of his own creative powers.

My 'Chronological table' also lists all of Henry James's novels and stories, and a few samples of his very large output of non-fictional work. The stories and novels selected here as representative samples to interest new readers may, I hope, send some of them in search of the titles omitted or barely mentioned.

In my 'Notes on further reading' I have limited myself to a handful of helpful works from among the vast outpourings of 'the James industry' which, in academic circles, begins to resemble 'the Shakespeare industry'. I would simply add that no commentator on Henry James can nowadays fail to mention our enormous debt to Professor Leon Edel. Anyone who has read his wonderful five-volume biography, or used his edition of *The Complete Tales of Henry James*, or the four-volume selection from the *Letters*, or his share in the authoritative James bibliography (all noted in the 'Notes on further reading'), not to speak of many other editions and collections, may be forgiven for saying to any new student of James's work: 'Once you have read Leon Edel on James, you will from then onwards need no further help in finding your way among all the other interpreters and expositors.'

A further introductory word: please do not overlook the following note about James's revision of his major fiction for the 'New York Edition'. Many current reprints of the novels and tales reproduce this later version. Some readers prefer the original texts, some the revised version—there is much to be said for both views. But it is obviously worthwhile to discover whether the book you are reading was written, say, by a promising young author of thirty, or had been largely rewritten and elaborated by the same man, with all his rich experience of a life's devotion to writing, some thirty years later. These late additions and qualifications, however excellent in themselves, sound strange indeed if we think of them, mistakenly, as the outpourings of a young man. I have tried in my 'Illustrative passages' to give samples of this novelist's way of dealing with dialogue, straight narrative, occasional set-piece character sketches and passages of external description. Except when acknowledgement is made to the New York Edition, these quotations may be assumed to come from first or early versions of the novel or story.

The 'Illustrative passages', which I have relegated for convenience to a separate section, are, in truth, an essential part of this introduction to Henry James. Several of the quotations are from the very large majority of his works not previously treated in the available space; but they are all intended to demonstrate the extraordinary range of James's lifetime labours. In a sense, these quotations and the comments thereon are equally part of his 'biography' as a writer, as for instance in the third section, which demonstrates how his technique of dialogue changed entirely during his writing career.

From the moment when young James, as an unenthusiastic law student at Harvard, decided to make writing his life career, the products of that writing profession supply almost all the essential biographical, as well as literary, material required for a study of his working life. Thus, in sketching the opening period of 'Young Harry of New York and New England', we are able to draw not only on his autobiographies and letters and notebooks, but also on the novels *Washington Square* and *The Bostonians* which were written years after he had ceased to think of New York and New England as his permanent home. Similarly, a strictly chronological survey of James's subsequent wanderings in Europe, and eventual decision to make his home in London, would in an introductory study of such small compass as the present work be of much less help to a reader of James's novels and stories than the briefest of comments on and quotations from those same written records of his *own* reactions (only thinly disguised in fictional form) to those journeys and those personal decisions. The brief chapter entitled 'I take possession of the old world' touches upon the writer's original responses to the old culture of his new continent. The chapter 'Bridging the Atlantic' has been expanded to offer several examples of his lifelong interest in the interactions of those cultures and continents. It is this 'appointed thematic doom' which won him his first success and fame as a writer, and although in his mature work his analysis of human motive and behaviour penetrates far below the level of 'cultural' or national habits and contrasts, nevertheless his major characters, over and over again, come from opposite sides of the Atlantic and their individual drama is always heightened and sometimes symbolized by these international differences. *The Portrait of a Lady* may embrace several of the themes already singled out for illustration, but deserves a chapter to itself as a novel near perfect in structure and so quintessentially 'James' in tone that any reader who cannot enjoy this particular novel may well be advised to abandon James altogether. My treatment of Henry James the Londoner limits itself to exhibiting a few of his literary responses to social and political disenchantments, not now so much as a visiting American as himself a full participating member of the society he shares and criticizes.

The brief selection of James's 'writing about writing' is included mainly as a warning to chance browsers in James's works; for however interesting they may be as samples of the novelist's own brooding over his chosen art, these stories should ideally be approached only by readers who have already enjoyed James's practice as a story-teller before turning to his attempts to turn his artistic theories into fiction. The sketch of *The Wings of the Dove* must, alas, serve as sole exponent of the 'later phase' of James's work, though extracts from and commentaries on *The Ambassadors* and *The Golden Bowl* appear in the 'Illustrative passages'. The last chapter mentions some of the writer's preoccupations when, after a period of disappointment and depression, he felt his creative powers reawakening.

I must end these introductory words with an explanation of my fairly sparse references to the external events of James's life (apart from the fact that they are so readily available in Leon Edel's five-volume biography). Many of our famous writers are as well remembered for their private lives, their wives and mistresses and romantic entanglements, as for their written work. To write of Thomas Carlyle without a mention of his wife Jane, or of Shelley without the various ladies who caused Matthew Arnold to cry out 'what a set!', or of Keats minus Fanny Brawne, would surely cripple any commentary on their written work as well as falsifying their life stories. With James it was quite different. He had no wife to share or influence his journeys, no mistresses to add spice to his biography or ask for identification in his written fiction. The kindest, most affectionate of men, he spread his sensibilities far and wide, as the amazing range of his intimate correspondence amply shows, even in the strictly selected volumes of his wonderful letters. Only for relatively brief periods, and those often coinciding with spasms of depression after some literary disappointment, would he pour out a more or less unreciprocated, if not always undeserved, flood of avuncular yearning, especially in his later years, upon younger people who seemed to share and understand the *meaning* of his life and work (see 'Illustrative passages', pp. 158–62). But he left no gossip behind him. We cannot speculate in him, as we can in most other writers, the degree to which one person or several persons who actually shared his physical and domestic existence contributed also to the nature of his creative work. Physically, James was always solitary. He may use extravagantly affectionate greetings in his letters, but the recurring '*mon bon*' he addresses in his notebooks is not a friend, but his lonely self. To quote from his story 'The Lesson of the Master': 'Nature had dedicated him to intellectual, not personal passion.'

Young Harry and 'the Master': the New York Edition

Henry James wrote twenty-two novels (two unfinished) and one hundred and twelve tales. Some of the novels were twice the length

The revised and the unrevised James (from an unpublished Max Beerbohm cartoon).

of ordinary novels; some of the tales were as long as a short novel. In his early sixties, James revised the main bulk of this immense output of novels and tales for the handsome New York Edition published in 1907–9, in twenty-four volumes. (The two novels left unfinished at James's death in 1916, *The Ivory Tower* and *The Sense of the Past*, were seen through the press the following year, and then added to the New York Edition.) It is from these revised texts that the majority of later reprints of James's fiction derive: a point very well worth noting in so far as the revisions and augmentations made by James in his sixties have given many readers an altogether distorted view of his *early* style. It was for this New York Edition, too, that James wrote the famous Prefaces—leisurely commentaries on his own work which enshrine James's 'garnered wisdom' as a consistently serious and self-aware writer of fiction. These much-quoted essays, like the New York Edition revisions themselves, have greatly affected readers' views of James and his intentions. They do not always offer an accurate account of the mind of the younger James. Just as his autobiographies (published in his seventies) recreate a marvellous picture of childhood in words and concepts a child could hardly have entertained, so the Prefaces to, and revisions of, James's early work must always be read with some degree of reservation. It was not until Leon Edel's splendid twelve-volume edition of *The Complete Tales of Henry James* that it was easily possible to read the impressive corpus of James's short stories in their earliest form—or, rather, the first appearance in book-form, containing the author's adjustments after their debut in periodicals on both sides of the Atlantic.

The first of James's novels to be revised for the New York Edition was *Roderick Hudson*, which was written in 1874, when Henry James was thirty-one. A few years later, for the English edition, James 'minutely revised' the novel, with 'a large number of verbal alterations'. But it is the extensively expanded version in the definitive New York Edition that is most often read today, together with its backward-looking Preface. It is true that this version contains, in Leon Edel's words, 'the richest and most improved form of this novel'; yet there is a freshness about the 1878 prose which, having already been 'minutely revised' by its young author, makes it the more attractive form of the novel which won him his early fame. A few samples of the later reworking of this text by the author in his sixties may show how to the richness of the final version something of the early quality was sacrificed. Indeed, after we have read the story and met its two chief characters, we may almost believe that the prose of the young artist Roderick Hudson had been rewritten by his cautious and more pedestrian friend, Rowland Mallet. The following examples are all from Chapter XX:

'Poor Miss Light!' she said at last simply. And in this it seemed to Rowland there was a touch of serious mockery.

(1878 text)

'Poor Miss Light!' she at last simply said. But it went, as for her ironic purpose, very far.

(1909 text)

'If I can in any way be of service to Mrs Light, I shall be happy', Rowland said.

(1878 text)

'If I can in any way be of service to Mrs Light I shall much rejoice', Rowland found himself a little recklessly articulating.

(1909 text)

Rowland greatly pitied her, for there is something respectable in passionate grief, even in a very bad cause; and as pity is akin to love he felt rather more tolerant of her fantastic pretensions than he had done hitherto.

(1878 text)

Rowland greatly pitied her—so respectable is sincerity of sorrow. She too was in the blighting circle of her daughter's contact, and this exposure, shared with the others who were more interesting, almost gave her, with the crudity of her candour, something of their dignity.

(1909 text)

'Puzzle them out at your leisure', said the Cavaliere, shaking his hand. 'I hear Mrs Light; I must go to my post. I wish you were a Catholic; I would beg you to step into the first church you come to and pray for us the next half-hour'.
'For 'us'? For whom?'
'For all of us. At any rate remember this—I delight in the Christina!'
Rowland heard the rustle of Mrs Light's dress; he turned away, and the Cavaliere went as he said to his post. Rowland for the next couple of days kept thinking of the sword of Damocles.

(1878 text)

The old man's face probed a moment the consciousness from which this question had sprung. 'Pray for her, dear sir', he at last simply said.
'I'll pray for *you*, Cavaliere', Rowland answered as they went.
He had become aware of Mrs Light's renewed approach and he slipped straight away. Yes, it was after this some providential support to her vague coadjutor that he found himself most invoking.

(1909 text)

The counsel of perfection, of course, is to read James in *both* versions—but, as Macaulay said in another context, that might be, for hopeful beginners, 'to demand from us so large a portion of so short an existence'!

Part One
The Early James

2 Young Harry of New York and New England

Family background

The Henry James who was born in the city of New York in 1843 was Irish Presbyterian by descent, a mixture we know only too well to be by no means a simple one. His grandfather, William James, was a severe Presbyterian who had arrived in America from Co. Cavan in 1789, settled in Albany, New York, and made a large fortune. The novelist's father, Henry, was one of William's eleven surviving children. Together with his share of the family fortune, this Henry inherited a permanent distaste for his strict Calvinist upbringing. A dreadful boyhood accident caused the amputation of one of his legs, and a rebellious nature caused him to endure throughout his early years as husband and father an 'insane terror' of a God whom he could only visualize as a hostile being, a terror culminating (while staying with his young family in Windsor Great Park, of all unlikely places for such an experience) in a horrific mental phenomenon which he later described as a 'vastation'. This term was borrowed from the works of the eighteenth-century Swedish theologian Emanuel Swedenborg, whose writings helped— together with those of the then fashionable French philosopher Charles Fourier—to restore him to mental health and wholeness. It is a remarkable tribute to the senior Henry that in spite of these physical and psychological wounds, he came to the conclusion that 'Every appetite and passion of man's nature is good and beautiful, and destined to be fully enjoyed.'

Father Henry, as an amateur philosophical theologian, became the sort of dictatorially vacillating open-minded liberal who insists on seeing several sides to every question. The young James boys, Henry and his elder brother William, were forced as children to bear the burden of their father's conscientious liberty. This carefully planned rootlessness, this almost orthodox heterodoxy, took physical as well as philosophical form: the elder Henry scorned national limitations as much as he scorned intellectual limitations—all categories and barriers were equally taboo. As a consequence, he and his young family were for ever on the move, seeking what the world in its variety had to offer, in daily life as well as in ways of thought. From infancy, the boys trailed about western Europe with their parents, briefly and erratically attending a variety of American and European schools. Whether in England,

Henry James senior and junior, 1854.

France, Switzerland or at home in New York or in the Boston area, Henry was free to soak himself in English and French, as well as American, life and literature. Although the 'passionate pilgrims' of his early novels and tales, like their young author, were capable of 'reeling and moaning' through the streets of Rome, every naked sense aquiver, they could also be, as he himself became, well read, given to mature comparisons and judgements, and silently sceptical. Young Henry was a reader and a brooder; but from his very earliest years it was on first-hand realities, things seen and heard and felt that he was to brood. It would be on the validity of his own first-hand impressions, and not on acquired generalizations (his father would never have encouraged those, and brother William would have countered them with larger and more authoritative systems!), that Henry would base his own 'revised wisdom'. It would be this quality in James, I believe, that later prompted T. S. Eliot, that other great Anglo-American literary master, to pay him the splendid compliment that he had 'a mind so fine that no idea could violate it'. (For a note on this often misunderstood remark, see p. 85.)

The elder Henry's wife, Mary Robertson Walsh, was also of Calvinist Scots/Irish descent. Husband and children alike testify over and over again, in letters home and to their friends, to her family devotion: to her, it would seem, devotion was a duty, and duty a delight. She certainly had need of both steadiness and adaptability, for her husband's determination to avoid all kowtowing to what we would now call 'the establishment', whether religious or educational or simply territorial, involved the family in endless travels, changes of houses, changes of school. His admirable penchant for intellectual and physical freedom could also be seen, by young Henry and his sister and three brothers, as an exasperating avoidance of any fixed role in life. What *was* he, what did he *do*, what did he *believe*?—this is what his children would wonder. Henry Senior stayed away from church but saw a loving Providence everywhere; he allowed his boys to read widely and he was himself a tireless author of open-ended religious writings; he whisked his family to and fro across the Atlantic (not so small a matter, in the 1840s and 1850s), always in response to some good-hearted plan which would be exchanged for another every month or two: a lovable, unpredictable, and to growing minds thoroughly unreliable father. One can see how, in contrast with this undisciplined genius, the mother of the family must have appeared, by default, a stable, if not dominant, figure. The novelist's biographer, Leon Edel, suggests that young Henry came very early in life to fear that marriage would inevitably weaken the man in relation to the woman. This fear may have been somewhat unfair to his father, whose reluctance to strike attitudes or demand orthodox behaviour was a positive article of faith in his own hard-won intellectual independence; but one way or another it certainly helped to nourish in the boy a close awareness of human relations, whichever way his own sympathies may have been moved.

During the family's return to an American base at Newport, Rhode Island, Henry, as a teenager, spent much time talking literature (including French literature) and literary ambitions with his friends Thomas Sergeant Perry and John La Farge, and later in the year 1859 found himself once again at Geneva—studying at yet another school. The following year saw the family in Switzerland and Germany before yet another retreat to Newport, where Henry continued to practise writing while brother William, hoping to become a painter, took lessons in art. It was at Newport, in the dreadful year 1861 when the American Civil War broke out, which would draw his two younger brothers Garth Wilkinson ('Wilky') and Robertson ('Bob') into the Union Army, that eighteen-year-old Henry suffered an 'obscure hurt' while helping to extinguish a small local fire. This injury he himself treated with such elaborate mystery (it certainly condemned him to recurrent and often incapacitating back-ache for many years) that commentators have seen in it a host of revealing possibilities. Was it an alibi for his own failure to play any part in the war? Was it a competitive effort to match the special consideration afforded to his father's amputated leg? Was it a dogged excuse for his determination, as apprentice writer, to choose the role of observer of life rather than actor in life? Was it even a real or imaginary rationale for sexual impotence? It is true that the family was no stranger to neurasthenia. William would have periods of depression approaching in intensity their father's famous 'vastation', and sister Alice became a prey to regular bouts of nervous breakdown and near-paranoiac withdrawal during which Henry himself became her most devoted nurse. Henry would make much of various physical ailments throughout his life; often enough, one suspects, in a carefully self-protective role. But on the whole he had a strong constitution and his regular feats of long-distance walking and horse-riding, together with a lifelong capacity for hard literary labour in the midst of ceaseless travel and an increasingly full social life, all contributed to a basic sturdiness of body as of mind. These resilient physical resources would bear him up through more than three score years and ten of resolute competence in ordering his celibate life, just as his highly organized consciousness would only very rarely fail to cope with the avalanches of sensuous and emotional experiences to which he exposed himself. Psychosomatic back-ache or no, sexual inhibitions or no, perilous imaginative flights or no, the Henry James who had withstood the rootless wanderings of his eccentric upbringing would almost always confront 'the wear and tear of discrimination' with disciplined sanity and a robust, if occasionally over-taxed, body.

A basically sound and sensible young man, then, who had survived an irregular upbringing and very early exposure to European schools and scenes and ways of life, determined quite early in life (after a year at the Harvard Law School) that he wished to become a writer. The New England scene was absorbed at a time when the Abolition fervour provided some sort of acceptable background to the dreadful Civil War into which his two younger brothers were swept up; but it was a New England viewed by a youngster who already had a more distinctive European background behind him. In the words of Leon Edel, in the first volume of his biography of James, 'Wordsworth's "plain living and high thinking" summed up New England for one who came to it with visions in his mind of the London of Dickens and the Paris of the Second Empire.' The older Henry remembered (in *Notes of a Son and Brother*) that on the brink of his twenties he had, at Harvard, to 'rinse [his] mouth of the European after-taste *in order* to do justice to whatever of the native bitter-sweet might offer itself in congruous vessels . . .'.

Washington Square

As the 'Chronological table' shows, for the first ten years of his writing life Henry James had produced well over a score of short stories. Some had American themes, some were the result of his European travels. His first full-length novel, *Watch and Ward* which appeared in serial form in 1871, was entirely American in its characters and its setting, and should be read as the work of an author still in his twenties. Then in 1875 three books were published, illustrating the various experimental efforts of the previous years. A volume of short stories appeared under the title of one of them, 'The Passionate Pilgrim', which exemplifies his first stage of willing absorption of his English and Continental discoveries; discoveries which are also commemorated in the collected volume of *Transatlantic Sketches*. The third book is his first published novel, *Roderick Hudson*, which foreshadows very many of his lines of future development, but may be most appropriately considered as a major result of his first 'passionate pilgrim' reactions to Europe, although the chief characters have a New England base and a varied set of New England characteristics.

The Europeans (1878) has a setting entirely in New England, but because of its mixed cast of characters it will be best appreciated as one of his larger group of 'international' studies. So that apart from a steady flow of shorter American tales, the two novels which most vividly present the responses of the young Henry James to his New York birthplace and his New England adolescence did not appear until later in his career—*Washington Square* in 1880 and *The Bostonians* in 1886—though it is quite obvious that their raw material had been digested long before. It is therefore not inappropriate to glance now at *Washington Square*, a novel in which a tense oppressive drama between father, daughter and a rejected potential son-in-law is played out on that New York social stage which, oddly enough, the elderly James would recall, in the wholly different prose of his memoirs of *A Small Boy and Others* (1913), as the early setting for the 'unconsciousness' of 'young naturalness':

> For it was as of an altogether special shade and sort that the New York young naturalness of our prime was touchingly to linger with us—so that to myself, at present, with only the gentle ghosts of the so numerous exemplars of it before me, it becomes the very stuff of the soft cerements in which their general mild mortality is laid away. We used to have in the after-time, amid fresh recognitions and reminders, the kindest 'old New York' identifications for it. The special shade of its identity was thus that it was not conscious—really not conscious of anything in the world; or was conscious of so few possibilities at least, and these so immediate and so a matter of course, that it came almost to the same thing.

> (Ch. IV)

Neither *Washington Square* nor *The Bostonians* figured among the works James so elaborately revised for the New York Edition, so we do not know how he would have expanded them in his sixties. The passage from *A Small Boy and Others* quoted above shows what he was capable of publishing in his seventieth year; and this following description, from the same source, of his memory of the smell of the ailanthus-trees near his childhood home—

> what I best recover in the connection is a sense and smell of perpetual autumn, with the ground so muffled in the leaves and twigs of the now long defunct ailanthus-tree that most of our own motions were a kicking of them up—the semi-sweet rankness of the plant was all in the air—and small boys pranced about as cavaliers whacking their steeds. There were bigger boys, bolder still, to whom this vegetation, or something kindred that escapes me, yielded long black beanlike slips which they lighted and smoked, the smaller ones staring and impressed; I at any rate think of the small one I can best speak for as constantly wading through an Indian summer of these *disjecta*, fascinated by the leaf-kicking process, the joy of lonely trudges . . .

> (Ch. VIII)

—is a pretty considerable cadenza on the early memory thus communicated in his description of the setting for the heroine of *Washington Square*:

it was here that you took your first walks abroad, following the nursery-maid and sniffing up the strange odour of the ailanthus-trees which at that time formed the principal umbrage of the square, and diffused an aroma that you were not yet critical enough to dislike as it deserved . . . It was here, at any rate, that my heroine spent many years of her life . . .

(Ch. III)

By 1880, at any rate, James was in his early maturity and immediately after *Washington Square* came his first incontestable masterpiece, *The Portrait of a Lady*. There is in *Washington Square* a concentration both of theme and tone which allows him to indulge an irony unmatched except by Jane Austen herself. The story concerns a New York widower, Dr Sloper, and his daughter Catherine. He is the most protective of fathers, with that excess of dutiful concern which has given 'paternalism' a bad name. At the very start of the novel, the irony which the martinet Doctor so frequently uses upon his disappointing daughter is aimed by his creator squarely at himself: 'He had in hand a stock of unexpended authority, by which the child, in its early years, profited largely.' The truncated household is completed by the figure of Dr Sloper's widowed sister, Mrs Penniman, a kindly but foolishly romantic-minded lady who 'was not absolutely veracious; but this defect was of no great consequence, for she never had anything to conceal'.

If Catherine was quiet, she was quietly quiet, as I may say, and her pathetic effects, which there was no one to notice, were entirely unstudied and unintended . . . But Mrs Penniman was elaborately reserved and significantly silent; there was a richer rustle in the very deliberate movements to which she confined herself, and when she occasionally spoke, she had the air of meaning something deeper than she said.

(Ch. XXII)

Into this grim temple of propriety and strict guardianship there ventures a young kinsman, Morris Townsend, who spies in the shy withdrawn figure of Catherine, her father's sole heiress, a solution to his own rootless improverishment. Nobody could blame the highly intelligent Dr Sloper for recognizing instantly that this charming young gentleman was obviously 'on the make':

The sign of the type in question is the determination—sometimes terrible in its quiet intensity—to accept nothing of life but its pleasure, and to secure these pleasures chiefly by the aid of your complaisant sex. Young men of this class never do anything for themselves that they can get other people to do for them, and it is the infatuation, the devotion, the superstition of others that keeps them going. These others in ninety-nine cases out of a hundred are women.

(Ch. XIV)

26

True enough. A great expert in morals, Dr Sloper's judgement is in its limited way correct; nor is the reader surprised when Morris, having had it made very plain to him that if the infatuated Catherine should venture to elope with him, she would be instantly disinherited, decides very quickly to absent himself. Yet is Catherine any happier for being protected? Was it not wrong to prevent her natural impulses from flowering? She had all the patient equipment for helping the handsome prodigal; perhaps, too, his probable ill treatment of her, much as it might have irritated the good Doctor to face competition in the polite exercise of sadism, would have supplied the missing significance in her life? In an indirect way, at any rate, the problem is resolved. Catherine's character, developed in spite of itself in the course of her sudden achievement of womanhood as she faces the implications of her choice, adjusts itself in the end quite naturally to spinsterhood. It might, but for a hair's breadth difference, have adapted itself equally easily to the lot of an ill-served wife.

Catherine's own feelings are driven deep within her, but they survive a trip to Europe with her father designed to allow her to forget the good-for-nothing Morris. On their return it is clear that he has often been staying at the home with her aunt Lavinia Penniman, who had stayed behind in Washington Square. A sample of James's assured dialogue, at this point, may illustrate both the technical rightness of Dr Sloper's judgements and the unveiled disdain with which he contemplates with his other sister, Mrs Almond, what he considers to be his daughter's weakness:

'I suppose she has had him there all the while,' he said. 'I must look into the state of my wine! You needn't mind telling me now; I have already said all I mean to say to her on the subject.'

'I believe he was in the house a good deal,' Mrs Almond answered. 'But you must admit that your leaving Lavinia quite alone was a great change for her, and that it was natural she would want some society.'

'I do admit that, and that is why I shall make no row about the wine; I shall set it down as compensation to Lavinia. She is capable of telling me that she drank it all herself. Think of the inconceivable bad taste, in the circumstances, of that fellow making free with the house—or coming there at all! If that doesn't describe him, he is indescribable.'

'His plan is to get what he can. Lavinia will have supported him for a year,' said Mrs Almond. 'It's so much gained.'

'She will have to support him for the rest of his life, then!' cried the Doctor. 'But without wine, as they say at the *tables d'hôte*.'

'Catherine tells me he has set up a business, and is making a great deal of money.'

The Doctor stared. 'She has not told me that—and Lavinia didn't deign. Ah!' he cried, 'Catherine has given me up. Not that it matters, for all that the business amounts to.'

'She has not given up Mr Townsend!' said Mrs Almond. 'I saw that in the first half minute. She has come home exactly the same.'

'Exactly the same; not a grain more intelligent. She didn't notice a stick or a stone all the while we were away—not a picture nor a view, not a statue or a cathedral.'

'How could she notice? She had other things to think of; they are never for an instant out of her mind. She touches me very much.'

'She would touch me if she didn't irritate me. That's the effect she has upon me now. I have tried everything upon her; I really have been quite merciless. But it is of no use whatever; she is absolutely *glued*. I have passed, in consequence, into the exasperated stage. At first I had a good deal of a certain genial curiosity about it; I wanted to see if she really would stick. But, good Lord, one's curiosity is satisfied! I see she is capable of it, and now she can let go.'

'She will never let go,' said Mrs Almond.

(Ch. XXVII)

It is true that the year in Europe with her father has not changed Catherine's intention to marry Morris. 'We have fattened the sheep for him before he kills it,' is Dr Sloper's summary. From this point on, the battle of wills between father and daughter reveals a temperamental likeness stronger even than their diametrically opposed opinions. We are reminded of the family likeness shared by another violently opposed father-and-daughter pair: King Lear and Cordelia. She declares quite openly to meddlesome Aunt Lavinia:

'Nothing is changed—nothing but my feeling about father. I don't mind nearly so much now. I have been as good as I could, but he doesn't care. Now I don't care either. I don't know whether I have grown bad; perhaps I have. But I don't care for that. I have come home to be married—that's all I know. That ought to please you, unless you have taken up some new idea; you are so strange. You may do as you please, but you must never speak to me again about pleading with father. I shall never plead with him for anything; that is all over. He has put me off. I am come home to be married.'

(Ch. XXV)

Ten very short concluding chapters (XXVI–XXXV) keep up a high tension, still charged with irony—and by no means all coming from Dr Sloper. Catherine's 'beautiful young man' continues to pay court, in spite of the young woman's assurance that their marriage will be undowered by any gift or legacy from her father: 'He is not very fond of me . . .It is because he is so fond of my mother, whom we lost so long ago. She was beautiful, and very, very brilliant; he is always thinking of her. I am not at all like her . . .'. Indeed no; she is too like her father. As for the Doctor, his remark to his sister Lavinia is deliberately, as ironically suited to this lady's sentimentality, couched in melodramatic phrase: 'Beware of the just resentment of a deluded fortune-hunter.'

The power of the last few chapters shows James at his most economically pitiless—each character plays out his or her part with the inevitability of nemesis itself: every mistaken decision reaps its painful reward; every revelation of the weakening effects of love on Catherine's side, and the cowardice of self-seeking treachery on Townsend's side, leads the reader on towards the conclusion he has for so long been hoping to evade. The novelist's skill is completely in control. By all means acknowledge a likeness in theme to Balzac's *Eugénie Grandet*, or a handling of irony equal to Jane Austen's own— these are not 'borrowings' or 'influences', but simply signs of equality and kinship with other novelists following their own type of mastery. After a gruesome scene in which Morris sidles away from his dispossessed heiress on a wholly trumped-up excuse, Catherine gives way to tears, 'It was almost the last outbreak of passion in her life; at least, she never indulged in another that the world knew anything about.' Grief-stricken, she tries to persuade herself, with the desperate illogicality of unrequited love, that Morris will come back and explain everything away:

> When it had grown dark, Catherine went to the window and looked out; she stood there for half an hour, on the mere chance that he would come up the steps. At last she turned away, for she saw her father come in. He had seen her at the window looking out, and he stopped a moment at the bottom of the white steps, and gravely, with an air of exaggerated courtesy, lifted his hat to her. The gesture was so incongruous to the condition she was in, this stately tribute of respect to a poor girl despised and forsaken was so out of place, that the thing gave her a kind of horror, and she hurried away to her room. It seemed to her that she had given Morris up.

> (Ch. XXX)

Dr Sloper's raised hat, and Catherine's Sloper-like resolution that *she* 'had given Morris up': this little moment says it all. The remaining pages are but a cruel insistent coda.

'Fortunately for Catherine, she could take refuge from her excitement, which had now become intense, in her determination that her father should see nothing of it.' Her last desperate note ('Dear Morris, you are killing me!') goes unanswered. Mrs Penniman's intrusions are repulsed with vigour: 'Catherine's outbreak of anger and the sense of wrong gave her, while they lasted, the satisfaction that comes from all assertion of force: they hurried her along, and there is always a sort of pleasure in cleaving the air.' From her silent resignation, as the days pass, Dr Sloper takes full satisfaction: 'To the pleasure of marrying a charming young man you add that of having your own way; you strike me as a very lucky young lady!' When Catherine volunteers 'I have broken off my engagement', her father vengefully comments: 'You are rather cruel, after encouraging him and playing with him for so long!' His other sister, Mrs Almond, 'guessed for herself that Catherine had been cruelly jilted', and the dialogue between her and Dr Sloper is so tensely revealing that one instinctively reads it as leading up to what, in a play, would be the brief 'final Act':

'I am by no means sure she has got rid of him,' the Doctor said. 'There is not the smallest probability that, after having been as obstinate as a mule for two years, she suddenly became amenable to reason. It is infinitely more probable that he got rid of her.'

'All the more reason you should be gentle with her.'

'I *am* gentle with her. But I can't do the pathetic; I can't pump up tears, to look graceful, over the most fortunate thing that ever happened to her.'

'You have no sympathy,' said Mrs Almond; 'that was never your strong point. You have only to look at her to see that, right or wrong, and whether the rupture came from herself or from him, her poor little heart is grievously bruised.'

'Handling bruises, and even dropping tears on them, doesn't make them any better! My business is to see she gets no more knocks, and that I shall carefully attend to. But I don't at all recognize your description of Catherine. She doesn't strike me in the least as a young woman going about in search of a moral poultice. In fact, she seems to me much better than while the fellow was hanging about. She is perfectly comfortable and blooming; she eats and sleeps, takes her usual exercise, and overloads herself, as usual, with finery. She is always knitting some purse or embroidering some handkerchief, and it seems to me she turns these articles out about as fast as ever. She hasn't much to say; but when had she anything to say? She had her little dance, and now she is sitting down to rest. I suspect that, on the whole, she enjoys it.'

'She enjoys it as people enjoy getting rid of a leg that has been

A courtship scene reminiscent of Washington Square (*from* Yale Wit and Humor, *Yale University, 1894*).

crushed. The state of mind after amputation is doubtless one of comparative repose.'

'If your leg is a metaphor for young Townsend, I can assure you he has never been crushed. Crushed? Not he! He is alive and perfectly intact; and that's why I am not satisfied.'

'Should you have liked to kill him?' asked Mrs Almond.

'Yes, very much. I think it is quite possible that it is all a blind.'

'A blind?'

'An arrangement between them. *Il fait le mort*, as they say in France; but he is looking out of the corner of his eye. You can depend upon it, he has not burnt his ships; he has kept one to come back in. When I am dead, he will set sail again, and then she will marry him.'

(Ch. XXXII)

That 'final Act' is brief indeed. Years have passed; the obstinate Catherine, now well advanced into middle age, had held out to the end, denying her father the pleasure of a promise that even after his death she would not marry Morris, and thus providing him only with the lesser satisfaction, before his death, of ratifying his intention to disinherit her. It is thus to a resigned spinster, still living in the Washington Square house (comfortably enough on an earlier maternal inheritance) that—with the connivance of a still incurably credulous old Aunt Penniman—Morris Townsend comes, much travelled and rootless as ever, to pay his final court. Catherine's long suffered wound has reopened, but her serenity in face of this almost unrecognizable plump and bearded Morris is, on the surface, complete:

> Morris stood stroking his beard, with a clouded eye. 'Why have you never married?' he asked, abruptly. 'You have had opportunities.'
>
> 'I didn't wish to marry.'
>
> 'Yes, you are rich, you are free; you had nothing to gain.'
>
> 'I had nothing to gain,' said Catherine.
>
> Morris looked vaguely round him, and gave a deep sigh. 'Well, I was in hopes that we might still have been friends.'
>
> 'I meant to tell you, by my aunt, in answer to your message—if you had waited for an answer—that it was unnecessary for you to come in that hope.'

(Ch. XXXV)

Her father's irony, at least, had not failed her, as 'Catherine . . . picking up her morsel of fancy-work, had seated herself with it again—for life, as it were.'

The Bostonians and The Princess Casamassima

Within its narrow compass, *Washington Square* leaves the reader with moral issues larger than can be dealt with in the book itself—again, as so often in the works of Jane Austen. While we ponder on the ethical problem posed by the action of one person denying to another person an experience which he or she thinks will cause harm, we can see that such matters may have a relevance to situations far more generalized than those concerning a particular father and a particular daughter. The second of James's novels here selected as echoing themes which first engaged his attention during his youthful years in New York and New England, namely *The Bostonians* (1886), is an altogether different matter. Like *The Princess Casamassima*, which was published in the same year, it deals overtly with public movements, with political attitudes and preconceived social beliefs, as they mingle with and come into conflict with the private lives of those people who hold such views. The first of this pair of novels deals with Bostonian women's suffrage struggles and similar liberating programmes in the years immediately succeeding the Civil War. The second, even more frankly confronting such unavoidably political issues as the exploits and murder plots of real life anarchists in London and elsewhere in the 1880s, must regrettably be neglected here (but see 'Illustrative passages', pp. 139–41) in favour of its companion work with a wholly American setting. *The Bostonians* is a very much longer novel than *Washington Square* and very much larger in scope. Its place in the James canon, along with *The Princess Casamassima*, is strange. Both books, gripping and wide-embracing as they are, came as disappointments to a reading public which by 1886 was looking to Henry James for still more variations on his American/European topic which had scored such a jackpot in 'Daisy Miller' of 1878 and was the chief attraction of the great achievement of *The Portrait of a Lady* of 1881, which had closely succeeded and greatly surpassed *Washington Square*.

Because *The Bostonians* was not included by James in his selective–definitive New York Edition, there is no late Preface to which we may turn for the author's reminiscent commentary. His Preface to the revised companion novel had made a very clear claim for its originality, based on the author's first-hand experience of London life: 'The simplest account of the origin of the *The Princess Casamassima* is, I think, that this fiction proceeded quite directly, during the first year of a long residence in London, from the habit and interest of walking the streets . . . the prime idea was unmistakably the ripe round fruit of perambulation.' For a precisely similar memory of the young Henry James's first-hand observations of Boston, we may turn to his recollection in the autobiographical *Notes of a Son and Brother* (1914), of how

I invoked, I called down the revelation of, new likenesses by the simple act of threading the Boston streets, whether by garish day (the afterglow of the great snowfalls of winter was to turn in particular to a blinding glare, an unequalled hardness of light,) or under that mantle of night which draped as with the garb of adventure our long-drawn townward little rumbles in the interest of the theatre or of Parker's—oh the sordid, yet never in the least deterrent conditions of transit in that age of the unabbreviated, the dividing desert and the primitive horse-car!

(Ch. X)

I am glad to stress those two eloquent confessions by Henry James himself of his 'walking the streets' of London and 'threading the Boston streets' as the 'simplest account' of the origins of these two wonderful novels. They should be treasured in mind against the over-literary comments of some critics who on the evidence of a touch of Dickens here or a dash of George Eliot there, would deny to this most original of creative writers (portly and ceremonious as he may have become in his late years) a genuine first-hand knowledge of the cities in which his plots are set.

There are two clear indications in Henry James's own words that the people and places he described in *The Bostonians* were based on his first-hand observations there some quarter of a century before the publication of the novel. One is yet another claim, in *Notes of a Son and Brother*, that

on the day, in short, when one should cease to live in large measure by one's eyes (with the imagination of course all the while waiting on this) one would have taken the longest step towards not living at all. My companions . . . were subject to my so practising in a degree which represented well-nigh the whole of my relation with them . . . since vision, and nothing but vision, was from beginning to end the fruit of my situation among them . . . to such an extent that . . . I was with all intensity taking in New England and that I knew no better immediate way than to take it in by my senses.

(Ch. X)

The other proof was more immediate—though just possibly as far-reaching in its effect. The early chapters of the novel had appeared in an American journal in the first months of 1885, and at once called forth from brother William and other intimates the charge that in his presentation of one of his Bostonian female activists, the ineffable Miss Birdseye, Henry had (in Leon Edel's summarizing words) 'lampooned a much respected Boston reformer, Miss Elizabeth Peabody, the elderly sister-in-law of Hawthorne, whose good works and crusading zeal were famous.' Henry at once protested, in reply, that 'Miss Birdseye was evolved entirely from my moral consciousness like every person I have ever drawn.' So whether this character was based on the fruit of 'vision, and nothing but vision', or was 'evolved entirely from my moral consciousness' presumably by creating a patchwork figure from the observation of several examples of a general type, the conclusion is the same: the character was James's own, and not wholly derived from a literary model.

Here is Miss Birdseye, in one of the many set-piece demonstrations of witty yet not wholly unsympathetic comic sketches of some of the Bostonian reforming ladies; with its companion piece on Mrs Farrinder it has at least one characteristic in common with the personalities of Dickens—it simply asks to be read *aloud*:

She was a little old lady, with an enormous head; that was the first thing Ransom noticed—the vast, fair, protuberant, candid, ungarnished brow, surmounting a pair of weak, kind, tired-looking eyes, and ineffectually balanced in the rear by a cap which had the air of falling backward, and which Miss Birdseye suddenly felt for while she talked, with unsuccessful irrelevant movements. She had a sad, soft, pale face, which (and it was the effect of her whole head) looked as if it had been soaked, blurred, and made vague by exposure to some slow dissolvent. The long practice of philanthropy had not given accent to her features, it had rubbed out their transitions, their meanings. The waves of sympathy, of enthusiasm, had wrought upon them in the same way in which the waves of time finally modify the surface of old marble busts, gradually washing away their sharpness, their details. In her large countenance her dim little smile scarcely showed. It was a mere sketch of a smile, a kind of installment, or payment on account; it seemed to say that she would smile more if she had time, but that you could see, without this, that she was gentle and easy to beguile.

She always dressed in the same way: she wore a loose black jacket, with deep pockets, which were stuffed with papers, memoranda of a voluminous correspondence; and from beneath her jacket depended a short stuff dress. The brevity of this simple garment was the one device by which Miss Birdseye managed to suggest that she was a woman of business, that she wished to be free for action. She belonged to the Short-Skirts League, as a matter of course; for she belonged to any and every league that had been founded for almost any purpose whatever. This did not prevent her being a confused, entangled, inconsequent, discursive old woman, whose charity began at home and ended nowhere, whose credulity kept pace with it, and who knew less about her fellow-creatures, if possible, after fifty years of humani-tary zeal, than on the day she had gone into the field to testify against the iniquity of most arrangements.

No one had an idea how she lived; whenever money was given her she gave it away to a negro or a refugee. No woman could be less invidious, but on the whole she preferred these two classes of the human race. Since the Civil War much of her occupation was gone; for before that her best hours had been spent in fancying that she was helping some Southern slave to escape. It would have been a nice question whether, in her heart of hearts, for the sake of this excitement, she did not sometimes wish the blacks back in bondage. She had suffered in the same way by the relaxation of many European despotisms, for in former years much of the romance of her life had been in smoothing the pillow of exile for banished conspirators. Her refugees had been very precious to her; she was always trying to raise money for some cadaverous Pole, to obtain lessons for some shirtless Italian. There was a legend that an Hungarian had once possessed himself of her affections, and had disappeared after robbing her of everything she possessed. This, however, was very apocryphal, for she had never possessed anything, and it was open to grave doubt that she could have entertained a sentiment so personal. She was in love, even in those days, only with causes, and she languished only for emancipations. But they had been the happiest days, for when causes were embodied in foreigners (what else were the Africans?), they were certainly more appealing.

(Ch. IV)

The portrait of Mrs Farrinder I have postponed to 'Illustrative passages' (pp. 138–39) alongside similar thumbnail-sketches from *The Princess Casamassima*, and the main theme of the novel, namely the struggle between Olive Chancellor and Basil Ransom for the possession, mental and physical, of the young girl Verena Tarrant is considered in 'Illustrative passages' (pp. 166–69) in the context of other purely emotional rather than 'American' studies. The American figures to note at present are structurally 'minor' characters, but will serve to illustrate how James's sharp satirical eye may nevertheless be used first to identify, and then to forgive, certain social types who are immediately amusing and ultimately pitiable.

Enjoying these wonderfully witty and entertaining thumb-nail sketches as Henry James, in full mastery of his mature creative powers, looks back on some of the rather pathetic figures who peopled the American scenes of his youth, we learn a great deal about the qualities of the man as well as those of the author. He was capable, to be sure, of straightforward disdain and dislike for the shoddier aspects of post-Civil War commercialism and its practitioners: his loathing for the popular gossip-press was given concentrated venom in his portrait of Matthias Pardon, a young journalist who is one of the contestants for the hand of Verena Tarrant:

> he had begun his career, at the age of fourteen, by going the rounds of the hotels, to cull flowers from the big, greasy registers which lie on the marble counters; and he might flatter himself that he had contributed in his measure, and on behalf of a vigilant public opinion, the pride of a democratic State, to the great end of preventing the American citizen from attempting clandestine journeys. Since then he had ascended other steps of the same ladder; he was the most brilliant young interviewer on the Boston press. He was particularly successful in drawing out the ladies; he had condensed into shorthand many of the most celebrated women of his time—some of these daughters of fame were very voluminous—and he was supposed to have a remarkably insinuating way of waiting upon *prime donne* and actresses the morning after their arrival, or sometimes the very evening, while their luggage was being brought up. He was only twenty-eight years old, and with his hoary head, was a thoroughly modern young man; he had no idea of not taking advantage of all the modern conveniences. He regarded the mission of mankind upon earth as a perpetual evolution of telegrams; everything to him was very much the same, he had no sense of proportion or quality; but the newest thing was what came nearest exciting in his mind the sentiment of respect. He was an object of extreme admiration to Selah Tarrant, who believed that he had mastered all the secrets of success, and who, when Mrs Tarrant remarked (as she had done more than once) that it looked as if Mr Pardon was really coming after Verena, declared that if he was, he was one of the few young men he should want to see in that connection, one of the few he should be willing to allow to handle her.
>
> (Ch. XVI)

Matthias Pardon may stand as an example of one of the propellant forces which complemented the magnetic forces of the kind of European civilization which had attracted young Henry James while he was ending his Harvard year. It was not only the artists and writers of Paris or Florence, populating their selected cafés, who would prove so attractive to Roderick Hudson and Rowland Mallet or to Clement Searle of 'A Passionate Pilgrim'—it was also the absence from these places of Matthias Pardon. Later, of course, Henry James (and his characters) would come to look upon the English and Continental scene with a more jaundiced eye and find that these attractive cultures could sprout their own crop of vulgarity and pretentiousness.

The more closely studied minor figures of Verena's parents, Selah Tarrant and his wife, are presented with equally vivid distaste; but the young Harvard student who had watched such people and their friends was already, by the time he came to write *The Bostonians*, prepared to give them the benefit of several doubts, and in his later sociological judgements came near to complete forgiveness. The Tarrants are a dismally insincere couple whose daughter Verena attracted to their company many Bostonians who would otherwise have spurned them. She it was who made bearable

> the bald bareness of Tarrant's temporary lair, a wooden cottage, with a rough front yard, a little naked piazza, which seemed rather to expose than to protect, facing upon an unpaved road, in which the footway was overlaid with a strip of planks. These planks were embedded in ice or in liquid thaw, according to the momentary mood of the weather, and the advancing pedestrian traversed them in the attitude, and with a good deal of the suspense, of a ropedancer. There was nothing in the house to speak of; nothing, to Olive's sense, but a smell of kerosene; though she had a consciousness of sitting down somewhere—the object creaked and rocked beneath her—and of the table at tea being covered with a cloth stamped in bright colours.

(Ch. XV)

Verena's mother is undeniably a comic figure—

> Mrs Tarrant, with her soft corpulence, looked to her guest very bleached and tumid; her complexion had a kind of withered glaze; her hair, very scanty, was drawn off her forehead *à la Chinoise*; she had no eyebrows, and her eyes seemed to stare, like those of a figure of wax. When she talked and wished to insist, and she was always insisting, she puckered and distorted her face, with an effort to express the inexpressible, which turned out, after all, to be nothing. She had a kind of doleful elegance, tried to be confidential, lowered her voice and looked as if she wished to establish a secret understanding, in order to ask her visitor if she would venture on an apple-fritter. She wore a flowing mantle, which resembled her husband's waterproof—a garment which, when she turned to her daughter or talked about her, might have passed for the robe of a sort of priestess of maternity.

(Ch. XIV)

—but via her Abolitionist parents and her 'mesmeric healer' husband Selah, she represents the more ludicrous side of many serious causes. It then comes as no surprise that the domineering Olive Chancellor (quite apart from her at first barely recognizable emotional infatuation with the girl) is prepared to buy Verena from these unworthy parents and make a serious and civilized feminist nest for her.

She was a queer, indeed . . . a flaccid, unhealthy, whimsical woman, who still had a capacity to cling. What she clung to was 'society' and a postion in the world which a secret whisper told her she had never had and a voice more audible reminded her she was in danger of losing . . . Verena was born not only to lead their common sex out of bondage, but to remodel a visiting-list which bulged and contracted in the wrong places, like a country-made garment. As the daughter of Abraham Greenstreet, Mrs Tarrant had passed her youth in the first Abolitionist circles, and she was aware how much such a prospect was clouded by her union with a young man who had begun life as an itinerant vendor of lead-pencils (he had called at Mr Greenstreet's door in the exercise of this function), had afterwards been for a while a member of the celebrated Cayuga community, where there were no wives, or no husbands, or something of that sort (Mrs Tarrant could never remember), and had still later (though before the development of the healing faculty) achieved distinction in the spiritualistic world.

(Ch. X)

There is one small contributory factor in the make-up of the Tarrant couple which connects them at one end of the scale of James's sensitive observation with the odious figure of Matthias Pardon, and at the other end with the innocent citizens of London who will comfort Minny Theale of *The Wings of the Dove* in her dire agony (see pp. 121–22), and that is their devotion to the cheap information provided by popular newspapers. When Mrs Tarrant is left at home to read the paper, 'from this publication she derived inscrutable solace'. For Selah himself, 'The newspapers were his world, the richest expression, in his eyes, of human life . . .'. Later in James's work, particularly in the novel *The Reverberator* where a family is devastated by a 'deluge of the lowest insult' from a 'recording, slobbering sheet', the novelist's own detestation of the invasion of privacy by the new journalism is wholehearted. There is all the more reason for a reader to notice how, in hating a particular kind of pandering deception, James reserves a tender sensibility for the victims of these aids to self-delusion. There may be villains abroad in novels like *The Bostonians* or *The Princess Casamassima* where James deals with political themes. But people like the Tarrants, absurd though they may be, are pitiable rather than despicable. Selah, once the 'itinerant vendor of lead-pencils' and later a bogus practitioner of 'manual activity' as a mesmeric healer, is ridiculed but not condemned. This careful discrimination of moral as well as aesthetic judgement in these passing accounts of minor characters will soon become, in James's most ambitious works, his most distinctive contribution to the art and practice of the novel.

3 'I take possession of the old world'

Dear People all—
  I take possession of the old world—I inhale it—I appropriate it!

Thus Henry James, aged thirty-two, opened a letter in November 1875 to his family from a hotel off Piccadilly, having arrived at Liverpool the previous day on what proved to be the beginning of the fruits of his now irreparable decision to live and work in Europe rather than in America. This rapturous letter over 'cold roast beef, bread and cheese and ale' after his train journey from Liverpool is that of a convinced and methodical 'passionate pilgrim'. That passionate stage he had already passed through— first during the Grand Tour year 1869–70 when he had wandered, without benefit of family companions, in England, Switzerland and Italy, gathering impressions which were written up at home in Cambridge, Massachusetts (including the significantly entitled tale 'A Passionate Pilgrim' itself), and again in the years 1872–4 when on a Continental tour largely in company with an aunt or a sister or a brother. This new pilgrimage starting at the end of 1875 would henceforth be less of a liberating *ex*patriation and more of a realistic (often, indeed, disillusioning) *re*patriation. Uncannily prescient, he was to become in effect not only the first great literary Anglo-American but also the first American with a cultural zeal for the Common Market, as well as the English-speaking Union.

A reader of the early tales, novels and travel sketches which must sadly be passed over at this point may perhaps spot from his now available letters of this period that James, living as always 'with my pen in my hand', often treated the old folks at home with suitable gobbets from drafts already lying on his hotel-room desk. For example, a striking passage from 'A Passionate Pilgrim' is embodied in a letter to his father from Malvern in March 1870. A few words from each version will indicate the new kind of detective games to which the recently released flood of James's letters will invite analysts of James's style. The letter includes the passage:

tasted too, as deeply, of the peculiar stillness and repose of the close—saw a ruddy English lad come out and lock the door of the old foundation school which marries its heavy Gothic walls to the basement of the Church, and carry the vast big key into one of the still canonical houses—and stood wondering as to the effect of a man's mind of having in one's boyhood haunted the Cathedral shade as a King's scholar and yet kept ruddy with much cricket in misty meadows by the Severn.

The tale itself prints the words:

> tasted, too, as deeply of the peculiar stillness of this clerical precinct; saw a rosy English lad come forth and lock the door of the old foundation school, which marries its hoary basement to the soaring Gothic of the church, and carry his big responsible key into one of the quiet canonical houses; and then stood musing together on the effect on one's mind of having in one's boyhood haunted such cathedral shades as a King's scholar; and yet kept ruddy with much cricket in misty meadows by the Severn.
>
> (Ch. I)

We may thankfully greet the transcriptions now available in his private letters as proof of James's affectionate receptivity of immediate first impressions, passed on first to his loved ones, then in 'international' paragraphs of fiction or travelogues, right up to the full flowering of his descriptive style in *The American Scene* (1907) when in his sixties he turned that same omnivorous scrutiny once again upon his native land.

That first independent wander-year, March 1869 to April 1870, had been crucial. Shunning the family preference for Germany (from which philosopher William had just returned), Henry set out for England, France, Switzerland, Italy—crossing the Simplon, comments Leon Edel, 'as if he had walked into his future'. He may soon have been 'reeling and moaning' through the streets of Rome, but Professor Edel is right to remind us that the Henry James who reeled and moaned had already become 'a mature and artistic young American singularly conscious of himself and his destiny'.

As will be seen in the following chapter, James's own estimate of his 'appointed thematic doom' was to be the activities of 'international young ladies', standing as living examples of the clashings and/or mergings of international cultures. But this lifelong interest could never have been developed if he himself had not, as a young traveller, first known the spontaneous enthusiasm of a more or less uncritical enjoyment of the European culture (mainly English, French and Italian) he had so thoroughly documented at second-hand during his early youth by studying the works not only of his fellow American Hawthorne, but also Dickens, George Eliot, Balzac, and others; and then during his solo wander-year and other conscientious tours, confirmed by first-hand observations. As we have already seen in sampling some of his American-based observations, it was their *quality* rather than their accidental geographical background that established his prime equipment as a novelist. The 'passionate pilgrim' years simply expanded the area of his exposed sensibility. Once he had shown himself capable of this larger scope, and only then, he was able to juggle his 'international' contrasts and comparisons with something approaching impartiality.

'A Passionate Pilgrim'

Purely on account of its revealing title, it is tempting to select 'A Passionate Pilgrim' from among a dozen other early tales to bear witness to the sheer infectious enthusiasm of the response of young Henry to his Old World. As he says through the mouth of his narrator: 'there are few sensations so exquisite in life as to stand with a companion in a foreign land and inhale to the depths of your consciousness the alien savour of the air and the tonic picturesqueness of things. This common relish of local colour makes comrades of strangers.' And as if to remind us that the 'exquisite sensations' do not exclude a strong sense of countervailing realistic commentary, this same American narrator, strolling with his new acquaintance and compatriot Clement Searle through Hampton Court, had already noticed that 'The tints of all things have sunk to a cold and melancholy brown, and the great palatial void seems to hold no stouter tenantry than a sort of pungent odorous chill', so that in front of dark royal portraits he can exclaim 'Poor mortalized Kings! ineffective lure of royalty.'

There are other reasons for selecting this story, apart from its substantial length and the confident youthful elegance of its style. It justifies the treatment of much of James's work as biographical signposts as well as literary documents. The immediate product of his 1869–70 wander-year, it was published in two issues of the *Atlantic Monthly* magazine in 1871, and it gave its title to James's first published book in 1875, in a collection of tales which contain the germs of several different kinds of future development. 'The Romance of Certain Old Clothes' is an entirely American story which plays with Hawthorne-like eeriness and ghostly horrors around the basic theme which is the fear of marriage; 'The Last of the Valerii' is another derivative fantasy now readable mainly for the attraction of its Italian setting; 'Eugene Pickering' introduces an early example of the innumerable James heroes with a markedly autobiographical 'split personality' attitude to human intimacies; 'The Madonna of the Future' is among the first of his many parables on the problems posed by the artistic profession; and 'Madame de Mauves' has the triple interest, for readers of James, for combining the 'international' theme with yet another example of a withdrawing American male, both made more acceptable by the freshness of its appreciation of an idealized French culture. It may be accepted as a further token of 'the shape of things to come' that the same year which launched these reprinted stories also launched James's first published novel, *Roderick Hudson*, in which the two contrasting sides of the author's nature, as sketched in the two 'passionate pilgrims' of our sample story, blossom out into two major characters in his first major work.

When later in life James wrote that these early tales were 'in the highest degree documentary for myself', he was telling the literal truth. The narrator in 'The Passionate Pilgrim' feels at Hampton Court that 'It was in this dark composite light that I had read all English prose; it was this mild moist air that had blown from the verses of English poets . . .', and *we* are listening to the autobiographical Henry who later recalled hiding under the table as a child, in order to go on listening to the reading aloud of Dickens. The narrator, like the author, had also just been travelling in Italy and France. Further, when he and the mortally ailing Clement Searle are on their way to visit the stately home in Hereford from which Searle's ancestor had emigrated to America, they spend some time soaking up their impressions from the slopes of the Malvern Hills whence 'A dozen broad counties, within the vast range of your vision, commingle their green exhalations'—and *we* are re-reading one of young Henry's letters to his parents in Massachusetts. We can even recognize the envy of the tourist–narrator as he in turn watches his sick friend in front of the ancestral castle 'like a proscribed and exiled prince, hovering about the dominion of the usurper'. This sort of thing is the language of the romantic novels, English and American, and the romantic histories Henry himself, as well as his narrator and Clement Searle, had read before setting out to see England and other European countries with his own eyes.

Nor does the 'literary and artistic influence' stop here. The second part of the tale is far more artificial than the first part. Clement Searle has become convinced that his own American ancestor had somehow been cheated out of his birthright, and that the present occupiers of Lockley Hall, Mr Searle and his spinster sister, are indeed interlopers. When the American visitors are shown the house, carefully noting the glowing Vandykes, Rubenses and a Rembrandt, and the gracious Claude, Murillo, Greuze and Gainsborough, we are not only turning over again with James the illustrations in histories of art, but repeating the inventories Henry had made on his own travels. It is a Reynolds portrait that finally pushes Clement Searle over the border between fantasy and mania: like some half-remembered character from Hawthorne or Edgar Allan Poe or the eighteenth-century 'Gothick' romancers, this poor dying personification of the rejected outsider comes to believe that he *is* his own ancestor—even to the extent of claiming, when the wandering pair later take refuge in Oxford, that Magdalen 'was my college, you know . . . the noblest in Oxford'. The poor man had from his first sight of the Lockley Hall treasures felt 'suddenly illumined with an old disused gallantry', even to the extent of seeing in 'Miss Searle, his maiden-cousin, prospective heiress of these manorial acres and treasures', a wife for himself as the future co-owner of Lockley. The semi-supernatural melodramatic tone of the story is maintained to the end: Miss Searle, summoned to attend the Oxford deathbed of Clement Searle, arrives dressed in mourning for her brother who has just been conveniently killed by a fall from his horse:

> She took my arm. A moment later we had entered the room and approached the bedside. The doctor withdrew. Searle opened his eyes and looked at her from head to foot. Suddenly he seemed to perceive her mourning. 'Already!' he cried, audibly; with a smile, as I believe, of pleasure.
> She dropped on her knees and took his hand. 'Not for you, cousin,' she whispered. 'For my poor brother.'
> He started in all his deathly longitude as with a galvanic shock. 'Dead! *he* dead! Life itself!' And then, after a moment, with a slight rising inflection: 'You are free?'
> 'Free, cousin. Sadly free. And now—*now*—with what use for freedom?'
> He looked steadily a moment into her eyes, dark in the heavy shadow of her musty mourning veil. 'For me,' he said, 'wear colours!'
> In a moment more death had come, the doctor had silently attested it, and Miss Searle had burst into sobs.

The above quotation is a sample of the derivative melodramatic vein from which James would soon free himself. True enough, mysterious ghost-like reincarnations of the living past would re-emerge in James's fiction in such late works as the story 'The Jolly Corner' of 1908 and the unfinished novel *The Sense of the Past* which would be posthumously dramatized, as play and film, as 'Berkeley Square', but in these works the ghostly element, as in the better known story 'The Turn of the Screw', would reach the reader via a sophisticated ambiguity wholly different from the borrowed simplicities of this early form. As it is, the title-story of James's first published book already demonstrates the great divide between his own first-hand impressions, set down in vivid and often lyrical clarity, and the clutter of the imitative. Whether in his response to the English countryside in his already tenderly understanding portraits of such timidly dignified people as Miss Searle, or even in the witty sharpness of such observations as the way in which 'Our host, with great decency, led the conversation to America, talking of it rather as if it were some fabled planet, alien to the

British orbit, lately proclaimed to have the proportion of atmospheric gases required to support animal life'—in all these instances we may see Henry James forming his own distinctive view of things, his own distinctive style.

But there is something more. A story like 'A Passionate Pilgrim' was for James 'in the highest degree documentary for myself' not simply as an emergent new writer, but more significantly as an individual whose own psychological make-up would be endlessly demonstrated in his fiction, sometimes heavily disguised and often quite overtly. This apparently uncomplicated story of an American's discovery of a new country and new people is already complex before the plot unfolds: it is not one American but *two* Americans who make the discoveries, and each is incomplete without the other. The American who feels so deprived of his romantic inheritance that he dies dispossessed in mind and body is also the unnamed American who befriends him and organizes his opportunities for meetings and departures, and who sees the world for what it is, rather than what it might become or ought to be. The Clement Searle half of this personality is also the first of a long series of James heroes who will in effect choose death as the more acceptable alternative to sharing their lives in an actual marriage, the first of a long line of 'weak' heroes whose instinct is for withdrawal. The other half of that double personality would become, of course, the wholly sane, immensely industrious, highly competent and relentlessly realistic creator of one of the largest and most idiosyncratic bodies of work in the English language.

Roderick Hudson

The briefest possible summary of *Roderick Hudson* would go something like this: Rowland Mallet, a well-to-do New Englander, considers that his young townsfellow Roderick Hudson is being cramped by his small-town puritanical background, and takes him as his guest for a sojourn in Rome where the young sculptor's promise may, in a more artistic ambience, blossom into a genuine creative achievement. This generous plan goes adrift when the superficially brilliant but morally weak young artist allows the social attractions of the Old World, and especially his infatuation for Christina Light, illegitimate daughter of an American mother and a broken-down Italian Cavaliere, to encourage him to think of himself as a genius. Coincident with the steady impoverishment of his creative powers, Christina finally jilts him by an unloving marriage to an Italian prince, after which Roderick is found dead in a ravine, whether by accident or suicide is not revealed. His sponsor and protector, Rowland, is heartbroken by this outcome, for which he feels himself morally responsible. The flight from New

England, the manifold diversions of Rome, the various pretensions and mostly modest artistic achievements of the Americans who have settled there to lead the 'artistic life', and the even greater danger threatening an artist's work when his attention is distracted by a personal sexual passion—all these aspects are as 'biographical' as one could wish, but none more so than the so close yet so contrasting natures of the sane competent uninspired Rowland and the gifted but feckless Roderick. One almost feels that it is this joint Rowland–Roderick figure, reassembled in one body, who has written the novel.

When James came to describe how his young New England character Roderick Hudson settled down in Rome to his work as a sculptor, he could certainly draw on first-hand experience. When he started to write the novel in Florence in 1874, he was full of the impressions of Rome gained the previous year, and a Rome not only an undying 'city of the soul' but also a Rome which a sizeable number of American artists and writers had made their adopted home. He had been a frequent welcome guest at the sumptuous suite in the Barberini Palace where the wealthy American William Wetmore Story, trained and eminent as a lawyer, had set himself up as a sculptor and as one of the recognized social focal points for the self-conscious American artistic colony. Indeed, very much later in his life James was persuaded by Story's family to write a large memoir of his old host and comrade—his only straightforward attempt at a biography. It was later in life, too, that James himself became enamoured of another expatriate sculptor, the Norwegian-born American Hendrik Andersen whom he would meet in Rome some twenty-five years later. Very strangely, it is Andersen, whom he had *not* met, who resembles Roderick Hudson, rather than Story, whom he *had*.

Once Rowland has introduced Roderick to Rome, the 'passionate pilgrim' magic operates immediately. He feels the need to establish himself in that wonderful sequence of creative artists:

'I have seen enough for the present; I have reached the top of the hill. I have an indigestion of impressions; I must work them off before I go in for any more. I don't want to look at any more of other people's works for a month—not even at Nature's own. I want to look at Roderick Hudson's! The result of it all is that I am not afraid. I can but try, as well as the rest of them! The fellow who did that gazing goddess yonder only made an experiment. The other day, when I was looking at Michael Angelo's Moses, I was seized with a kind of defiance—a reaction against all this mere passive enjoyment of grandeur. It was a rousing great success, certainly, that sat there before me, but somehow it was not an inscrutable mystery, and it seemed to me,

not perhaps that I should some day do as well, but that at least
I *might!*'

'As you say, you can but try,' said Rowland. 'Success is only
passionate effort.'

(Ch. V)

And passionate effort, for a time, it is; exhausting and exhilarating
for sponsoring Rowland as well as creative Roderick: 'Rowland felt
the need for intellectual rest, for a truce to present care for
churches, statues and pictures on even better grounds than his
companion, inasmuch as he had really been living Roderick's intellectual life the past three months as well as his own' (Ch. V). The
Rowland in James watches the Roderick in James with rapturous
fulfilment at second hand:

> Rowland took a generous pleasure in his companion's confident
> *coup d'oeil*; Roderick was so much younger than he himself had
> ever been! Surely youth and genius hand in hand were the most
> beautiful sight in the world. Roderick added to this the charm
> of his more immediately personal qualities. The vivacity of his
> perceptions, the audacity of his imagination, the picturesqueness
> of his phrase when he was pleased—and even more when he was
> displeased—his abounding good humour, his candour, his
> unclouded frankness, his unfailing impulse to share every
> emotion and impression with his friend; all this made comrade-
> ship a high felicity and interfused with a deeper amenity the
> wanderings and contemplations that beguiled their pilgrimage
> to Rome.

(Ch. V)

The young creator is, at first, a rewarding pupil:

> Roderick's first fortnight was a high aesthetic revel. He declared
> that Rome made him feel and understand more things than he
> could express; he was sure that life must have there for all one's
> senses an incomparable fineness; that more interesting things
> must happen to one than anywhere else. And he gave Rowland
> to understand that he meant to live freely and largely and be as
> interested as occasion demanded.

(Ch. V)

While Roderick is sculpting away, Rowland is happy to enjoy the
pleasures of appreciation:

> But Rowland had two substantial aids for giving patience the air
> of contentment; he was an inquisitive reader and a passionate
> rider. He plunged into bulky German octavos on Italian history,
> and he spent long afternoons in the saddle, ranging over the
> grassy desolation of the Campagna. As the season went on and

the social groups began to constitute themselves, he found that he knew a great many people and that he had easy opportunity for knowing others.

(Ch. V)

Before long, Roderick begins to relax:

He interrupted, he contradicted, he spoke to people he had never seen and left his social creditors without the smallest conversational interest on their loans; he lounged and yawned, he talked loud when he should have talked low and low when he should have talked loud. Many people in consequence thought him insufferably conceited and declared that he ought to wait till he had something to show for his powers before he assumed the airs of a spoiled celebrity. But to Rowland and to most friendly observers this judgment was quite beside the mark, and the young man's undiluted naturalness was its own justification. He was impulsive, spontaneous, sincere . . .

(Ch. V)

His fellow artists begin to have doubts, but his admirers are more in love with the sculptor than with his sculptures:

All this was what friendly commentators (still chiefly feminine) alluded to when they spoke of his delightful freshness, and critics of harsher sensibilities (of the other sex) when they denounced his damned impertinence. His appearance enforced these impressions—his handsome face, his radiant unaverted eyes, his childish unmodulated voice. Afterwards, when those who loved him were in tears, there was something in all this unspotted comeliness that seemed to lend a mockery to the causes of their sorrow.

(Ch. V)

What this sorrow became, and how it affected all those nearest and dearest to Roderick, is studied in 'Illustrative passages' (pp. 162–66). These are human problems, with little or no contribution from their national characteristics either as expatriates or passionate pilgrims. All the main characters are American, including the fascinating Christina Light herself who passes for one, though her American mother hid from her illegitimate offspring until late in the story the news that her real father was the pathetic Cavaliere who is their humble guide and attendant. There are, as yet, no 'international' problems to solve, like those to be studied in the following chapter. Whatever happens, most of the characters are happy to be in Europe most of the time. True enough, Roderick's foolish mother may attribute his downfall to 'this wicked, infectious, heathenish place!' and he himself will grumble that 'If I had not come to Rome I shouldn't have risen, and if I had not risen I shouldn't have fallen'; but by that time everyone knows that his downfall is one of character. Rome, Florence, Switzerland—none of these shared any blame. The puritanical Mary Garland herself had felt, in Rome, a beauty that 'penetrates to one's soul and lodges there and keeps saying that man was made not to suffer but to enjoy. This place has undermined my stoicism . . . I love it!'

So, very obviously, did Henry James. If some of his characters come to grief after leaving America, it will be partly because of the clash of different social conventions, and partly because the very enrichment from which they have profited may render them a larger prize for corruption. 'Lilies that fester smell far worse than weeds.'

4 Bridging the Atlantic: 'my appointed thematic doom'

When Henry James came to write the Preface to Volume XVIII of his revised New York Edition (which contained his most famous story, 'Daisy Miller'), it must have been with something of a satisfied sigh that he recalled 'The international young ladies, felt by me once more . . . my appointed thematic doom. . .'. It was this 'doom' more than anything, that had marked him out as a distinguished and distinguishable writer of fiction and had captured for him such success among the general reading public as he always coveted. The first of his novels to be published, *Roderick Hudson* (1875), had treated the plight of an inexperienced young American artist when exposed to the impact of Europe. A year to two later appeared two novels the very titles of which seemed to stake his claim as a trans-Atlantic interpreter: *The American* (1877) and *The Europeans* (1878), the first again planting a straightforward American among European sophisticates, and the second transplanting into a staid New England family a pair of long-lost cousins who had been thoroughly and temptingly Europeanized. At the other end of his lifelong output, the three major novels *The Wings of the Dove*, *The Ambassadors* and *The Golden Bowl* (1902–4) all have Americans and Europeans struggling significantly with trans-Atlantic attractions and antipathies as they are embroiled in the major problems of life. It was indeed his 'thematic doom'.

In the major fiction, of course, the trans-Atlantic theme is only one aspect of the plot, only one ingredient of the drama. In the earlier novels and in dozens of his stories, James often allowed the contrasts and clashes of American–European relations to provide the main, sometimes the only, interest for his readers. It is for this reason that we may nowadays need some effort of historical imagination to recapture that sense of fascinated outrage which once thrilled social conservatives on both sides of the Atlantic when they read (in the words of Forrest Reid) 'one of those *amours de voyage* that Henry in his youth was so fond of treating'.

The trans-Atlantic balance has shifted so radically in the last hundred years or so that the manners and attitudes of James's trans-Atlantic pilgrims may sometimes seem to be those of some distant millennium rather than of one short century. Even some of the plots ring false to us, as they did not in James's time. What modern mother would whistle her son back to London at the news that he was becoming interested in an American heiress? And some speeches seem to come from the wrong lips. It is more likely to be an American than an English lady, nowadays, who could express the hope, in considering Anglo-American reciprocity, 'that an ultimate fusion was inevitable'. Perhaps the best way to allow for the interest taken by James's readers in the 1870s and 1880s in actual, as well as fictional, Anglo-American marriages is to recall that the fruit of one such union, solemnized in 1874, was Winston Churchill.

The American

The American is so melodramatic a treatment of the American/ European theme, the American hero Christopher Newman so 'new' and the noble French Bellegarde family so well 'guarded', that it comes as no surprise that some thirteen years after publication this novel was the first to be dramatized by James and staged at Southport, of all unlikely places, before running for a respectable seventy nights at a London theatre in 1891. The novel's plot pattern may seem over-simple in its confrontation of the New World's commercial direct assertions on the one hand, and the Old World's aristocratic inbred assumptions on the other, but a reading of *The American* in its first published form (for the revised New York Edition version, almost thirty years later, was so radically rewritten as to become almost another book) shows a confident narrative style fully competent to sweep the reader along.

How Henry James came to find himself in a position to be a fictional spokesman for the contrasting American and French outlooks on life and rules of social behaviour makes an amusing story in its own right. After Henry's first independent European tour in 1869–70, he returned to Massachusetts with his head full of new impressions and enough material for innumerable travel sketches and stories peopled by characters from both sides of the Atlantic. He had also experienced the first deeply affecting bereavement of his life; the early death of his dearly beloved cousin Minny Temple in 1870, that 'young and shining apparition' who lived for only twenty-five years but was to re-emerge in Henry James's memory and in his written work for the rest of his long life.

And then, in 1875–6, he had set out alone to make Paris his base, with what now seems to be an astonishingly inappropriate job: a commission to supply a New York newspaper, the *Tribune*, with regular entertaining news-letters describing Parisian life. Alas, whatever merits the young writer had by then developed, a facility for chatty news snippets was not among them. His employers were wonderfully patient as James's slices of elaborate and brooding observations continued to arrive; but the end could not be long postponed. His essays were not suitable for a New York daily newspaper. When he surrendered the commission, he did so with a Parthian shot that has often been quoted, and that would figure

THE AMERICAN. 173

... to his mother, who is very fond of the old traditions. But you must remember that he speaks for no one but himself."

"Oh, I don't mind him, ..."

"... I know what ... amount to."

"In the good old times," ... "marquises and counts used to have their appointed ... and jesters to crack jokes for them. Nowadays we see a great strapping democrat keeping ... about him to play the fool. It's a good situation, but I certainly am very degenerate."

M. de Bellegarde fixed his eyes for some time on the floor. "My mother ... me," he ... presently, "of the announcement that you made ... her the other evening."

"That I ... marry your sister?"

"That you ... The proposal ... required, on my mother's part, a great deal of ... She naturally took me into her counsels, and ... There was a great deal to be considered; more than you ... We have viewed the question on all its faces, we have weighed one thing against another. Our conclusion has been that we ... My mother has desired me to inform you ... She will have the honour of saying a few words to you on the subject herself. Meanwhile ... heads of the family, ..."

Newman got up and came nearer, ...

"I will recommend my sister to accept you."

Newman passed his hand over his face, and pressed it for a moment upon his eyes. This promise had a great sound, and yet the pleasure he took in it was embittered by his having to sta... there so and receive ...

The American *revised*: 'almost another book'.

again, with remembered disappointment, more than once in his future writing life: 'If my letters have been "too good" I am honestly afraid that they are the poorest I can do, especially for the money.' So, one way and another, the Henry James whose novel *The American* appeared serially in an American magazine in 1876–7 had been professionally vexed by his own countrymen and sufficiently critical of the kind of Paris handed on by his adored mentor Balzac, to allow his earlier rapturous reactions to England and the Continent to be corrected by afterthoughts. Young Henry was now in his thirties—he had seen and felt enough to enable him to set American values against European values, to embody them in representative fictional characters and allow the conflict to work itself out. This kind of maturing process always has a sadness about it: *The American* makes disillusion a subject for theatrical demonstration.

In presenting Christopher Newman as an unconsciously crude discoverer of Europe, James had to make the effort to disguise, while sketching his main figure, his own richness of observation. For example, nothing could be less like James's own travel essays and wonderfully vivid letters than Newman's early report to the American lady who had launched him into European society:

I supposed you knew I was a miserable letter-writer, and didn't expect anything of me. I don't think I have written twenty letters of pure friendship in my whole life; in America I conducted my correspondence altogether by telegrams. This is a letter of pure friendship; you have got hold of a curiosity, and I hope you will value it. You want to know everything that has happened to me these three months . . . I have seen some very pretty things, and shall perhaps talk them over this winter by your fireside. You see, my face is not altogether set against Paris. . .
Do you ever hear from that pretty lady? If you can get her to promise she will be at home the next time I call, I will go back to Paris straight. I am more than ever in the state of mind I told you about that evening; I want a first-class wife. I have kept an eye on all the pretty girls I have come across this summer, but none of them came up to my notion, or anywhere near it. I should have enjoyed all this a thousand times more if I had the lady just mentioned by my side. The nearest approach to her was a Unitarian minister from Boston, who very soon demanded a separation, for incompatibility of temper. He told me I was low-minded, immoral, a devotee of 'art for art'—whatever that is: all of which greatly afflicted me, for he was really a sweet little fellow. But shortly afterwards I met an Englishman, with whom I struck up an acquaintance which at first seemed to promise well—a very bright man, who writes in the London papers and

knows Paris nearly as well as Tristram. We knocked about for a week together, but he very soon gave me up in disgust. I was too virtuous by half; I was too stern a moralist. He told me, in a friendly way, that I was cursed with a conscience; that I judged things like a Methodist, and talked about them like an old lady. This was rather bewildering. Which of my two critics was I to believe? I didn't worry about it, and very soon made up my mind they were both idiots.

(Ch. V)

Tucked away in this naive recital is the germ of the story: Newman wants 'a first-class wife', someone who will complete, and bring to life, his bought collection of strange artefacts and new attitudes. That he should have chosen as his pretty lady the young widowed member of the family of the unbending Marquis de Bellegarde is at once a mark of his ambition, his foolhardiness and his simple optimism.

A similar naiveté is assumed by James the narrator when we are asked to imagine Newman's courtship:

> . . . during the next six weeks he saw Madame de Cintré more times than he could have numbered. He flattered himself that he was not in love, but his biographer may be supposed to know better. He claimed, at least, none of the exemptions and emoluments of the romantic passion. Love, he believed, made a fool of a man, and his present emotion was not folly but wisdom—wisdom sound, serene, well directed. What he felt was an intense all-consuming tenderness, which had for its object an extraordinarily graceful and delicate, and at the same time impressive, woman, who lived in a large gray house on the left bank of the Seine. This tenderness turned very often into a positive heartache; a sign in which, certainly, Newman ought to have read the appellation which science has conferred upon his sentiment. When the heart has a heavy weight upon it, it hardly matters whether the weight be of gold or of lead; when, at any rate, happiness passes into that place in which it becomes identical with pain, a man may admit that the reign of wisdom is temporarily suspended. Newman wished Madame de Cintré so well that nothing he could think of doing for her in the future rose to the high standard which his present mood had set itself. She seemed to him so felicitous a product of nature and circumstance that his invention, musing on future combinations, was constantly catching its breath with the fear of stumbling into some brutal compression or mutilation of her beautiful personal harmony. This is what I mean by Newman's tenderness: Madame de Cintré pleased him so, exactly as she was, that his desire to interpose between her and the troubles of life had the

55

quality of a young mother's eagerness to protect the sleep of her first-born child. Newman was simply charmed, and he handled his charm as if it were a music-box which would stop if one shook it.

(Ch. XIII)

The unreality of their relationship persists, though by the time the Bellegardes are persuaded to allow Newman to 'buy' Claire, the strangely shy young widow, we are persuaded that she and Christopher Newman have developed a hankering for one another which, though far indeed from romantic love, does at least sustain their story until we reach its melodramatic conclusion.

Meanwhile, our closer attention has been reserved for Newman's other acquaintances, especially the friendship which develops between him and Claire's younger brother, the highly sophisticated yet dangerously rootless Valentin de Bellegarde. A somewhat factitious mutual interest is invented for them in the person of a little female copyist, Noémie Nioche, whose routine pictures Newman ignorantly admires, and whose more evident coquettishness involves Valentin in an 'affair of honour', a wholly pointless duel which allows the author the luxury of a moving deathbed scene. We may later recall it as a rehearsal for the even more moving sickroom drama between Ralph Touchett and his cousin Isabel Archer in *The Portrait of a Lady*: and with that parallel in mind we may—as so often in James—note how often in a scene of high emotional force the affection so accurately conveyed seems to have no relevance to the sex of the character, so that while in *The American* the death of Valentin is moving enough to remind us of Henry's cousin Minny Temple, so in the opening pages of *The Portrait of a Lady* the travel yearnings and adolescent longings of Isabel Archer may be traced to Minny or to the young Harry James himself. However moving in itself, the record of the last moments of Valentin's thrown-away life reveals to Newman the guilty secret of the Bellegarde family, thus placing in his hands the ultimate means of revenge or forgiveness.

The trivial origin of the fatal duel had been told with witty asides in the opera-house where Christopher Newman and Valentin met just after the young Vicomte had challenged little Noémie's 'jealous votary . . . a tall robust young man with a thick nose, a prominent blue eye, a Germanic physiognomy, and a massive watch chain':

'She is immensely tickled,' he said. 'She says we will make her fortune. I don't want to be fatuous, but I think it is very possible.'

'So you are going to fight?' said Newman.

'My dear fellow, don't look so mortally disgusted. It was not my own choice. The thing is all arranged.'

'I told you so!' groaned Newman.

'I told *him* so,' said Valentin, smiling.

'What did he do to you?'

'My good friend, it doesn't matter what. He used an expression—I took it up.'

'But I insist upon knowing; I can't, as your elder brother, have you rushing into this sort of nonsense.'

'I am very much obliged to you,' said Valentin. 'I have nothing to conceal, but I can't go into particulars now and here.'

'We will leave this place, then. You can tell me outside.'

'Oh no, I can't leave this place; why should I hurry away? I will go to my orchestra stall and sit out the opera.'

'You will not enjoy it; you will be preoccupied.'

Valentin looked at him a moment, coloured a little, smiled, and patted him on the arm. 'You are delightfully simple! Before an affair a man is quiet. The quietest thing I can do is to go straight to my place.'

(Ch. XVII)

How different in tone is the sequel:

Newman went back to Valentin's room, which he found lighted by a taper on the hearth. Valentin begged him to light a candle. 'I want to see your face,' he said. 'They say you excite me,' he went on, as Newman complied with this request, 'and I confess I do feel excited; but it isn't you—it's my own thoughts. I have been thinking—thinking. Sit down there and let me look at you again.'. . .

'They have stopped it,' said Newman. Now that he had spoken out, he found a satisfaction in it which deepened as he went on. 'Your mother and brother have broken faith. They have decided that it can't take place. They have decided that I am not good enough, after all. They have taken back their word. Since you insist, there it is!'

Valentin gave a sort of groan, lifted his hands a moment, and then let them drop.

'I am sorry not to have anything better to tell you about them,' Newman pursued. 'But it's not my fault. I was, indeed, very unhappy when your telegram reached me; I was quite upside down. You may imagine whether I feel any better now.'

Valentin moaned gaspingly, as if his wound were throbbing. 'Broken faith, broken faith!' he murmured. 'And my sister—my sister?'

'Your sister is very unhappy; she has consented to give me up. I don't know why. I don't know what they have done to her; it must be something pretty bad. In justice to her you ought to know it. They have made her suffer. I haven't seen her alone, but only before them! We had an interview yesterday morning. They came out flat, in so many words. They told me to go about my business. It seems to me a very bad case. I'm angry, I'm sore, I'm sick.'

Valentin lay there staring, with his eyes more brilliantly lighted, his lips soundlessly parted, and a flush of colour in his pale face. Newman had never before uttered so many words in the plaintive key, but now, in speaking to Valentin in the poor fellow's extremity, he had a feeling that he was making his complaint somewhere within the presence of the power that men pray to in trouble; he felt his out-gush of resentment as a sort of spiritual privilege.

'And Claire', said Bellegarde, 'Claire? She has given you up?'

'I don't really believe it,' said Newman.

'No, don't believe it, don't believe it. She is gaining time; excuse her.'

'I pity her!' said Newman.

'Poor Claire!' murmured Valentin. 'But they—but they'—and he paused again. 'You saw them; they dismissed you, face to face?'

'Face to face. They were very explicit.'

'What did they say?'

'They said they couldn't stand a commercial person.'

(Ch. XIX)

For the sake of the plot, the scene must end with a scarcely credible revelation:

For some time, however, the dying man said nothing more. He only lay and looked at his friend with his kindled, expanded, troubled eye, and Newman began to believe that he had spoken in delirium. But at last he said:

'There was something done—something done at Fleurières. It was foul play. My father—something happened to him. I don't know; I have been ashamed—afraid to know. But I know there is something. My mother knows—Urbain knows.'

'Something happened to your father?' said Newman, urgently.

Valentin looked at him, still more wide-eyed . 'He didn't get well.'

'Get well of what?'

But the immense effort which Valentin had made, first to decide to utter these words, and then to bring them out, appeared to have taken his last strength. He lapsed again into silence, and Newman sat watching him. 'Do you understand?' he began again presently. 'At Fleurières. You can find out. Mrs Bread knows. Tell her I begged you to ask her. Then tell them that, and see. It may help you. If not, tell every one. It will—it will'—here Valentin's voice sank to the feeblest murmur—'it will avenge you!'

(Ch. XIX)

Between these quoted dialogues, of course, the crux of the novel had occurred. The old dowager Marquise and her stolid elder son had reneged on the acceptance of Newman as a suitor for Claire, and the too-easily manipulated widow had been spirited away to a convent. Somehow the death of Valentin is more memorable, more painful, than the effective obliteration of Claire. The reader is scarcely concerned with Newman's loss of the unlikely lady who had come to embody his desire to corner a wife as he had previously cornered some financially attractive commodity: 'I want to do the thing in handsome style. . . I want to make a great hit. I want to possess, in a word, the best article on the market.' Our remaining interest is in how he will even up the score with the noble but disingenuous Bellegardes.

A twenty-page chapter (XXII) of highly competent Victorian narrative and dialogue between Newman and Mrs Bread, the disaffected Bellegarde housekeeper, puts us in possession of the family secret: the old Marquis had opposed the marriage of his daughter to the odious nobleman de Cintré, but his wife and heir had been so determined on the alliance that when the old man was struggling for life, his wife had denied him his prescribed medicine and so, by negative means, murdered him –but not before the suspicious Mrs Bread had revived him for long enough for him to scribble a dying condemnation:

> My wife has tried to kill me, and she has done it: I am dying horribly. It is to marry my dear daughter to M. de Cintré. With all my soul I protest—I forbid it. I am not insane—ask the doctors, ask Mrs B—. It was alone with me here, to-night; she attacked me and put me to death. It is murder, if murder ever was. Ask the doctors.
>
> HENRI-URBAIN DE BELLEGARDE.

(Ch. XXII)

With this paper in his possession, Newman had his power of black-mail. How would he use it?

Strangely enough, in the novel he magnanimously destroys the evidence—and loses Claire; in the later dramatized version, he reveals the evidence and allows it (and his vengeance) to be destroyed, after claiming Claire from confinement in her convent. Either way, with a noble wife or without a noble wife, Newman has his moral triumph. The brash confident American who had been humiliated by Europeans would himself humiliate his humiliators by forgiving them, by withholding his power to demolish them. It sounds like the solution of a dream-like reverie. The Western materialist who had striven to conquer by means of marriage (a strangely Old World dynastic aim for a Californian profiteer?) is shown at the end of this international parable to demonstrate a finer moral tone than the Parisian inheritors and protectors of established 'consideration'. Up to this point, he had attempted to conquer (without ever understanding or appreciating) European 'culture'. The new man who had been introduced as a character with 'an eye in which innocence and experience were singularly blended', who had sought the more or less anonymous Claire as the crown jewel of his Europe-raiding booty, had finally shown them all that the cowboy was superior in fine sensibility, as well as in wealth. It was a serial story which the subscribers to the *Atlantic Monthly*, for twelve months of 1876–7, could read with patriotic relish.

The Europeans

Because of its balancing title and its appearance so soon after *The American*, it might be expected that the short novel *The Europeans* (named 'A Sketch' by the author, and not revised by him for inclusion in the New York Edition thirty years later) would be a complementary account of the struggles of a group of Old World representatives trying to come to grips with a hostile reception in the New World. But there the likeness stops. In place of the uncompromisingly foreign and modern Newman, we are treated to the spectacle of a brace of native-born Americans who have been living the 'high life' or 'artistic life' in Europe for long enough to have absorbed its cultural assumptions, and who give themselves the amusing experience of returning to visit, for a spell, their stay-at-home New England cousins. What follows is not a sharply contested fight to the death like that of Newman and the Bellegardes, but rather a basically good-natured treatment of slowly melting incomprehensions as the cousins, so unlike in their daily habits and expectations, come to enjoy a kind of mutual respect. There is plenty of light-hearted satire of the grim rigidity of New England life—but it is written by a writer born in New York and brought up in New England, so there is an affectionate understanding behind the light scorn. Although the contrasting trans-Atlantic parties find it quite difficult to forge any permanent links as they stretch out tentative hands to touch and caress, they can at least 'agree to differ' without anything in the nature of permanently wounding heartbreak. There are no duels or convent walls or skeletons in the family cupboard. The rooted Americans and their expatriate kin may be ready at some moments to part more in sorrow than in anger, and at other moments to decide to 'make a go of it'. Either way, they end up 'wiser' rather than 'sadder'.

The contrasting characters, for so short a novel, are plentiful, variegated and so unlike in their trans-Atlantic habits as to be, at first meeting, almost caricatures. To his young nephew Felix Young, the wandering bohemian who has been at home with actors and musicians in Europe and now hopes to earn his way in America by the only slightly less respectable trade of portrait-painting, old Mr Wentworth appears 'a tremendously high-toned old fellow; he looks as if he were undergoing martyrdom, not by fire, but by freezing'. Felix's sister Eugenia is even more misplaced in New England: she is no less a personage than the morganatic wife of a German princeling, glorying in the courtesy title of Baroness Münster. What devastation will *she* wreak in the Wentworth household? In the end, very little. Not only does she withdraw from the possibility of renouncing her German rights in favour of yet another rich kinsman, Robert Acton, but she cannot even influence the young Wentworth son, Clifford, to stray far from the strait and narrow path leading him to Acton's sister Lizzie. As for Wentworth's daughters, Charlotte and Gertrude, they at first seem indistinguishable to jolly feckless Felix: 'They are sober; they are even severe. They are of a pensive cast; they take things hard. I think there is something the matter with them; they have some melancholy memory or some depressing expectation. It's not the Epicurean temperament.' No, indeed. And although Gertrude will in fact marry Felix, and Charlotte content herself with a local young Unitarian minister, one somehow feels that their sisterly likeness will outlive the markedly contrasted natures of their husbands.

In short, the whole affair reads like a gentle charade. There is an understated kinship which forbids too sharp a sense of distaste on the part of the puritan stay-at-homes, or too easy a readiness to write them off as a bunch of bores on the part of their romantic exotic visitors. This surprising tolerance of opposites is occasionally quite explicitly stressed by the young novelist who is now beginning to feel himself at home on either side of the Atlantic; even the frozen Mr Wentworth could be made to melt:

It appeared to him that he could get much nearer, as he would have said, to his nephew; though he was not sure that Felix was altogether safe. He was so bright and handsome and talkative that it was impossible not to think well of him; and yet it seemed as if there were something almost impudent, almost vicious—or as if there ought to be—in a young man being at once so joyous and so positive. It was to be observed that while Felix was not at all a serious young man there was somehow more of him—he had more weight and volume and resonance—than a number of young men who were distinctly serious. While Mr Wentworth meditated upon this anomaly his nephew was admiring him unrestrictedly. He thought him a most delicate, generous, high-toned old gentleman, with a very handsome head, of the ascetic type, which he promised himself the profit of sketching. Felix was far from having made a secret of the fact that he wielded the paint-brush, and it was not his own fault if it failed to be generally understood that he was prepared to execute the most striking likenesses on the most reasonable terms. 'He is an artist—my cousin is an artist,' said Gertrude; and she offered this information to every, one who would receive it. She offered it to herself, as it were, by way of admonition and reminder; she repeated to herself at odd moments, in lonely places, that Felix was invested with this sacred character. Gertrude had never seen an artist before; she had only read about such people.

(Ch. V)

For modern readers who can take the Atlantic in their stride more readily than readers of the 1870s, a story like *The Europeans* may be valued for its deft lightness of touch and for its flowing passages of accomplished dialogue of the comedy of manners (see 'Illustrative passages', pp. 149–50). This quality has endured longer than the more dramatic clash of cultures celebrated in the dramatic passages of *The American*. When, for example, Felix is asking for Charlotte's help in his surprising project of marriage to her sister Gertrude, the subtle interplay of affectionate yet reticent confessions on both sides has become a point in the relationship between two interesting *people*, rather than between an American girl and a Europeanized man:

> Charlotte sat mutely staring at the floor, and Felix presently added, 'Do go on with your slipper. I like to see you work.'
>
> Charlotte took up her variegated canvas, and began to draw vague blue stitches in a big round rose. 'If Gertrude is so—so strange,' she said, 'why do you want to marry her?'
>
> 'Ah, that's it, dear Charlotte! I like strange women; I always have liked them. Ask Eugenia! And Gertrude is wonderful; she says the most beautiful things!'
>
> Charlotte looked at him, almost for the first time, as if her meaning required to be severely pointed. 'You have a great influence over her.'
>
> 'Yes—and no!' said Felix. 'I had at first, I think; but now it is six of one and half a dozen of the other; it is reciprocal. She affects me strongly—for she *is* so strong. I don't believe you know her; it's a beautiful nature.'
>
> 'Oh yes, Felix; I have always thought Gertrude's nature beautiful.'
>
> 'Well, if you think so now,' cried the young man, 'wait and

see! She's a folded flower. Let me pluck her from the parent tree and you will see her expand. I'm sure you will enjoy it.'

'I don't understand you,' murmured Charlotte. 'I *can't*, Felix.'

'Well, you can understand this—that I beg you to say a good word for me to your father. He regards me, I naturally believe, as a very light fellow, a Bohemian, an irregular character. Tell him I am not all this; if I ever was, I have forgotten it. I am fond of pleasure—yes; but of innocent pleasure. Pain is all one; but in pleasure, you know, there are tremendous distinctions. Say to him that Gertrude is a folded flower and that I am a serious man!'

Charlotte got up from her chair, slowly rolling up her work. 'We know you are very kind to every one, Felix,' she said. 'But we are extremely sorry for Mr Brand.'

'Of course you are—you especially! Because,' added Felix hastily, 'you are a woman. But I don't pity him. It ought to be enough for any man that you take an interest in him.'

'It is not enough for Mr Brand,' said Charlotte simply. And she stood there a moment, as if waiting conscientiously for anything more than Felix might have to say.

'Mr Brand is not so keen about his marriage as he was,' he presently said. 'He is afraid of your sister. He begins to think she is wicked.'

Charlotte looked at him now with beautiful appealing eyes—eyes into which he saw the tears rising. 'Oh, Felix, Felix!' she cried, 'what have you done to her?'

'I think she was asleep; I have waked her up!'

But Charlotte, apparently, was really crying; she walked straight out of the room. And Felix, standing there and meditating, had the apparent brutality to take satisfaction in her tears.

(Ch. XI)

In the final chapter, when Mr Wentworth consents to the unforeseen match (and Charlotte herself picks up the Rev. Mr Brand), it is the rightness of touch shown by Gertrude in her assessment of Brand's psychology that quite clearly absorbs our attention more than the now taken-for-granted international marriage:

'Father,' repeated Charlotte, '*consent*.'

Then at last Mr Brand looked at her. Her father felt her leaning more heavily upon his folded arm than she had ever done before; and this, with a certain sweet faintness in her voice, made him wonder what was the matter. He looked down at her and saw the encounter of her gaze with the young theologian's; but even this told him nothing, and he continued to be bewildered. Nevertheless, 'I consent,' he said at last, 'since Mr Brand recommends it.'

'I should like to perform the ceremony very soon,' observed Mr Brand, with a sort of solemn simplicity.

'Come, come, that's charming!' cried Felix, profanely.

Mr Wentworth sank into his chair. 'Doubtless, when you understand it,' he said, with a certain judicial asperity.

Gertrude went to her sister and led her away, and Felix having passed his arm into Mr Brand's and stepped out of the long window with him, the old man was left sitting there in un-illumined perplexity.

Felix did no work that day. In the afternoon, with Gertrude, he got into one of the boats, and floated about with idly-dipping oars. They talked a good deal of Mr Brand—though not exclusively.

'That was a fine stroke,' said Felix. 'It was really heroic.'

Gertrude sat musing, with her eyes upon the ripples. 'That was what he wanted to be; he wanted to do something fine.'

'He won't be comfortable till he has married us,' said Felix. 'So much the better.'

'He wanted to be magnanimous; he wanted to have a fine moral pleasure. I know him so well,' Gertrude went on. Felix looked at her; she spoke slowly, gazing at the clear water. 'He thought of it a great deal, night and day. He thought it would be beautiful. At last he made up his mind that it was his duty, his duty to do just that—nothing less than that. He felt exalted; he felt sublime. That's how he likes to feel. It is better for him than if I had listened to him.'

(Ch. XII)

It is at such moments in the 'international' novels and tales that one feels the superiority of Henry James the novelist over Henry James the sociologist of international cultures. The 'international' interest is itself undeniable, as Philip Grover points out in his comment on James's story 'A London Life' (1888) (in *Henry James and the French Novel*). The treatment of a Balzacian theme of the contrast between provincial and metropolitan morals and manners is made more striking because in this case the 'provincial' United States and the 'metropolitan' London are separated by national frontiers and a great ocean. 'Therefore', writes Dr Grover, 'although James could later say in his preface that there was no reason why Laura Wing and Wendover had to be Americans, in the actual composition of this story he had been well aware of the structural uses he could make of their nationality for the purposes of anti-thesis.' True enough. But in selecting such examples as *The Europeans* and 'A London Life', we admit that a purely thematic antithesis of American and trans-Atlantic social habits would fail to involve the reader unless the chief characters, as in these cases, had already captured his attention at psychological levels far deeper than those explicable in terms of national variants in social conventions. As Dr Johnson remarked in his 'Preface to Shakespeare': 'His story requires Romans or Kings, but he thinks only on men.' And to make a point which may be closely applied to the best of James's international stories, Johnson clinches the matter thus: 'a poet overlooks the casual distinction of country and condition, as a painter, satisfied with the figure, neglects the drapery'.

It remains, for our present purpose, to select a few of the dozen or so 'international' stories James wrote in the late 1870s and early 1880s, while his 'thematic doom' was uppermost in his mind while he began to settle down (see 'Chronological table') on the European side of the Atlantic. The young Henry James who has been seen earlier, in 'passionate pilgrim' mood, 'reeling and moaning' through the storied streets of Rome was the same man who, at this time of a major group of international tales, had announced in his critical study of Nathaniel Hawthorne (1879) that 'the flower of art blooms only where the soil is deep, that it takes a great deal of history to produce a little literature, that it needs a complex social history to set a writer in motion'. Already something of the fresh propagandist enthusiasm of a story like 'A Passionate Pilgrim' (1871) had been mildly moderated by the young writer's perception that 'the England of my visions', beneath whose 'acres of rain-deepened greenness a thousand honoured dead lay buried', could also shelter the not so honoured living who had added precious little to their heritage. Much, much later, when returning to his native New York in his sixties, he would discover that even that shallower soil of America he had effectively spurned in his Hawthorne biography could itself sprout a late growth of colourful pretentious weeds such as clustered around a fashionable hostess in his disillusioned story 'Crapy Cornelia' (1909), whose smile could

> twinkle not only with the gleam of her lovely teeth, but with that of all her rings and brooches and bangles and other gew-gaws, to curl and spasmodically cluster as in emulation of her charming complicated yellow tresses, to surround the most animated of pink-and-white, of ruffled and ribboned, of frilled and festooned Dresden china shepherdesses with exactly the right system of curves and convolutions and other flourishes, a perfect bower of painted and gilded and moulded conceits.

The social criticism in the selective group of tales now to be considered is much less savage; but it is there, and it gives liveliness and bite to what might otherwise have been too schematic a balancing of superficial international characteristics.

'Daisy Miller'

Pride of place in this brief selection must be given to 'Daisy Miller' (1878), a simple little story which was an instant topic of comment and debate immediately after its publication in the *Cornhill* magazine, and became over the years probably the most popular of all James's productions. In the month of its publication, Henry wrote to brother William: 'I am very glad indeed that you were pleased with "Daisy Miller", who appears (*literally*) to have made a great hit here. "Every one is talking about it" etc., and it has been much noticed in the papers.' Indeed, to quote another letter, if his Daisy had 'been, in fact, so harshly treated by fate and public opinion, she has had it made up to her in posthumous honours'. To a modern reader of this witty little period piece with nothing in the way of a plot and merely an unexpected purely accidental sad ending, it is very difficult to see what all the fuss was about.

Daisy Miller is simply a bright, uncomplicated, friendly young American girl who finds herself trailing after her stolid mother on a European tour, when she would much prefer to be back at home in Schenectady, N.Y., with her easy-going boy-friends. Henry James must have observed dozens of well-dressed, laughing, attractive and inexperienced American Daisies during his own quite staid ramblings in France and Switzerland and Italy. Indeed, the chief male character in the story, the very proper post-graduate student Winterbourne who runs across Daisy and her mother and brother at a Swiss resort, reacts to her much as we might have expected young Henry James to have done. Winterbourne is amused by her freshness, her insouciance, her carelessness about prim European insistence on chaperones and the like. He himself is quite happy to accompany her on an unchaperoned sight-seeing trip to the local castle. He had quickly 'thought it very possible that Master Randolph's sister was a coquette; he was sure she had a spirit of her own, but in her bright, sweet, superficial little visage there was no mockery, no irony'. This being so, it was perhaps imperceptive for the young gentleman to shake off as teasing raillery her repeated indications that she wished to see more of him. In Schenectady and New York, 'I have always had', she said, 'a great deal of gentlemen's society.' Winterbourne was simply 'inclined to think Miss Daisy Miller was a flirt—a pretty American flirt'. They would meet again in Rome, where Winterbourne (as one might expect) would be visiting an aunt, and the homesick Miller trio bravely pursuing their European tour.

Whatever may have been the standards of social life in Schenectady, the social rules of the ladies of the American colony in Rome were most severe. Miss Miller's tendency to stroll about sight-seeing either alone or—even worse—in company with a young Italian escort becomes the main delicious talking point of the officially horrified American matrons. It is worth noticing that at no time, in Switzerland or in Rome, does any native European comment on Daisy's behaviour: she is judged and condemned by her own expatriate countrywomen. Perhaps this is one reason for the endless debate about Daisy's 'problem' among Anglo-Saxon readers? Jealous disapproval from the American ladies, friendly timid disapproval from the hovering Winterbourne, a negligent tolerance from her vulgarian mother, but daily faithful adoring attendance from her captivated *cavaliere* Giovanelli—Daisy flits lightly within these circling opinions, not by any means ignorant of them, but quite sure of her own rectitude and determined to play out her own part as a young unhampered American girl. Still no 'plot'!

No plot, but a likeable character emerging mainly from her effect on other people. 'She goes on from day to day, from hour to hour, as they did in the Golden Age', says Winterbourne's aunt, adding: 'I can imagine nothing more vulgar.' Vulgarity, indeed, is what they were all imagining. For Winterbourne, 'it was painful to hear so much that was pretty and undefended and natural assigned to a vulgar place among the categories of disorder'. It is difficult to find anything to admire in this potential husband for Daisy who was so studiously aware of her merits and so loath to share them:

Winterbourne wondered how she felt about all the cold shoulders that were turned towards her, and sometimes it annoyed him to suspect that she was too light and childish, too uncultivated and unreasoning, too provincial, to have reflected upon her ostracism, or even to have perceived it. Then at other moments he believed that she carried about in her elegant and irresponsible little organism a defiant, passionate, perfectly observant consciousness of the impression she produced. He asked himself whether Daisy's defiance came from the consciousness of innocence or from her being, essentially, a young person of the reckless class. It must be admitted that holding oneself to a belief in Daisy's 'innocence' came to seem to Winterbourne more and more a matter of fine-spun gallantry. As I have already had occasion to relate, he was angry at finding himself reduced to chopping logic about this young lady; he was vexed at his want of instinctive certitude as to how far her eccentricities were generic, national, and how far they were personal. From either view of them he had somehow missed her, and now it was too late. She was 'carried away' by Mr Giovanelli.

(Ch. IV)

Daisy had *not*, of course, been 'carried away' by her Italian admirer. She had failed to be carried away by Winterbourne himself; she would suddenly, and with dreadfully fascinated publicity, expose herself to be carried away by nothing more romantic than 'the Roman fever'.

As *deus ex machina*, the malarial infections of the 'villainous miasma' of the Colosseum at midnight bring a sudden end to it all. Winterbourne, fretful, wanders there by moonlight and, in the one melodramatic moment in so subtly developed a situation, finds Daisy and her Italian escort already there, together, 'at the great cross in the centre'. There are strained words, and as usual Winterbourne retreats ambiguously:

> They passed under one of the dark archways: Giovannelli was in front with the carriage. Here Daisy stopped a moment, looking at the young American. '*Did* you believe I was engaged the other day?' she asked.
>
> 'It doesn't matter what I believed the other day,' said Winterbourne, still laughing.
>
> 'Well, what do you believe now?'
>
> 'I believe that it makes very little difference whether you are engaged or not!'
>
> He felt the young girl's pretty eyes fixed upon him through the thick gloom of the archway; she was apparently going to answer. But Giovanelli hurried her forward. 'Quick, quick,' he said; 'if we get in by midnight we are quite safe.'
>
> (Ch. IV)

A paragraph or two, and Daisy is dead. 'It's going round at night', says young brother Randolph, 'that's what made her sick. She's always going round at night.' From Daisy's mother Winterbourne learns that 'she was never engaged to that handsome Italian ... she told me to ask if you remembered the time you went to that castle, in Switzerland'. We twitch with the remembrance that Daisy's innocent visit to Chillon with Winterbourne was precisely as innocent as her visit to the Colosseum with Giovanelli. But it was the Italian, not the American, who spoke these words at her graveside: 'She was the most beautiful young lady I ever saw, and the most amiable ... And she was the most innocent.'

So Daisy died. Nobody killed her. She transgressed the social rules of people for whom she had no respect or regard. She was not the deliberate victim of gossip but the accidental victim of 'bad air'—which, like a bad reputation, she underestimated. In his Preface, thirty years later, to the volume of the New York Edition containing this story, James harks back to the days when some American readers considered it 'an outrage on American girlhood'. He protests 'that my supposedly typical little figure was of course pure poetry, and had never been anything else; since this is what helpful imagination, in however slight a dose, ever directly makes for'. He had patiently set down Daisy's plight in a letter of 1880, written to an American bluestocking who had written to ask whether his heroine had been 'obstinate and defying, or superficial and careless':

> The whole idea of the story is the little tragedy of a light, thin, natural, unsuspecting creature being sacrificed as it were to a social rumpus that went on quite over her head and to which she stood in no measurable relation. To deepen the effect, I have made it go over her mother's head as well. She never had a thought of scandalising anybody—the most she ever had was a regret for Winterbourne.

'An International Episode'

If we modern readers find all this pother mystifying, we must remember the validity of certain social assumptions of more than a century ago which nowadays strike one as outmoded if not positively discordant. James's '*pendant* or counterpart' to Daisy and her mistakes was the more plausible story of how an American girl, as fresh as Daisy but far less naive, was able to keep at bay and rise above the suspicious snobbery of a whole ducal family, in 'An International Episode' (1878). It is by no means a simple tit-for-tat reversal of the Daisy situation, for no tragedy hovers over the elegant social comedy which treats of the charming welcome a couple of aristocratic Englishmen received in New York and Newport, and the decidedly unwelcoming attitude of their English female relations when the Americans are foolhardy enough to return the visit.

The light elegance of this story shows James, now in his mid-thirties, at his confident best in the ability to make use of his own travel observations and endow his characters with vivid personal life. When young Lord Lambeth, heir to the dukedom of Bays-water, finds himself in New York with his young kinsman Percy Beaumont, their first sight of the city and its strange inhabitants is sheer comedy, with Henry James transferring to his young adventurers his own oft-expressed disdain for the American hotel-lounges of his day:

> The ground-floor of the hotel seemed to be a huge transparent cage, flinging a wide glare of gaslight into the street, of which it formed a sort of public adjunct, absorbing and emitting the passers-by promiscuously. The young Englishmen went in with every one else, from curiosity, and saw a couple of hundred men sitting on divans along a great marble-paved corridor, with their legs stretched out, together with several dozen more standing in a *queue*, as at the ticket-office of a railway station, before a

brilliantly-illuminated counter, of vast extent. These latter persons, who carried portmanteaux in their hands, had a dejected, exhausted look; their garments were not very fresh, and they seemed to be rendering some mysterious tribute to a magnificent young man with a waxed moustache and a shirt front adorned with diamond buttons, who every now and then dropped an absent glance over their multitudinous patience. They were American citizens doing homage to an hotel-clerk.

(Ch. I)

By the kindness of an American business man they are whisked away from the stifling New York of August to the seaside delights of Newport where they readily accept the hospitality of their new friend's wife, and the amused and amusing company of her younger sister and her friends. The change of scene is economically represented by

> . . . images of brilliant mornings on lawns and piazzas that over-looked the sea; of innumerable pretty girls; of infinite lounging and talking and laughing and flirting and lunching and dining; of universal friendliness and frankness; of occasions on which they knew every one and everything and had an extraordinary sense of ease; of drives and rides in the late afternoon, over gleaming beaches, on long sea-roads, beneath a sky lighted up by marvellous sunsets; of tea-tables, on the return, informal, irregular, agreeable; of evenings at open windows or on the perpetual verandahs, in the summer starlight, above the warm Atlantic.

(Ch. III)

Their younger co-hostess, Bessie Alden, had been educated at Boston—in which city, according to her brother-in-law, 'you have to pass an examination at the city limits; and when you come away they give you a kind of degree'. When Bessie has plied Beaumont with questions about his cousin's title and responsibilities, she wishes to invest the unscholarly modest young aristocrat with the qualities such people had possessed in the English novels she had read. In her educated Boston way she is as direct as Daisy from Schenectady:

> 'Lord Lambeth,' said Bessie Alden, 'are you an hereditary legislator?'
> 'Oh, I say,' cried Lord Lambeth, 'don't make me call myself such names as that.'
> 'But you are a member of Parliament,' said the young girl.

Newport, Rhode Island ('An International Episode') – but it could as well be Rotten Row, London ('The Lady Barberina').

71

'I don't like the sound of that either.'

'Doesn't your father sit in the House of Lords?' Bessie Alden went on.

'Very seldom,' said Lord Lambeth.

'Is it an important position?' she asked.

'Oh dear no,' said Lord Lambeth.

'I should think it would be very grand,' said Bessie Alden, 'to possess simply by an accident of birth the right to make laws for a great nation.'

'Ah, but one doesn't make laws. It's a great humbug.'

'I don't believe that,' the young girl declared. 'It must be a great privilege, and I should think that if one thought of it in the right way—from a high point of view—it would be very inspiring.'

'The less one thinks of it the better,' Lord Lambeth affirmed.
(Ch. III)

Such innocent inquisitions were misinterpreted by Beaumont, who communicated his doubts to Lambeth's mother, who immediately recalled him (by means of a bogus telegram) to London.

The second side of the diptych is presented as lightly and freshly as the first. The May London of Hyde Park and Rotten Row, 'the famous avenue whose humours had been made familiar to the young girl's childhood by the pictures in *Punch*', is as charming to Bessie and her sister Mrs Westgate as Newport had been to the British visitors. The difference is that the American ladies are not rescued from *their* hotel. After they have stumbled upon Lambeth and Beaumont almost by accident, the young men certainly call upon them—but only after a long very audible silence do the Duchess and her married daughter call to quiz them, on the brink of their planned visit to the Marquis of Lambeth at his own subsidiary Castle. Bessie has received from her married sister just the sort of warnings delivered to Daisy Miller in Rome: '"Remember", she said, "that you are not in your innocent little Boston . . ."'. Then she went on to explain that there were two classes of American girls in Europe—those that walked about alone and those that did not. '"You happen to belong, my dear," she said to her sister, "to the class that does not."' There had been little need for such a lecture. After all the entertainment they had offered their English guests at Newport, what had *they* to confess to his lordship?

'No one has sent us cards.' said Bessie.

'We are very quiet,' her sister declared. 'We are here as travellers.'

'We have been to Madame Tussaud's,' Bessie pursued.

'Oh, I say!' cried Lord Lambeth.

'We thought we should find your image there,' said Mrs Westgate—'yours and Mr Beaumont's.'

'In the Chamber of Horrors?' laughed the young man.

'It did duty very well for a party,' said Mrs Westgate. 'All the women were *décolletées*, and many of the figures looked as if they could speak if they tried.'

(Ch. IV)

Like 'Daisy Miller', this story hurries to what the reader expects to be a logical (and in this case, happy) ending—but instead, it just stops. Just as Giovanelli, whose escorting of Daisy caused such scandal, was the one to pronounce her 'innocent', so it is Lord Lambeth himself who declares of Bessie Alden: 'She's not afraid, and she says things out, and she thinks herself as good as any one. She is the only girl I have ever seen that was not dying to marry me.' In both stories, the American girl surprises her censorious countrywomen by being quite above their suspicions. In both stories, the possible hero-figures fail to capture the prize, Winterbourne because he was a young fogey, and Lambeth because the literate girl, with her Boston-bred notions of political responsibilities, found him, the future Duke, deficient in *noblesse oblige*.

'The Pension Beaurepas'

In none of James's 'international' tales is his treatment of Americans abroad more woundingly severe than in 'The Pension Beaurepas' (1879), where all the important characters are themselves Americans abroad: the satire is not from a European point of view at all, it is simply one James-like American observing with different kinds of distaste his own countrymen and countrywomen abroad. Nobody is betrayed, nobody falls foul of misunderstood signals from an alien culture. We are allowed merely to watch how the differently interpreted sense of 'liberty', brought about by residence abroad, may exaggerate and somehow force from pathos into near-tragedy the entirely different temperamental flaws of two small wandering American families. In their case the *pension* life of lakeside Geneva acts as a forcing-house for qualities already lodged within them before they crossed the Atlantic. Nothing violent 'happens' in this quiet piece of observation of contrasted American expatriate types; but there is a violence of disgust, of outraged compassion, lying just beneath the surface of the limpid narrative prose and the light assured dialogue. Quiet though it is, the tale exposes a loathing for crude acquisitiveness on the one hand and cultural snobbery on the other, together with pity for the victims of both sets of false values.

To the *pension* of the neutral recorder come two American families. The Rucks—father, mother and daughter—are comparatively fresh to the delights of travel; the Churches—mother and daughter—are irremediably steeped in the staler experiences of the European ethos. Both little groups are pathetically inadequate to respond naturally to their good fortune. After watching the Ruck trio, the narrator explains:

> Mr Ruck is a broken-down man of business. He is broken-down in health, and I suspect he is broken down in fortune. He has spent his whole life in buying and selling; he knows how to do nothing else. His wife and daughter have spent their lives, not in selling, but in buying; and they, on their side, know how to do nothing else. To get something in a shop that they can put on their backs—that is their one idea; they haven't another in their heads. Of course they spend no end of money, and they do it with an implacable persistence, with a mixture of audacity and of cunning. They do it in his teeth and they do it behind his back; the mother protects the daughter, and the daughter eggs on the mother. Between them they are bleeding him to death.
>
> (Ch. VIII)

For James the author, such people as the Rucks were by this time sitting birds. Mother and daughter are vulgarian spendthrifts, and happy in their joint lack of interest in any products of European culture outside the shop-loads of dresses, lace and jewellery: it is usually inside such Geneva stores that we meet them. Father Ruck may be described as a soft-headed business man; he does nothing to curb the selfish extravagance of his ladies, while moaning each day as news from New York signifies his steady collapse into bankruptcy.

The full savagery of James's observant irony is reserved not for the obviously inadequate Rucks, but for new arrivals at the *pension*, the self-satisfied Mrs Church and her pathetic daughter Aurora. Madame Beaurepas herself is well aware that Mrs Church's elegant pretensions have their seamy side:

> 'Two *Américaines*—a mother and a daughter. There are Americans and Americans: when you are *difficiles*, you are more so than any one, and when you have pretensions—ah, *par exemple*, it's serious. I foresee that with this little lady everything will be serious, beginning with her *café au lait*. She has been staying at the Pension Chamousset—my *concurrent*, you know, farther up the street; but she is coming away because the coffee is bad. She holds to her coffee, it appears. I don't know what liquid Madame Chamousset may have invented, but we will do the best we can for her. Only, I know she will make me *des histoires* about some-

thing else. She will demand a new lamp for the salon; *vous allez voir cela*. She wishes to pay but eleven francs a day for herself and her daughter, *tout compris*; and for their eleven francs they expect to be lodged like princesses. But she is very "ladylike"—isn't that what you call it in English? Oh, *pour cela*, she is ladylike!'

(Ch. IV)

This lady's absurdly inflated notions might have gained from James and his readers the compassionate pity he would bestow, for example, upon such another self-deluded misfit as Mrs Tarrant of *The Bostonians*. But it is Mrs Church's more intelligent daughter who claims our compassion, for the brutal damage done to her young claims on life by her mother's falsities and petty snobbery. So callously indifferent is this self-styled sensitive lady to the misery she is wreaking on her daughter, that she boasts of her own prowess as an educator, in passages which show the quality of Henry James's disdainful irony—not simply as a narrator, but also as a listener: for the young author must have observed, on his own patient, absorbing and modestly enriching European travels, many a Mrs Church:

'Always at your studies, Mrs Church,' I ventured to observe.

'Que voulez-vouz? To say studies is to say too much; one doesn't study in the parlour of a boarding-house. But I do what I can; I have always done what I can. That is all I have ever claimed.'

'No one can do more, and you seem to have done a great deal.'

'Do you know my secret?' she asked, with an air of brightening confidence. And she paused a moment before she imparted her secret—'To care only for the *best*! To do the best, to know the best—to have, to desire, to recognise, only the best. That's what I have always done, in my quiet little way. I have gone through Europe on my devoted little errand, seeking, seeing, heeding, only the best. And it has not been for myself alone; it has been for my daughter. My daughter has had the best. We are not rich, but I can say that.'

'She has had you, madam.' I rejoined finely.

'Certainly, such as I am, I have been devoted. We have got something everywhere; a little here, a little there. That's the real secret—to get something everywhere; you always can if you *are* devoted. Sometimes it has been a little music, sometimes a little deeper insight into the history of art; every little counts you know. Sometimes it has been just a glimpse, a view, of a lovely landscape, an impression. We have always been on the look-out. Sometimes it has been a valued friendship, a delightful social tie.'

(Ch. VIII)

This *credo* is a more substantial version of her earlier philosophical confession to the patient narrator:

> 'Yes, we like Europe; we prefer it. We like the the opportunities of Europe; we like the *rest*. There is so much in that, you know. The world seems to me to be hurrying, pressing forward so fiercely, without knowing where it is going. "Whither?" I often ask, in my little quiet way. But I have yet to learn that any one can tell me.'
>
> (Ch. V)

Aurora herself is desperate enough to contemplate playing truant with the vulgar Rucks, if this is the only way she can manage to get back to the America she longs to see, a wish always denied by her mother, whose claim it is that 'My daughter and I are not pushers; we move with little steps. We like the old, trodden paths; we like the old, old world.' Aurora's own view is rather different:

> Have you been all over Europe,' I asked—'in all the different countries?'
>
> She hesitated a moment. 'Everywhere that there's a *pension*. Mamma is devoted to *pensions*. We have lived, at one time or another, in every *pension* in Europe.'
>
> 'Well, I should think you had seen about enough,' said Miss Ruck.
>
> 'It's a delightful way of seeing Europe,' Aurora rejoined, with her brilliant smile. 'You may imagine how it has attached me to the different countries. I have such charming souvenirs! There is a *pension* awaiting us now at Dresden,—eight francs a day, without wine. That's rather dear. Mamma means to make them give us wine. Mamma is a great authority on *pensions*; she is known, that way, all over Europe. Last winter we were in Italy, and she discovered one at Piacenza,—four francs a day. We made economics.'
>
> 'Your mother doesn't seem to mingle much,' observed Miss Ruck, glancing through the window at the scholastic attitude of Mrs Church.
>
> 'No, she doesn't mingle, except in the native society. Though she lives in *pensions*, she detests them.'
>
> 'Whey does she live in them, then?' asked Miss Sophy, rather resentfully.
>
> 'Oh, because we are so poor; it's the cheapest way to live. We have tried having a cook, but the cook always steals. Mamma used to set me to watch her; that's the way I passed my *jeunesse*— my *belle jeunesse*. We are frightfully poor,' the young girl went on, with the same strange frankness—a curious mixture of girlish grace and conscious cynicism. 'Nous n'avons pas le sou. That's

one of the reasons we don't go back to America; mamma says we can't afford to live there.'

(Ch. IV)

Here is the unvarnished truth. Poor Aurora's one longing is to learn to behave like an ordinary American girl (how Daisy Miller would have loved her!):

'You are not an American girl,' I ventured to observe.

My companion almost stopped, looking at me; there was a little flush in her cheek. 'Voilà!' she said. 'There's my false position. I want to be an American girl, and I'm not.'

'Do you want me to tell you?' I went on. 'An American girl wouldn't talk as you are talking now.'

'Please tell me,' said Aurora Church, with expressive eagerness. 'How would she talk?'

'I can't tell you all the things an American girl would say, but I think I can tell you the things she wouldn't say. She wouldn't reason out her conduct, as you seem to me to do.'

Aurora gave me the most flattering attention. 'I see. She would be simpler. To do very simple things that are not at all simple— that is the American girl!'

(Ch. VII)

The narrator would hardly be a Jamesian young gentleman of the fiction of this period if he were not conscious that 'this insidiously mutinous young creature was looking out for a preserver', that 'she might do something reckless and irregular—something in which a sympathetic compatriot, as yet unknown, would find his profit'. He would certainly not be a Jamesian young gentleman of this period if he did not instinctively flinch from being himself the preserver. We are left to watch both families moving relentlessly to their doom—the Rucks to bankruptcy in New York, the Churches to another frugal *pension* at Dresden. Aurora, whose one harmless desire had been 'To do very simple things that are not at all simple that is the American girl', fails in her protest. She is the other side of the medal of, and hence a sort of propitiation for, poor Daisy Miller who *did* succeed, and died for her success.

'The Siege of London'

Our third American 'heroine' in this selected group may be considered as a very much older and more experienced Daisy Miller type of social misfit who, rather to their discredit than to her credit in the strictest terms of the game, managed finally to 'make good' among members of a London society as vulgarly snobbish as she herself was vulgarly egalitarian. 'The Siege of London'

(1883) is a substantial novelette more than half the length of the novel *The Europeans*. Something of the innocence of appreciation of New England scenery and mode of life in *The Europeans* is still present here and there in this far more sophisticated metropolitan tale, as in the enjoyment of the Parisian scene in the early pages where the young American diplomat Waterville and his Anglicized American friend Littlemore first meet Mrs Headway and her infatuated English baronet; or later in the Warwickshire setting of the baronet's impressive country seat where the main characters play out their social drama while enjoying 'that rural hospitality which is the great invention of the English people and the most perfect expression of their character'. When we are told how much Waterville himself values 'those fine old houses, surrounded with hereditary acres, which from the first of his coming to England he had thought of with such curiosity and such envy', then we are gently reminded that if Mrs Headway was a lady with a questionable past, she had had the wit to select for herself a truly appreciated future.

That the outrageously blatant yet irresistible female besieger happened to be not only American but in addition a brassy product of the south-western frontier, added to the piquancy of the situation and allowed James to indulge yet another series of leisurely observations on current disparities in Anglo-American social customs—but the incompatibilities to be resolved are first a matter of social class, secondly an issue of conventional morality and only in the third place a by-product of international differences. Mrs Nancy Headway (ex-Mrs Beck, ex-Mrs—who knows who?) was as much a challenge to the classifications of her own countrymen as she was to the imagination of British hostesses: 'She was a charming woman, especially for New Mexico; but she had been divorced too often—it was a tax on one's credulity; she must have repudiated more husbands than she had married. . . She had gone in mainly for editors—she esteemed the journalistic profession. . . "The elegant and accomplished Mrs Beck", the newspapers called her— the other editors, to whom she wasn't married.' It is made very clear, as she sets her cap at the Old World, that Mrs Headway had never been 'received' in New York society. It is mainly for this reason that she declares: 'I have taken a great fancy to this old Europe; I feel as if I should never go back.' Her final success in becoming the wife of an English baronet is achieved against the resistance, partly active and partly passive, of her two American men friends, one a diplomat and one an old acquaintance from the frontier days. Class is stronger than morality in this tale, and moral judgement more severe than national pride.

Yet although Mrs Headway's triumphant scaling of the class barriers of Victorian London is a more remarkable feat than her ability to over-ride the social disadvantages both of her shady past life and her Far Western origins, it is a sign of Henry James's splendid assurance as a social satirist that he allows us to see, in passages of high social comedy, that it was precisely the attraction to her English hosts of those other two 'disadvantages', social and national, that really enabled her to conquer. Henry James, the inveterate London diner-out, knew that the mixture of aristocrats and plutocrats who constituted the 'upper class' of the 1880s contained many people who were indifferent, if not hostile, to genuine cultural standards, and were only too thankful to welcome the entertainment provided by Mrs Headway:

> She was alone against many, and her opponents were a very serried phalanx; those who were there represented a thousand others. They looked so different from her that to the eye of the imagination she stood very much on her merits. All those people seemed so completely made up, so unconscious of effort, so surrounded with things to rest upon; the men with their clean complexions, their well-hung chins, their cold, pleasant eyes, their shoulders set back, their absence of gesture; the women, several very handsome, half strangled in strings of pearls, with smooth plain tresses, seeming to look at nothing in particular, supporting silence as if it were as becoming as candlelight, yet talking a little, sometimes, in fresh, rich voices. They were all wrapped in a community of ideas, of traditions; they understood each other's accent, even each other's variations. Mrs Headway, with all her prettiness, seemed to transcend these variations; she looked foreign, exaggerated; she had too much expression; she might have been engaged for the evening. Waterville remarked, moreover, that English society was always looking out for amusement and that its transactions were conducted on a cash basis. If Mrs Headway were amusing enough she would probably succeed, and her fortune—if fortune there was—would not be a hinderance.

> (Ch. VI)

Mrs Headway herself, the same Nancy Beck whom her still half-fascinated Anglicized countryman Littlemore can remember entertaining him so freely on the back patio at San Diego, 'knew of course that as a product of fashionable circles she was nowhere, but she might have great success as a child of nature'. Littlemore's own sister, who had married an English squire and has become *plus royaliste que le roi*, can be scandalized at the ease with which the members of her newly acquired social circle can flout their own declared standards: 'If they think there's something bad about you they'll be sure to run after you. It's like the decadence of the Roman Empire.' The sharpness of the besieger's own perceptions is presented with a wholly attractive honesty:

She pretended to be surprised at her good fortune, especially at its rapidity; but she was really surprised at nothing. She took things as they came, and, being essentially a woman of action, wasted almost as little time in elation as she would have done in despondence. She talked a great deal about Lord Edward and Lady Margaret and about such other members of the nobility as had shown a desire to cultivate her acquaintance; professing to understand perfectly the sources of a popularity which apparently was destined to increase. 'They come to laugh at me,' she said; 'they come simply to get things to repeat. I can't open my mouth but they burst into fits. It's a settled thing that I'm an American humorist; if I say the simplest things, they begin to roar. I must express myself somehow; and indeed when I hold my tongue they think me funnier than ever. They repeat what I say to a great person, and a great person told some of them the other night that he wanted to hear me for himself. I'll do for him what I do for the others; no better and no worse. I don't know how I do it; I talk the only way I can. They tell me it isn't so much the things I say as the way I say them. Well, they're very easy to please. They don't care for me; it's only to be able to repeat Mrs Headway's "last". Every one wants to have it first; it's a regular race.'

(Ch. VIII)

Such a person is obviously eminently worthy to be the wife of any baronet in the kingdom. Among all the chatterers and surmisers and assessors, English and American alike, who are appalled by or secretly admire her campaign, it is the self-effacing young Sir Arthur Demesne himself who wins the reader's approval. Nancy Headway finally arranges for him to ask Littlemore, face to face, if he knows of any just cause or impediment to their marriage. To Littlemore's embarrassed 'Have you any question to ask me?', Sir Arthur's 'hesitation was probably extremely brief; but Littlemore heard the ticking of the clock while it lasted. "Certainly, I have no question to ask", the young man said in a voice of cool, almost insolent surprise.' One closes this beautifully told, highly intelligent study of social pretensions and human qualities with the cheering assurance that one old Warwickshire family will be all the better for its rich new blood.

'Lady Barberina'

The last of our five representative 'international' tales is 'Lady Barberina' (1884). (James changed the spelling of the lady's name to Barbarina, incidentally, in his revision of the story.) In this particular story the social scales seem at first to be well balanced between the two main characters, an American husband and an English wife. Whereas in 'An International Episode' an English marquis had been rejected by an American girl, and in 'The Siege of London' a vulgar American divorcée had captured a wealthy English baronet, in 'Lady Barberina' we are invited to consider the consequences of national and personal idiosyncrasies on the union of a pair who in their respective societies were each sitting on the top of the pile—Jackson Lemon, a professional man of good repute who is also an American millionaire, and the daughter of the Marquis of Canterville. There had been enough real alliances between such members of the two acknowledged American and English social *élites* by 1884 for the major tensions of the plot to lie elsewhere—and here 'Lady Barberina' is more akin to the overwhelmingly psychological problems already brilliantly expounded in *The Portrait of a Lady* as only marginally, almost accidentally, affected by national backgrounds.

Like 'The Siege of London', this novelette could well have been expanded to a full-size volume, so tensely interesting is the human situation. The early sections are as wittily observant as anything Henry James ever wrote. Once again, Hyde Park serves as a convenient meeting place for urbane pleasantries between English and American social critics. This mood sharpens to an initial contest of wills between Jackson Lemon and the Canterville family, vividly readable because one can see right on both sides. Lemon is no piratical Newman, but as a notable medical scholar and also a millionaire he is insulted and affronted by the preliminary business of a 'marriage settlement' for his nobly born wife. Some pages are occupied by polite skirmishes which, with the best of good manners on both sides, nevertheless give some hint at storms ahead:

> Jackson Lemon looked from one of his companions to the other; he coloured a little, and gave a smile that was perhaps a trifle fixed. 'Settlements? We don't make them in the United States. You may be sure I shall make a proper provision for my wife.'
>
> 'My dear fellow, over here—in our class, you know, it's the custom,' said Lord Canterville, with a richer brightness in his face at the thought that the discussion was over.
>
> 'I have my own ideas,' Jackson answered, smiling.
>
> 'It seems to me it's a question for the solicitors to discuss,' Lady Canterville suggested.
>
> 'They may discuss it as much as they please,' said Jackson Lemon, with a laugh. He thought he saw his solicitors discussing it! He had indeed his own ideas. He opened the door for Lady Canterville, and the three passed out of the room together,

walking into the hall in a silence in which there was just a tinge of awkwardness. A note had been struck which grated and scratched a little. A pair of brilliant footmen, at their approach, rose from a bench to a great altitude, and stood there like sentinels presenting arms.

(Ch. III)

Such anthropological niceties apart, the Lemon–Canterville alliance wins general approval, especially from the American-born Lady Marmaduke, friend of the Lady Barberina's sister, who called herself Lemon's 'social godmother' but who might in addition have lived on to be a founder member of the English-Speaking Union:

She wished to add an arch or two to the bridge on which she had effected her transit from America, and it was her belief that Jackson Lemon might furnish the materials. This bridge, as yet a somewhat sketchy and rickety structure, she saw (in the future) boldly stretching from one solid pillar to another. It would have to go both ways, for reciprocity was the keynote of Lady Marmaduke's plan. It was her belief that an ultimate fusion was inevitable, and that those who were the first to understand the situation would gain the most.

(Ch. II)

Dr Jackson Lemon would, after all, gain much from his 'marriage settlement'. His valuation of his new bride is entirely just:

There was something simple and robust in her beauty; it had the quietness of an old Greek statue, without the vulgarity of the modern simper or of contemporary prettiness. Her head was antique; and though her conversation was quite of the present period, Jackson Lemon had said to himself that there was sure to be in her soul a certain primitive sincerity which would match with her facial mould. He saw her as she might be in the future, the beautiful mother of beautiful children, in whom the look of race should be conspicuous. He should like his children to have the look of race, and he was not unaware that he must take his precautions accordingly. A great many people had it in England; and it was a pleasure to him to see it, especially as no one had it so unmistakably as the second daughter of Lord Canterville. It would be a great luxury to call such a woman one's own; nothing could be more evident than that, because it made no difference that she was not strikingly clever. Striking cleverness was not a part of harmonious form and the English complexion; it was associated with the modern simper, which was a result of modern nerves. If Jackson Lemon had wanted a nervous wife, of course, he could have found her at home; but this tall, fair girl, whose character, like her figure, appeared mainly to have been formed by riding across country, was differently put together. All the same, would it suit his book, as they said in London, to marry her and transport her to New York?'

(Ch. II)

In the answer to that last question hangs the pathetic failure of an international marriage which, for once in these tales, had looked almost entirely propitious, well balanced. One of Jackson Lemon's professional friends guessed that 'Lady Barb, in New York, would neither assimilate nor be assimilated.' While we watch her flinching from meeting the New York ladies who flock to greet her and afford her every mark of precedence in their own different yet internally well stratified system, her creator is at hand to remind us, with one of those ironical comments which go to the very heart of the matter, that 'it was not in the least of American barbarism that she was afraid; her dread was of American civilization'. Jackson Lemon had hoped to help his wife launch a New York *salon*: he was a serious professional man with an international scientific reputation as well as unexpectedly inherited wealth. But Lady Barb had been educated as a horsewoman in 'firm, tailor-made armour', not a *salonnière*; 'so long as she didn't hunt, it didn't much matter what she did'. For the civilized arts she had no taste, and no desire to learn. Nor would she even act as a non-playing neutral hostess, simply because her own version of her own inherited social code was so limited, so infantile, that without the help of titles and formal precedence she was all at sea—quite ignorantly and innocently so. 'I don't know what I miss, I think I miss everything!' There was no malice, no shrinking from 'barbarism', but simply lack of curiosity:

> 'How do you know what people are?' he said in a moment. 'You have seen so few; you are perpetually denying yourself. If you should leave New York tomorrow you would know wonderfully little about it.'
> 'It's all the same,' said Lady Barb; 'the people are all exactly alike.'
> 'How can you tell? You never see them.'
> 'Didn't I go out every night for the first two months we were here?'
> 'It was only to about a dozen houses—always the same; people, moreover, you had already met in London. You have got no general impressions.'
> 'That's just what I have got; I had them before I came. Every one is just the same; they have just the same names—just the same manners.'

(Ch. V)

She could explain nothing, because 'in her own class the business was not to express, but to enjoy; not to represent, but to be represented'.

Slowly, through pages of faultless cultural and personal insight, with the reader's pity shared between disappointed husband and uncomprehending wife, we are guided to a conclusion that if Lady Barb could not 'rise at all to his conception, and had not the least curiosity about the New York mind', it was not simply from loyalty to national or cultural or aristocratic preconceptions that she 'thought it would be extremely disagreeable to have a lot of people tumbling in on Sunday evening without being invited', but because she herself was a basically stupid person 'of a dense, patient, imperturbable obstinacy'. Here as if to prove the point, we are treated to the spectacle of Lady Barb's sister Lady Agatha, who had come to visit the Lemons, taking an immediate fancy to her new surroundings, adapting herself with such delighted acquiescence that she falls in love with a young American and promptly marries him without parental consent, and follows him out to the Far West where her elopement makes her instantly popular and accepted. With precisely the same family upbringing, the same cultural and social assumptions as her sister, this young Canterville daughter becomes a kind of Daisy Miller in reverse, and with evident success.

We take leave of Jackson Lemon and his wife in London, riding still in Hyde Park. It is clear that she will never return to her husband's country. He, for his part, fades away as the typical Jamesian hero of such tales is doomed to fade; his money supports the flighty Lady Agatha and her Far West husband, while he himself scans the face of his and Lady Barberina Lemon's baby girl 'for the look of race—whether in hope or fear, to-day, is more than my muse has revealed'. The Lemons have become a mutually uncomprehending man and wife.

The confident assurance of Henry James's now fully mature power as a writer had presented readers with highly entertaining and wholly persuasive passages of dialogue and narration based on the observations James had made, first as a 'passionate pilgrim' and later as an increasingly sceptical participant in the life of several countries. The earlier black-versus-white simplifications of national differences had given place to a more judicious balancing of various national and cultural comparisons and contrasts. But behind all this notable development in the novelist's technique as spokesman for his 'appointed thematic doom', there has been developing even more significantly—for his future career as a creative writer—the power of analysing and conveying the essential qualities of individual human beings.

Henry James himself took pleasure in admitting this same development when he came to write the Preface to the volume of the New York Edition containing the last four of our quintet of selected stories. He admits that he seemed to have been 'struck with no possibility of contrast in the human lot as great as that encountered as we turn back and forth between the distinctively American and the distinctively European outlook'. Yet in looking back over a career which by that time had included the publication of *The Wings of the Dove* and *The Golden Bowl*, he adds that his later subject matter had 'not been the exhibited behaviour of certain Americans as Americans, of certain English persons as English, of certain Romans as Romans. Americans, Englishmen, Romans are, in the whole matter, agents or victims. . .'. He asks us to recognize that 'the subject in each case could have been perfectly expressed had *all* the persons concerned been only American or only English or only Roman or whatever'. Yet looking back on his work of thirty-odd years ago, we can now see that what he is hankering after is a full Jamesian elaboration of poor Lady Marmaduke's naive but warm-hearted belief that in the case of England and the United States, at any rate, 'an ultimate fusion was inevitable'. James's own quixotic vision is of an international 'sublime consensus of the educated'.

These few sentences of the later James, incidentally, testify to a lifelong sensitivity to significant external stimuli as well as to his own developing consciousness, wherever it may lead him. It is that quality of self-awareness in James which, in studying his artistic career, makes it of less value than usual for us to poke about for 'influences' and 'models'. A touch of Dickens here, of Balzac there? Yes, yes. Or we may wish to pause to note, in 'The Siege of London', how far that story may or may not resemble the play *L'Aventurière* by Emile Augier which Waterville and Longmore and Nancy Headway had been watching in the opening pages of that story? Such clues for footnotes are as nothing, unless we can relate them to reveal afresh the quality of James's *own* power of selection and discrimination at various points in his career. It is surely this quality that T. S. Eliot had in mind when he made his celebrated remark that James had a mind 'so fine that no idea could violate it'. The word to underline here is '*violate*', not 'idea'. James's mind buzzed with ideas, including political ideas and cultural borrowings. But until they had been absorbed, and could re-emerge from what he called 'the deep wells of unconscious cerebration', he could not allow raw theories or cultural manifestations simply to bruise, rather than percolate into, his ability to select and judge.

Three minor signals may be repeated at this point, as we leave these samples from the much larger total of works with 'international' themes as their main characteristic. The first signal will also apply to almost the whole of James's other fiction as well: it is simply a reminder that social comedy of the type displayed by James cannot function unless certain patterns of 'decent behaviour' are taken for granted, any more than tennis can be played without a net or without lines drawn on the court. Half the skill, the fun even, of many characters in James's 'international' tales consists simply in the degree to which they cheat or defy social expectations, whether American or European. We who tend to admit few conventional rules in the social games we now play may need to make a conscious effort to take seriously, even if we (like the author) recognize them as hypocritical, the dividing lines crossed by James's wanderers across social or national assumptions.

The second signal is more positive. We have an opportunity to detect even in these less ambitious works of art the abiding presence of James's compassionate concern for life's victims, whether they be victims of social or economic systems or simply of the unfairness of human life itself. This tenderness towards those who humbly oil the wheels of life or stand ineffectually aghast at man's inhumanity to man is a quality not often prominent, or even present at all, in 'the comedy of manners'. We may recall that the pretty young Newport girls who attracted the admiration of Lord Lambeth are a very far cry from that other American girl, the poor submissive Aurora Church who had lived 'at one time or another, in every *pension* in Europe'. They are all in another world from that inhabited by Lord Canterville who, if his 'fortune was more ancient than abundant', was himself nevertheless 'visibly, incontestably, a personage'. To some extent they are all, Americans and Europeans, rich and poor alike, victims of the tribal dances they have been called upon to play; but Henry James the diner-out and honoured guest at country house parties always seemed to have a special eye open for those who played subsidiary and usually unrecognized roles—Mrs Bread the Bellegarde's housekeeper, Madame Beaurepas conning her guests, or Jackson Lemon's quiet but perceptive old mother in New York.

The third signal can hardly have gone unobserved. The one thing Henry James's important male characters in these novels and stories have in common is their tendency to withdrawal, self-abnegation, sacrifice. Christopher Newman in *The American*, Mr Brand in *The Europeans*, Winterbourne in 'Daisy Miller', Lord Lambeth in 'An International Episode,' the narrator in 'The Pension Beaurepas'—they either lose their girls or recognize the loss too late. Jackson Lemon won Lady Barb, but he had to lose his homeland to keep her. The sidelines baronet of 'The Siege of London' is the one exception, as 'Mrs Headway's "latest".' We shall meet many more such men in the later James.

5   *The Portrait of a Lady*

A year or so before their brief and disastrous marriage, Lord Byron was favoured by his confidante, Lady Melbourne, with a composition by his future wife, Annabella Milbanke, in which she had set out a priggish list of specifications for a husband. The poet sent back this recipe for a 'spouse elect' to Lady Melbourne with the comment: 'She seems to have been spoiled—not as children usually are—but systematically Clarissa Harlowed[†] into an awkward kind of correctness, with a dependence upon her own infallibility which will or may lead her into some egregious blunder.' Shortly afterwards, he wrote of Annabella: 'I do admire her as a very superior woman, a little encumbered with Virtue . . .'. It was just such a kind of young lady, courageous and independent enough to capture the reader's admiration, yet so unluckily headstrong as to engage his shocked sympathy, who is the heroine of *The Portrait of a Lady*, Isabel Archer.

From New York to England

Very early in *The Portrait of a Lady* there is a strange little scene which betrays a brooding indwelling of creator and created figure so intense as to be almost an effort at identification. Mrs Touchett, the independent-minded wife of a wealthy American living mainly in Europe, is revisiting New York State and 'takes up' her niece, Isabel Archer. This lonely intelligent girl has a mind 'a good deal of a vagabond' and an imagination 'by habit ridiculously active'. She accepts her aunt's fairy-Godmother offer of a new life in Europe, a considerable advance on the 'history of German Thought' which, like a youthful George Eliot, she is reading on the occasion of Aunt Lydia Touchett's irruption. She and her sisters had 'no regular education and no permanent home—they had been at once both spoiled and neglected'. By the time Isabel was fourteen, she and her sisters had been 'transported . . . three times across the Atlantic'. She was familiar with 'the London *Spectator*, the latest publications, the music of Gounod, the poetry of Browning, the prose of George Eliot'. She 'liked to be thought clever, but she hated to be thought bookish'. She was jealous of her more socially active sister. 'Her deepest enjoyment was to feel the

---

[†] Clarissa Harlowe was the consciously virtuous, much tempted heroine of Samuel Richardson's novel of the same name.

continuity between the movements of her own soul and the agitations of the world.' She was inactive but excited throughout the Civil War. And suddenly we realize that in our first introduction to Isabel Archer we are gazing at a detailed portrait not of Minny Temple, the dead but beloved cousin to whom she has been likened—but of young Henry James himself.

Isabel is to face the most gruelling fate of all James's 'international young ladies' as she resigns herself to life with a detestable husband, whom misjudgement in her zest for experience had brought her to marry, and to whom pride will keep her faithful. 'The agitations of the world', so thinks Isabel in her innocent if presumptuous folly, can be tamed to keep pace with 'the movements of her own soul'. In *The Portrait of a Lady*, the stay-at-home observer is represented by Isabel's cousin, Ralph Touchett. It is Ralph who is called upon not only to give his cousin financial liberation, 'to put a little wind in her sails', but also to weep in prescient impotence as he watches her using that liberty to march into a prison far worse than any from which his generosity had released her. Ralph, perhaps the most thoroughly likeable and credible of all James's sensitive invalids, whose 'serenity was but the array of wild flowers niched in his ruin', is presented as being himself fully conscious of his *own* attempts, muted though they must necessarily be, to profit by a double nature. Recognizing in Isabel a similar but potentially more active sensibility, he quite explicitly reveals to his cousin his wry social deceptions:

> 'I keep a band of music in my ante-room', he once said to her. 'It has orders to play without stopping; it renders me two excellent services. It keeps the sounds of the world from reaching the private apartments, and it makes the world think that dancing's going on within.'

Isabel's complementary fault, from which a larger dose of Ralph in her make-up might have saved her, was that

> . . . she was always planning out her development, desiring her perfection, observing her progress. Her nature had, in her conceit, a certain garden-like quality, a suggestion of perfume and murmuring boughs, of shady bowers and lengthening vistas, which made her feel that introspection was, after all, an exercise in the open air, and that a visit to the recesses of one's spirit was harmless when one returned from it with a lapful of roses.

—and at this point there follows the ironic comment about her consciousness that 'there were other gardens in the world than those of her remarkable soul'.

Isabel's introduction to English country-house life, at her wealthy gentle uncle's house Gardencourt, is compassed in the mood, and the prose, of a passionate pilgrim beautifully mellowed (see 'Illustrative passages', pp. 142–45). Old Touchett, at his tea-table on the lawn, provides the appropriate tone of unflamboyant wealth: his face 'seemed to tell that he had been successful in life, yet it seemed to tell also that his success had not been exclusive and invidious, but had had much of the inoffensiveness of failure'. It is his wife who has the sharper edge; indeed, 'the edges of her conduct were so very clear-cut that for susceptible persons it sometimes had a knife-like effect'. Launched gently into English society under these most favourable auspices, Isabel soon attracts the notice of the Touchetts' eligible neighbour, Lord Warburton, one of 'the radicals of the upper class', with a hundred thousand a year.

Isabel was 'very liable to the sin of self-esteem; she often surveyed with complacency the field of her own nature . . .' and she had 'an unquenchable desire to think well of herself'. So far, so good; a very proper wish. But more specifically, 'it was one of her theories that Isabel Archer was very fortunate in being independent, and that she ought to make some very enlightened use of that state'. After a few terse words with her aunt over some minor social lapse, Isabel declares herself in words that promise all, and foreshadow her tragedy:

'But I always want to know the things one shouldn't do!'
'So as to do them?' asked her aunt.
'So as to choose,' said Isabel.

Ralph Touchett finds a daily interest in watching her progress and imagining the chart of her boundless future. He is unsurprised when she gently rejects a proposal of marriage from the super-eligible Lord Warburton, for he has enough cousinly imagination to divine Isabel's view that 'the "splendid" security so offered her was *not* the greatest she could conceive'. She makes it clear to the baffled nobleman that to marry him would be somehow to escape her fate, even though the act of renouncing so magnificent a capture made Isabel 'really frightened at herself'. Meanwhile her interfering friend Henrietta Stackpole, noticing the *rapport* between cousins, tries to enlist Ralph's support for the claims of Caspar Goodwood, an American suitor who had pursued Isabel across the Atlantic. Isabel had earlier felt Goodwood's appeal, for he represented all that was most energetic and creative in the American commerical myth and had at times 'seemed to range himself on the side of her destiny . . .'. He was, certainly, a more active combatant than Lord Warburton: 'she saw the different fitted parts of him as she had seen, in museums and portraits, the different fitted parts of armoured warriors—in plates of steel handsomely inlaid with gold'. Ralph devotes himself to a deeper understanding of Isabel.

'You're exacting', he tells her, 'without the excuse of thinking your-self good'—and he adds: 'I shall have the thrill of seeing what a young lady does who won't marry Lord Warburton.' This senti-ment is echoed in louder tones by Caspar Goodwood, who has pursued Isabel to her London hotel and is once again rejected, but only by Isabel's wilful swerve against his undeniable attraction. He is made to feel, in his straightforward sexual drive, 'a strong man in the wrong'. Isabel's sole reason for rejecting him is that 'I don't want to be a mere sheep in the flock; I want to choose my fate.' She is, at the same time, callously willing to treat him as a second-best reserve:

'You'll get very sick of your independence.'
'Perhaps I shall; it's even very probable. When that day comes I shall be very glad to see you.'

Isabel returns to Gardencourt. The temptations of aristocratic consideration and physical passion have been mastered—but for what? Ralph, more intrigued than ever, persuades his dying father to leave Isabel half his own inheritance, 'I should like to put a little wind in her sails', he explains to the old man. 'She wishes to be free, and your bequest will make her free.' It is a magnificent stroke of construction that James should present this scene guaranteeing Isabel's final financial liberation, immediately after the girl has met, and found herself strangely attracted by, a visiting friend of her aunt's, by name Madame Merle. For Madame Merle, sophis-ticated and generous, competent and manipulating, cultivated and rapacious, will be the one to act as representative of the temptress to the third and final impediment to Isabel's true freedom. In ignorance alike of her coming fortune (from old Touchett) and of her coming doom (via Madame Merle), Isabel awaits in apparent serenity, among her friends, the death of her kindly uncle. And with the heroine poised on her confident flight towards the unknown, the opening third of the novel is completed.

What is so striking about these eighteen chapters, quite apart from their effortless groundwork of plot, is their liveliness. There are long passages of ratiocination, but they are broken up by vivid dialogue and laced throughout with wit. In the mellow comfort of Gardencourt, at any rate, even such edgy characters as Mrs Touchett and Henrietta Stackpole are softened by an amused tolerance. Her hostess may speculate that Henrietta as a journalist 'has lived all her life in a boarding-house, and I detest the manners and liberties of such places', but Ralph and Isabel, who had more to fear from her inquisitiveness, see her in more indulgent imagery, borrowed from the careers in which this energetic feminist does, or might, channel her talents:

She rustled, she shimmered, in fresh, dove-coloured draperies
. . . she was as crisp and new and comprehensive as a first issue
before the folding. From top to toe she had probably no misprint.
She was wanting in distinction, but . . . she was brave: she
went into cages, she flourished lashes, like a spangled lion-tamer.

As for Mrs Touchett herself, she exhibits, even before the advent
of the professionally competent Madame Merle, all those qualities
of serenity which Henry James, from far back, had valued—and
celebrated—in womankind:

> Mrs Touchett had a great merit; she was as honest as a pair of
> compasses. There was a comfort in her stiffness and firmness;
> you knew exactly where to find her and were never liable to
> chance encounters and conclusions. On her own ground she was
> perfectly present, but was never over-inquisitive as regards the
> territory of her neighbour.

It is in this mood of relaxed vigilance, in the paradoxical urbanity
of country-house life, that Isabel makes her vitally important
assessment of Madame Merle: 'She was in a word a woman of
strong impulses kept in admirable order. This commended itself to
Isabel as an ideal combination.'

We are to have many more aspects of Isabel Archer's nature
steadily unveiled, as we overhear her talking with Madame Merle
and her cousin, or are made privy to her long, private musings. At
one point she concludes that 'the supreme good fortune', 'the
essence of the aristocratic situation', was 'to be in a better position
for appreciating people than they are for appreciating you'—the
word 'appreciate' denoting, in this freshly observed novel of
James's early maturity, an activity which in his later novels would
come to be expressed more bitterly by some such concept as
'dominate' or simply 'devour'. She is uncritically impressed by
Madame Merle's competence, all morning letter-writing and afternoon water-colours and evening piano-playing or embroidery, plus
a general capacity for manipulation which seems at first to be
entirely for the benefit of the persons manipulated. Isabel's observation of her produces some admirable judgements:

> . . . she had rid herself of every remnant of that tonic wildness
> which we may assume to have belonged even to the most amiable
> persons in the ages before country-house life was the fashion
> . . . She existed only in her relations, direct or indirect, with her
> fellow mortals . . . One always ended, however, by feeling that
> a charming surface doesn't necessarily prove one superficial; this
> was an illusion in which, in one's youth, one had but just escaped
> being nourished.

Chatting of her cosmopolitan friends, Madame Merle promises

Isabel an introduction to Gilbert Osmond, an American living in Italy, who is 'exceedingly clever' but 'very indolent'. Meanwhile, her scornful sweeping aside of the claims of straight boy-meets-girl affairs is in line with James's own persistent shrinking from the treatment of normal courtship. Just as Olive Chancellor in *The Bostonians* will show an envious contempt for Verena's probable liking for 'a young man in a white overcoat and paper collar', so Madame Merle snorts about 'a young man with a fine moustache going down on his knees'. Yet when Madame Merle explicitly confesses her 'great respect for *things* . . . one's home, one's furniture, one's garments, the books one reads, the company one keeps—these things are all expressive', Isabel disagrees, and in her disagreement is economically pin-pointed the rigidity—the frigidity, almost—of a heroine too prudently headstrong not to be felt by the reader, this time, to be courting disaster: 'I don't know whether I succeed in expressing myself, but I know that nothing else expresses me.' We feel momentarily grateful for the memory of the assurance that in Isabel 'the love of knowledge coexisted with the finest capacity for ignorance'.

From England to Europe

When Madame Merle hears from Mrs Touchett of Isabel's legacy, her first impulse is to cry out: 'Ah, the clever creature!' As for Miss Archer herself: 'The acquisition of power made her serious; she scrutinized her power with a kind of tender ferocity, but was not eager to exercise it.' Her widowed aunt takes her off to Paris, where the young woman is contemptuous of the 'inane' American colony and may be presumed to share the author's view-point of Ned Rosier, a young effeminate *déraciné*, who 'had some charming rooms . . . decorated with old Spanish altar-lace, the envy of his female friends, who declared that his chimney-piece was better draped than the shoulders of many a duchess'. She continues to brood over her nature and her destiny, until cousin Ralph, visited at his invalid's retreat at San Remo, accuses her in turn: 'Don't try so much to form your character—it's like trying to pull open a tight, tender young rose.' We are, by these reiterated but subtly variegated monologues and conversations, gradually made apprehensive for the fortunate young woman's oft-rehearsed fate.

The scene changes to Florence, to the hill-top house of Gilbert Osmond. The master of the house, aged forty, is receiving back his daughter, Pansy, from her convent. His friend Madame Merle wishes to put Isabel 'in your way'—and 'I want you of course to marry her'. This sudden directness between a pair who are so very oblique in company speaks of an intimacy taken for granted, of 'knowing each other well and each on the whole willing to accept the satisfaction of knowing as a compensation for the inconvenience—whatever it might be—of being known'. Osmond is presented as a self-centred vaguely discontented connoisseur who, when in low spirits, behaves like 'a demoralized prince in exile'—or, as Ralph puts it, 'a prince who has abdicated in a fit of fastidiousness and has been in a state of disgust ever since'. Ralph also tries gently to open his cousin's eyes to the character of Madame Merle ('She's too complete, in a word'), for he knows her to fall into that dangerous category of persons who had achieved 'perfect training, but had won none of the prizes'.

Ignoring Ralph's hint, Isabel visits Gilbert in company with his married sister, the sensible but over-experienced Countess Gemini, and begins to feel his strange fascination. He is an unashamed dilettante, but it is his elegant non-competitiveness that seems to attract her: 'I've a few good things', Mr Osmond allowed; 'indeed I've nothing very bad. But I've not what I should have liked.' Moreover:

> It was not so much what he said and did, but rather what he withheld, that marked him for her as by one of those signs of the highly curious that he was showing her on the underside of old plates and in the corner of sixteenth-century drawings: he indulged in no striking deflection from common usage, he was an original without being an eccentric.

When Osmond speaks of 'my studied, my wilful renunciation', the reader is alerted at the danger: with her new confidence, her new fortune, her new consciousness of having turned down two splendid *offers*, Isabel now feels the attraction of a *claim*. One is strangely reminded of Portia's Belmont in *The Merchant of Venice*, with Caspar Goodwood and Lord Warburton figuring as the Princes of Morocco and Aragon, and Osmond as an unworthy Bassanio linked with the attractions—for an heiress—of the leaden casket. Mrs Touchett simply writes off Osmond as 'an obscure American dilettante, a middle-aged widower with an uncanny child and an ambiguous income'. Ralph, who 'had a kind of loose-fitting urbanity that wrapped him about like an ill-made overcoat, but of which he never divested himself', is too distressed, at first, to speak out of turn. Perversely, Isabel–Portia carries away an image of her Osmond–Bassanio as of 'a quiet, clever, sensitive, distinguished man . . . holding by the hand a little girl whose bell-like clearness gave a new grace to childhood'. The fact that Isabel had turned down such a prize as Lord Warburton naturally increases her value, in Osmond's eyes, as a collector's item. 'He had never forgiven his star for not appointing him to an English dukedom', and to succeed where the great Lord Warburton failed is a special delight to him.

The manner in which one's pleasure in the company of Ralph and Warburton is revived just before the chilly Osmond's proposal of marriage is a skilful weighting of the scales. When *he* detects the feel of success—'the most agreeable emotion of the human heart'—the reader shudders.

Six more chapters unfold before the choice is made irrevocable. Before giving Osmond her answer, Isabel absents herself (in one of those abrupt Jamesian foreshortenings of time: another long journey taken, so to say, within a parenthesis) for a year of Near Eastern travel. On returning, she receives in Florence another appeal from Caspar Goodwood. He, too, is sent about his business: Isabel had written to him about her engagement, but his instant rocketing to her side flatters her power without changing her course. Mrs Touchett is angered by the engagement and blames Madame Merle. Ralph, now perilously ill, is grieved deeply enough to say outright 'I think he's narrow, selfish': and from Isabel comes, during a conversation of great restraint and beauty on both sides, the surprising claim that life with Osmond will represent, for her, the 'one ambition—to be free to follow a good feeling'. We suddenly recognize that Isabel, who has been steadily diminishing the store of regard a reader has built up for her earlier in the novel, is falling for the one allowable temptation for a person in her position—the temptation to *give*. She, who won our interest in the selfish days of her education for life, when all her judgement was consecrated to what she might *want* from life, comes parlously near losing it at the very point when she decides on a course of sacrifice. Ralph, cousinly antennae more sensitive than ever, grasps the high tragic nature of her mistake: 'She was wrong, but she believed; she was deluded, but she was dismally consistent.' She loved Osmond 'for his very poverties dressed out as honours'. It is to this that her vaunted imagination has led her. Isabel's superior amusement at her imagination of her own unenlightened sisters' disapproval 'at her not having chosen a consort who was the hero of a richer accumulation of anecdote' is matched by Osmond's icy jubilation: 'Contentment, on his part, took no vulgar form; excitement, in the most self-conscious of men, was a kind of ecstasy of self-control.' He has the conceit to inform his bride-to-be: 'You're remarkably fresh, and I'm remarkably well-seasoned.' For him, the capture is that of a living soul. There is a horrible knell—so far, so wonderfully have we been worked upon—in the notion of this impotent life-sucking mannikin teasing his captured prey: 'he could tap her imagination with his knuckle and make it ring'.

The last twenty chapters of the fifty-five-chapter novel set forth, with a variation of pace and a wealth of creative power that raise James from the level of virtuoso to that of serene master of fiction, the consequences of Isabel's blunder, the full payment exacted for that tragic flaw which had been displayed earlier in the book: 'the love of knowledge coexisted in her mind with the finest capacity for ignorance'. The Osmonds are discovered in their Roman palazzo after an interval of nearly three years, during which we are told that they had, and lost, a baby. Pansy, now nineteen, is being sought in marriage by—of all people—Ned Rosier. Osmond desires a far better match for Pansy than Rosier, who may see her as the perfect American *jeune fille* but can offer her and her father no worldly distinction. When Lord Warburton turns up again in Rome, Osmond masters his jealousy of his wife's former suitor and his envy of the Warburton prestige and welcomes him to the palazzo parties, hoping that the noble lord will fall for Pansy. As usual, it is cousin Ralph, now mortally sick in Rome, who has the sensibility to crystallize and elucidate, as he ponders with his friend Warburton the awful domestic situation of the girl he himself had freed for great flights: 'The free, keen girl had become quite another person; what he saw was the fine lady who was supposed to represent something . . . she represented Gilbert Osmond. Good heavens, what a function!'

Osmond's vice is not only gross egotism, but an egotism morbidly concerned with the world's opinion, which he takes such pains to appear to despise. Ralph, who hardly ever sees him (for Osmond returns his detestation), senses that 'under the guise of caring only for intrinsic values Osmond lived exclusively for the world', his highest delight being 'to please himself by exciting the world's curiosity and then declining to satisfy it'. Ralph's ethical judgement of Osmond is couched in terms of artistic taste: 'He always had an eye to effect, and his effects were deeply calculated. They were produced by no vulgar means, but the motive was as vulgar as the art was great.'

During the first three years of Isabel's marriage she has seen little of Madame Merle. When they meet to discuss, obliquely, the policy to be pursued in the matter of Ned Rosier's play for Pansy and the superior attractions of Lord Warburton, Isabel feels at first the old admiration. Contrasted with the 'revulsions and disgusts' to which she had become the domestic victim, 'it was a pleasure to see a character so completely armed for the social battle'. She agrees, at any rate, to support any bid Lord Warburton may make for Pansy. When the same topic is raised by Osmond, he makes the offensive suggestion that Isabel still has it in her power to influence her old suitor's selection of her step-daughter as the future Lady Warburton. Osmond's lust for the Warburton connexion is nakedly exposed. He loathes *her* because she has not brought him the self-fulfilment, the self-advertisement he had desired of her: 'he despised her; she had no traditions and the moral horizon of a Unitarian minister'. His disappointment is as sharp as her own, and hers is complete: 'She had taken all the first steps in the purest confidence, and then she had suddenly found the infinite vista of a multiplied life to be a dark, narrow alley with a dead wall at the end.' He thought of himself, she now sees, as 'the first gentleman in Europe', but 'under all his culture, his cleverness, his amenity, under his good-nature, his facility, his knowledge of life, his egotism lay hidden like a serpent in a bank of flowers'. Isabel Archer, the innocently amusing little egotist of the early chapters, is seeing the full blossoming of that quality.

Poor little Pansy resigns herself to a long siege, knowing perfectly well that Lord Warburton is not in love with her, and determined to preserve herself, against her father's wishes, for Ned Rosier. The amiable nobleman, having failed in his last sidelong rescue attempt, takes leave of the Osmonds and returns to England, to the furious bitterness of Gilbert who accuses his wife, in vile words, of having plotted against his plans for Pansy. Standing before his venomous self-pity, 'She might have represented the angel of disdain, first cousin to that of pity. "Oh, Gilbert, for a man who was so fine—!" ' And one is reminded, yet again, that although in *The Portrait of a Lady* one's sympathies are enlisted on a full tragic scale, yet the old hackneyed Jamesian theme that marriage is an avoidable disaster still abides as the kernel of the plot.

Henrietta's American cavalry, so to say, swoops to make a fruitless gesture of rescue: Caspar calls on the Osmonds, makes yet another protestation of love to Isabel, finds himself patronizingly 'taken up' by a malicious Osmond who delights in making fun of his wife's friends, and used by Mrs Osmond (who has conceded that though he may not love, he is now permitted to 'pity' her) to act as fellow-courier with Henrietta for Ralph's safe conduct back to Gardencourt and death. The unsubtle ironclad Henrietta herself becomes, momentarily, a minor irritant to make visible the Osmonds' friction; and nothing is more effective, among all the varied descriptions of and surmises about the Osmonds' domestic hell, than Gilbert's vain attempt to parade a masochistic patience in enduring Miss Stackpole's presence (so that Isabel's loyalty to her friend gains 'a spice of heroism'), an attempt countered by Isabel's restraint in keeping her friend away from her husband: 'Her immediate acceptance of his objections put him too much in the wrong—it being in effect one of the disadvantages of expressing contempt that you cannot enjoy at the same time the credit of expressing sympathy.' The withering touch of Osmond is almost visibly demonstrated at such comparatively unimportant moments, or in passing references such as that to the formal parties which he 'still held for the sake not so much of inviting people as of not inviting them'. His vileness, we are made in various ways to see, lies not in what he does but in what he is.

So far, although our attention has been riveted upon the chief characters in the drama, the pace and tone of the novel have not greatly varied: the slow development of the 'ado' over Isabel's destiny is matched by the slow revelation of her appalling miscalculation. But the last seven chapters of the novel show a remarkable quickening. Brooding monologues give place to confrontations which verge on the melodramatic. Pretences vanish; secrets are revealed; sudden wilful decisions are taken. Of the three important facts that are yet to be revealed to Isabel, one has been known to readers from the time of its commission, the second has been taken for granted and the third has probably been guessed. It is all but laid bare when Madame Merle arrives to discover how far the wretched scheme for Pansy and Lord Warburton had miscarried, and whether Isabel herself had set the noble suitor against it. As the strained dialogue continues, 'a strange truth was filtering into her soul. Madame Merle's interest was identical with Osmond's: that was enough'. Isabel grasps the first simple truth that it was Madame Merle who had arranged her marriage and that Gilbert had married her for her money. We then watch a brief scene between Madame Merle and Osmond himself in which their long complicity is taken for granted and his present disdain for her made manifest.

News comes that Ralph is dying and Osmond, on grounds of propriety, forbids his wife to travel to England to be at her cousin's deathbed. In face of such malignity she hesitates—and it is at this crucial point that Countess Gemini, eager to encourage her sister-in-law in one act of defiance, reveals to her the second truth that Madame Merle and Osmond had been lovers, some time ago, for a period of six or seven years, and that Pansy is their daughter. This 'aid to innocent ignorance' from so unexpected a quarter knocks out of Isabel's sails, so to say, whatever breath of wind the generosity of Ralph had originally put behind them. Suddenly the astounding if perverse grandeur of Madame Merle's own role is laid bare, and for an instant it almost seems that it is she whose stature is worthy of a 'portrait'. For paragraphs at a time, the writing glows with a kind of muted excitement. Isabel, of course, will now travel to England in defiance of Gilbert's ban. Madame Merle, arch-priestess of competence, stands revealed as a pathetically unsuccessful loser in life's battle. There had been no question of Gilbert's marrying his devoted mistress: she had no money for him. The chattering Countess pats Madame Merle back again into non-heroic dimensions: 'She hoped she might marry a great man; that has always been her idea . . . The only tangible result she has ever achieved—except, of course, getting to know everyone and staying with them free of expense—has been her bringing you and Osmond together.' So far, after all, from being tragic, she has been pathetically cheated of meagre hopes: 'She has worked for him, plotted for him, suffered for him; she has even more than once found money for him; and the end of it is that he's tired of her.'

'No possibility of a happy ending'

In the four remaining chapters James has not so much stepped up the pace as changed gear altogether. They throb, these final resolutions of character already revealed, with all the accumulated life of a brilliantly sustained and always witty control of the patiently achieved narrative of the main novel. We know now, readily enough, what will *happen*. Yet, curiously, the desire to see just *how* the main characters will be true to the natures we now so completely know, is vividly insistent. When Isabel meets Madame Merle at Pansy's convent, just before she leaves for England, it is as if the reader, along with Isabel Archer, had 'been thinking all day of her falsity, her audacity, her ability, her probable suffering . . .'. The contrast between the imprisoned Pansy and her two visitors, her unknown mother who is about to depart for America and her known step-mother who promises to return to her in Rome—all this is almost too much to be handled. The temptation to melodrama, as the two women meet to part for ever, is brilliantly avoided, is replaced by a moment of psychological truth so categorically right that only a major novelist in full control could have identified it and then had the art to bring it off. Isabel, being a James heroine, keeps silent about her new knowledge. Madame Merle, plunging on, suddenly feels, suddenly knows that her long secret has been laid bare:

> She had not proceeded far before Isabel noticed a sudden break in her voice, a lapse in her continuity, which was in itself a complete drama. This subtle modulation marked a momentous discovery—the perception of an entirely new attitude on the part of her listener. Madame Merle had guessed in the space of an instant that everything was at an end between them, and in the space of another instant she had guessed the reason why. The person who stood there was not the same one she had seen hitherto, but was a very different person—a person who knew her secret. This discovery was tremendous, and from the moment she made it the most accomplished of women faltered and lost her courage. But only for that moment. Then the conscious stream of her perfect manner gathered itself again and flowed on as smoothly as might be to the end . . .

She has after all, if only by her own worldly standards, her moment of tragic stature. For Isabel, the shock of complete truth is curiously deflating:

. . . the dry staring fact that she had been an applied handled hung-up tool, as senseless and convenient as mere shaped wood and iron. All the bitterness of this knowledge surged into her soul again; it was as if she felt on her lips the taste of dishonour. There was a moment during which, if she had turned and spoken, she would have said something that would hiss like a lash. But she closed her eyes, and then the hideous vision dropped. What remained was the cleverest woman in the world standing there within a few feet of her and knowing as little what to think as the meanest. Isabel's only revenge was to be silent still—to leave Madame Merle in this unprecedented situation.

There is one last twist of the knife before Madame Merle disappears. She tells Isabel that it was Ralph who induced old Mr Touchett to make her an heiress. This is the third missing truth, for Isabel. And her only revenge is to reply: 'I believed it was you I had to thank!'

Madame Merle dropped her eyes; she stood there in a kind of proud penance. 'You're very unhappy, I know. But I'm more so.'

'Yes; I can believe that. I think I should like never to see you again.'

From this point onwards, to borrow Mr Graham Greene's words about this novel, 'There is no possibility of a happy ending: this is surely what James always tells us, not with the despairing larger-than-life gesture of a romantic novelist, but with a kind of bitter precision.' By this time, the reader knows the characters so well that his question is not 'What will happen?' but simply 'How will they play out the remaining cards in their hands?' In a strange way, thinking of Isabel's cousin almost as if he were a living commentator, the reader's question might be 'What will Ralph Touchett make of it all?' What he has made of it will appear only when Isabel sits at his deathbed, in a most moving scene (see 'Illustrative passages', pp. 156–58) which shows that he has loved her more steadfastly than any of her three suitors. Of those three, Lord Warburton had been rejected by Isabel and had failed to offer Pansy an alternative to her convent. The faithful Caspar Goodwood appears on a final rescue attempt, begging Isabel to join him rather than return to Italy and her detestable husband Osmond who had been sadistic enough to forbid Isabel to visit her dying cousin. Her return to him would be to a now wholly antagonistic husband with a technical grievance of insubordination by the wife who had at first hoped to use her Touchett legacy to 'free' him for higher things, and was still his disappointing chattel. Caspar Goodwood's strong sexual magnetism is like that of Morris Townsend in *The*

American, but Isabel is proof against it, as Catherine Sloper had been:

> 'Ah, be mine as I'm yours!' she heard her companion cry. He had suddenly given up argument, and his voice seemed to come, harsh and terrible, through a confusion of vaguer sounds.
>
> This however, of course, was but a subjective fact, as the metaphysicians say; the confusion, the noise of waters, all the rest of it, were in her own swimming head. In an instant she became aware of this. 'Do me the greatest kindness of all,' she panted. 'I beseech you to go away!
>
> 'Ah, don't say that. Don't kill me!' he cried.
>
> She clasped her hands; her eyes were streaming with tears. 'As you love me, as you pity me, leave me alone!'
>
> (New York Edition)

Isabel, like Catherine, had taken on in this novel the role more often occupied by one of James's withdrawing gentlemen. She must endure her chosen fate as Mrs Osmond as Catherine faced her chosen fate of spinsterhood, 'for life, as it were'.

Part Two
The Later James

6 Henry James the London-based professional

The social critic

The design of this Preface has understandably stressed the 'international' aspects of Henry James the Anglo-American writer, and later sections (particularly the 'Illustrative passages') must unavoidably glance, however briefly, at the full flowering of his developed (some would say overdeveloped) style in the early years of this century. This pattern demands a compensating sacrifice of the space which would have been filled by coverage of that substantial block of James's work which deals mainly with the social life of his adopted country. In a curious way, James's series of novels and tales based on his observation of late-Victorian class distinctions, marriage patterns, domestic tensions and the privations suffered by the unsuccessful players in an elaborate social life which took inequality for granted—all these products of his acute observation of a London-based life may strike a modern reader as more distant, more foreign, than his tacklings of 'international' problems. The puzzling differences in various national habits, though they may often be considered superficial and may diminish with the speed and frequency of modern travel, are still nevertheless with us today. They may be acknowledged and faced without any great sense of shame. To put it at its lowest ethical level, a foreigner cannot *help* being a foreigner. We may be amused, or irritated, when a Frenchman does things in this particular odd manner, or an American adopts that particular un-English outlook; but one can hardly *blame* them. Their alibi, like the alibis of James's blundering Americans in Europe, or bewildered Europeans in America, is simply our own recognition of an unavoidable fact of international life.

How otherwise when English readers nowadays read James's stories of English life at about the turn of the century! Whatever one's personal or doctrinal views may be on the subjects of divorce and birth-control, there is no doubt whatever that the widespread acceptance of both practices in the world at large has completely changed that automatic obloquy which a late-Victorian novelist could assume to be the fate of those active sinners who indulged in adultery, and those unfortunates who suffered the passive besmirchment of illegitimacy. When, as now, the marriage vow is no longer automatically sacred, and the possession of a pair of legitimate parents may no longer be taken for granted, then a modern 'novelist of manners' must find that at least half the plots available to his predecessors less than a century ago have become invalid. Some of the more dreadful plights faced by James's Londoners at the turn of the century, whether in town or country, no longer strike terror into a reader's heart. The desperate expedients risked by some of his characters, such as child-murder in *The Other House*, or the ghoulish emotional cannibalism attributed to members of his social set by the Peeping-Tom narrator of *The Sacred Fount*—all these and similar reactions are now completely out of date and seem far more melodramatic than any equally old-fashioned views of international behaviour.

The two best-known novels of this phase of James's treatment of the social world, *What Maisie Knew* and *The Awkward Age*, reflect very faithfully that uncertain period at the turn of the century when the loose behaviour of 'the naughty nineties' was still being judged (whether as outrageous or enlightened) by the steadily receding standards of full Victorian rectitude (or hypocrisy). There is rich social comedy, as well as harsh personal suffering, in these ambiguous situations. Underneath all the elaborate quadrille of divorced and remarried parties in *What Maisie Knew* there has been active the unchanging ravages of sexual infatuation. Yet the consequent patterns are as farcical as those of Restoration comedies. 'A' (male) and 'B' (female) are divorced. 'A' remarries 'C' (female) and 'B' remarries 'D' (male). Before long, 'C' and 'D' begin to form a third regrouping. All very entertaining and 'knowing'? Yes; unless we view it all, as James asks us to do, through the eyes of the innocent yet sensitive and intelligent eyes of little Maisie, deserted child of 'A' and 'B'. In her eyes, as innocence comes to terms with squalid ever-changing self-indulgence, the jealousies and greed of the grown-ups seem more hurtful than the sexual licence itself. *The Awkward Age* setting is that of a similar but rather more self-conscious set of London worldlings who strive to create a pseudo-aristocratic enlightened *salon* where the fashionable arts, as well as the current trendy marital liberation, are wittily discussed. It is a London version of the sort of *demi-monde* pretensions which, at the same time, were fascinating in Paris the novelist Marcel Proust.

It has sometimes been wondered how the expatriate Henry James, for all his celebrated feats of dining-out at the tables of those who needed an entertaining bachelor to balance their lists, could have combined these transient activities with his self-imposed role of theorist and practitioner of the higher literature. At this point, it is well to remember that the clever hostess of the day strove to leaven the leading lights of 'society' with generous helpings of fashionable Bohemia. Painters, poets, musicians, playwrights, actors

and actresses—these, too, were available for more serious conversational gambits.

One such hospitable household was the home of Sir George and
Lady Lewis in Portland Place—where the Prince and Princess of
James's *The Golden Bowl* would set up their handsome London
establishment (see also 'Illustrative passages', pp. 147–49 and 156),
based very clearly on first-hand knowledge. Sir George, the most
famous solicitor of his day, is tactfully described in the *Dictionary
of National Biography* as having enjoyed 'for more than a quarter of
a century the practical monopoly of those cases where the seamy
side of society is unveiled, and where the sins and follies of the
wealthy classes threaten exposure and disaster'. His legal handling
of various predicaments suffered by close personal friends of the
Prince of Wales would be rewarded by a baronetcy when that
leader of society came to the throne as King Edward VII. From
the point of view of a London-based novelist like James, the
outstanding characteristic of the Lewises' dinner parties is that they
included not only wealthy socialites but also the more successful
representatives of the current world of literature, painting, the
theatre and music. It was James's complete acceptance by this sort
of milieu that enabled him to keep in touch with social scandals
and speculations which would emerge in stories like 'In the Cage'
and novels like *The Sacred Fount*, as well as the problems by his
fellow artists which would be treated at length in *The Tragic Muse*
or in particular aspects in such tales as 'The Death of the Lion',
'The Figure in the Carpet' or 'The Lesson of the Master' (see
pp. 113–16).

By the kindness of the Lewises' grand-daughter, Mrs Elizabeth
Wansborough, I have turned the pages of a surviving notebook
containing their dinner-lists for the period 1885–98. In 1885,
James's table-mates included social luminaries like Lady Shrews-
bury and Alfred de Rothschild, plus the painter Edward Burne-
Jones and the poet Robert Browning—so when, shortly after
Browning's death, he concocted the esoteric little parable 'The
Private Life', in which the character based on Browning (to quote
Leon Edel) 'had been all "private life" and had no life in public,
save the usual and the expected', he knew what he was writing
about. The Burne-Jones couple often shared James's company
(they became Sir Edward and Lady after the painter's baronetcy
in 1894); and so did the popular painter Laurence Alma-Tadema
(knighted in 1899) and his family, who were present with James
at a bumper evening in 1890 which (as so often at the Lewises'
parties) was graced musically by Joachim and Sir Charles and
Lady Hallé, plus the Shakespearean actor Frank Benson and, as
notorious representative of near-the-throne society, Mrs Langtry
herself. Later in the same year his co-diners included painters John

S. Sargent (who would paint portraits of the host and of James himself) and Whistler, with Mr Cassel (later Sir Ernest) and Mr and Mrs Asquith from the world of finance and politics. On New Year's Eve 1892 a large party included the actor-manager Henry Irving (soon to be knighted) and financier Otto Kahn. During the following year, Sir John Everett Millais the painter joins the regular Burne-Jones couple and conductor Hallé, and James again joins the Lewises' New Year's Eve festivities.

So it continues. On the evidence of this one little notebook alone, James was repeatedly meeting men and women from the worlds of power and the polite arts—the Alfred Lyttletons would coincide in 1895 with Elizabeth Robins the actress (whose collection of letters from Henry James, *Theatre and Friendship*, revived in 1932 her memories of their long association against the background of theatrical hopes and disasters) and the Beerbohm Trees; the more famous actress Mrs Patrick Campbell would turn up in 1896, and again with the actress Ellen Terry in 1898, along with Johnston Forbes-Robertson (with which actor-manager James had several professional contacts, ending with the production in 1907 of his play *The High Bid*, based on the story 'Covering End') and the popular playwright J. M. Barrie and wife plus the Beerbohm Tree family—all these again, on New Year's Eve.

The above named diners, merely a few samples from the family cum politics cum the professions cum the arts who graced one hostess's table during a period which included 'the naughty nineties', when Henry James happened to be present, do at least show that the novelist's knowledge of the social and artistic world of the time was as genuinely first-hand as his Dickens-like absorption of London's shabbier life had been, when he indulged his lifelong habit of prowling urban streets by day and by night. He himself would ceaselessly protest that 'The artist was what he *did*—he was nothing else.' But the theories he would air in prefaces and note-books, and his disposition to 'rank as an apostle in the high aesthetic band' (to quote Gilbert's operetta *Patience* of 1881), would alike be very firmly based on the social experiences and contacts he himself naturally took for granted, but which we his readers a century later need some effort to reconstruct. It is good to remember that James the rigorous social and aesthetic critic was also a popular recurring figure, in his late fifties, at a whole sequence of the Lewises' New Year's Eve frolics. The cross-fertilization on such occasions must have been remarkable. For example, the popular novelist Anthony Hope (Hawkins) is now remembered as the creator of the fictional kingdom of Ruritania in *The Prisoner of Zenda* (1894) and *Rupert of Hentzau* (1898), but his *Dolly Dialogues* (1894) have much in common with James's lighter passages of the comedy of manners. He, too, frequented the

Lewises' parties, and there is no doubt that in his later attempts at more serious social studies his novels can be unexpectedly Jamesian in both theme and style. He had obviously read 'the Master' closely, and like George du Maurier whose *Trilby* also graced that productive year 1894, he had dined at the same all-embracing Lewis table and probably made a note of Jamesian mannerisms as well as Jamesian manners.

More extended opportunities for these social and artistic observations and debates were available, of course, at the splendid weekend house parties at which the ever courtly American novelist was by this time so frequent a guest (see 'Domestic and social geography', pp. 189–90). Reference has been made to those 'Illustrative passages' which give examples of James's close scrutiny, usually critical enough to please the most radical taste, of this kind of life. It was during such sophisticated country visits, too, that he could penetrate beneath the propaganda of political parties to the actual behaviour of elected politicians. To quote from a recent essay by Mr A. N. Wilson (*Essays by Divers Hands*, Vol. XLIII, Royal Society of Literature, 1984): 'Arthur Balfour and H. H. Asquith might shout at each other across the floor of the House of Commons, but they attended the same house parties, shot the same grouse and tried to commit adultery with the same women.'

Of James's negative criticism of the end-of-century society of his adopted country—its greed hidden under inherited possessions, as in *The Spoils of Poynton*, or its power to injure its young children by negligence or corrupt examples, as in *The Awkward Age* or *What Maisie Knew*—there are plenty of examples scattered throughout these pages. A brief word remains to be said about his more positive disapproval: his angered compassion for the lowlier members of society, the servants and governesses and humble folk of various kinds who oiled the wheels but rarely profited by the working of the machine; and especially his repeated exposure, throughout his whole range of novels and tales, of the deprived state of women who could find no outlet for their skills and interests save by the sordid bargains, often enough leading to a polite form of servitude, of the marriage market. A few examples may suffice to remind us that the same Henry James who in *The Bostonians* could find a rich field for satire in the public propaganda of the Women's Rights movement, could also present, with a compassion at times verging on militancy, the plight of women who were devoid of the pleasures men could find in their professional careers.

At the same time, he celebrated as no other novelist has so consistently done, the unrecognized services of those ladies who *did* occupy the few jobs open to them. Those widows and spinsters who mysteriously 'turned up' when a family was in need of a 'spare

The Reform Club, where James became a resident member. It was in such clubs that James's London gentlemen discussed the London scene.

wheel' 'nobody knew if other people paid them: they only knew that *they* did', whose role was to 'pick up the stitches' in other people's knitting—these anonymous ministrants were often graciously acknowledged in such metaphors as these. Yet it adds insult to injury, for one of the unsuccessful unsaleable offerings in James's marriage market, to know that she will be condemned to become (as Mrs Touchett reminds Isabel Archer in *The Portrait of a Lady*) 'a companion—some decayed gentlewoman with a darned cashmere and dyed hair, who paints on velvet'. It is to avoid such a fate that the poor girl in the story 'Glasses', whose beautiful face is her only fortune, stumbles about trying to disguise her increasing blindness, rather than wearing spectacles which would give her game away. Poor Mrs Wix, the housekeeper in *What Maisie Knew*, who is as cruelly neglected in her profession as is her little charge Maisie in her innocent person, has gone beyond the plight of the young lady in 'Glasses', for she has become a companion *with* spectacles 'which, in humble reference to a divergent obliquity of vision, she called her straighteners', which, as she 'explained to Maisie, were put on for the sake of others, whom, as she believed, they helped to recognize the bearing, otherwise doubtful, of her regard . . .'. Behind the clever teasing of such words one may recognize not only pity, but a hatred for the 'fast set' who took such servitors for granted. Nor is every such victim female: an entire story, 'Brooksmith', is devoted to a retired butler who tries to maintain, in his unpensioned retirement, the old-world standards he had helped to support while in the service of a mean employer. One could readily recruit Henry James not only for Women's Rights, but for the first campaigns for a Welfare State. What he did *not* forget, however, was that the less scrupulous people who joined such admirable crusades could themselves be as carelessly callous as anyone else. Two sardonic sentences from the story 'Georgina's Reasons' manage to show that servitude can co-exist with the most liberal sentiments: 'She used to read to the blind, and, more onerously, to the deaf. She looked after other people's children while the parents attended anti-slavery conventions.'

Perhaps the tale which most exhibits the tragi-comic possibilities, for a novelist of James's sensibility, of the different strands of social life he observed as a Londoner was 'In the Cage' (1898). The scene of all its action is the telegram counter of a small branch post and telegraph office, in a screened-off section of a grocer's shop pervaded by the smells of 'hams, cheese, dried fish, soap, varnish, paraffin, and other solids and fluids'. At this neutral counter, 'in framed and wired confinement', sits a young woman whose own life is deprived and commonplace; there are passages of venomous compassion which describe the daily range of experience enjoyed by her domestic neighbours who borrowed coals and umbrellas that were repaid in potatoes and postage-stamps. It had been a questionable help, at that time, to ladies submerged, floundering, panting, swimming for their lives, that they *were* ladies; but such an advantage could come up again in proportion as others vanished, and it had grown very great by the time it was the only ghost of one they possessed.

Her fiancé, Mr Mudge, has a life bounded by the small change of the other half of the shop, the grocery. As is customary with James, the writer is as sharp-eyed in spotting craven subservience as in spotting careless tyranny: though sharing the girl's poverty and her exclusion from the pleasures of the life at which they gaze out through their cages and window-panes, Mr Mudge is a staunch supporter of the social system which oppressed them both: he adores 'the charm of the existence of a class that Providence had raised up to be the blessing of grocers'. Their very prodigalities pleased him: 'The more flirtations . . . the more cheese and pickles.'

The *real* life of the telegram-girl 'in the cage' is the vicarious imaginary life she leads while piecing together, via their constant 'wires' to one another, the intricate yet feckless social affairs of the toffs, male and female, who are forever dashing into the office to arrange, or postpone, or cancel, their ever-changing assignations and evasions. One recalls that the sort of house parties described in *The Sacred Fount* and a dozen or so tales of marriage and/or adultery, passion and/or withdrawal, could only have been assembled in the first place via the nimble tapping fingers of young ladies 'in the cage'. So, the girl takes a fancy to a certain Captain Everard via whose raffish if incompetent telegrams she can trace his philanderings. Such 'plot' as the story holds concerns her silent emendations which aim to further the Captain's amatory escapades, but help him instead towards a compromised marriage. All this, too complicated for unravelling here, is of less interest than the Captain's complete inability to see beyond the class barriers separating them when he makes a clumsy effort to thank the anonymous ministrant who (in a curiously prophetic adumbration of 'the medium is the message') has been trying to help her romantic hero. On one occasion, when she has been working overtime on his behalf, he meets her, after office hours, in Hyde Park. After a few awkward remarks she admits that she has not yet had time to eat. 'Then you haven't eaten—?' asks the Captain. His ignorance of the daily habits of clerks is complete. She enlightens him: 'Yes, we do feed once.' In kindness, she fibs across the social barrier: 'I'm not a bit hungry.' His reply is, for him, equally kindly: 'Ah, but you *must* be, awfully?' I know of no passage of equal length, in any work by novelists more notable than James for socio-political attitudes, that so neatly exposes the 'two worlds' of late Victorian and

Edwardian life. It is this same penetration which enlivens the otherwise oppressive greenhouse atmosphere created by Henry James the novelist when he comes to describe the life of his London-based characters on the other side of the fence, *outside* the cage.

Self-communing: writing about writing

I have earlier sounded two introductory notes of caution for new readers of James: the need to know the young Henry James before trying to come to terms with 'the Master', and the need to recognize that for a person of his temperament and his point in history the treatment of sexual passion was, to our present notion, very guarded. There is one other possible pitfall to indicate—less important in the long run than the other two, but still capable of 'putting off' unlucky readers who happen too early upon James's self-conscious stories and parables concerning the artistic predicaments of a writer like himself.

In his later years, James revised the bulk of his earlier work and wrote that great sequence of eighteen long Prefaces to the New York Edition of his works, which when gathered up into a volume of their own as *The Art of the Novel* (edited by R. P. Blackmur, 1934) have for the last fifty years been among the most quoted of all pronouncements by creative writers on their own literary art. But long before the famous Prefaces, James had produced a flood of literary criticism of a very high order, ranging from book reviews to long essays; he thought well enough of them to publish four selections in book form (ranging from *French Poets and Novelists* of 1878 to *Notes on Novelists* of 1914). We now know that his private *Notebooks* (edited by F. O. Matthiessen and K. B. Murdoch in 1947) were also crammed with self-communing monologues on the subject of his own lifelong profession; and his letters to his family and friends, now so abundantly available in the four volumes of selections edited by Leon Edel (1974–84), could themselves be combed through for fascinating examples of insight into his own and other writers' failings and successes.

With all this wealth of critical commentary to his credit, it may be wondered why James allowed these professional interests to spill over into providing the actual subject matter of some of his 'creative' work. Before coming to any conclusion about the wisdom or unwisdom of these artistic themes as subject matter for novels and stories, it is fair for us to acknowledge how much, during James's writing lifetime, the art of fiction had loomed over all other forms of domestic entertainment. The circulating libraries were booming; the age of 'cheap editions' and 'pocket editions' had dawned; large fortunes could be made by purveyors of popular fiction for the vastly expanded reading public who were beneficiaries of education reforms. Never before had the population been so literate; never before had so many avid new readers awaited the next books by their favourite authors, sometimes full of thrilling adventures, sometimes of love affairs, more often full of both. There was, therefore, some excuse for James's belief that readers of stories might be interested in the professional problems of the authors who produced them.

In our own day, it is taken for granted that the people who produce the films, television programmes, radio and video cassettes and all the other swiftly changing methods for capturing entertaining sounds and sights, are themselves of personal interest to us. Not only are we expected to have keen personal interest in the private lives, taken as entertainment in themselves, of the people who are seen and heard on the various versions of mass media; we are often invited to share their artistic preferences. The professional tastes of authors, song-writers, producers, as well as actors and actresses, and their choice of 'Desert Island Discs', are deemed to be as entertaining as the artistic products (often lowly enough) which first brought their names to our attention. This profuse use of by-products of the entertainment industry as raw material for that same industry reaches (for some listeners) the point of ultimate absurdity when we are invited, on television or radio, to watch one unknown comedian pretending to be another unknown comedian, imitating a programme we had not ourselves even seen or heard.

These current habits may perhaps be borne in mind when we happen upon one of James's (often sour or disgruntled) stories about the writer's trade. However much we may cling to the view that novelists at their most creative may be expected to find better subject matter than themselves as they sit at their desks writing sad stories about themselves as writers sitting at their desks, it must at once be admitted that James's own inexhaustible store of freshly observed commentary is usually vivid enough to endow with lively humour even his most schematic arrangements of contrasting literary or artistic type-figures. Thus, in the story 'The Next Time' (1895), he invented a novelist who (like his creator) is the master of a subtle and distinguished style, whose books are always praised by the critics but do not sell well, and who therefore tries hard to produce a vulgar best-seller. Alas, his programme of 'writing down' to please the novel-buying public never comes off. Try as he may, the result of his efforts at saleable vulgarity always emerges as a 'shameless, merciless masterpiece'. He simply cannot learn the art of making sow's ears out of silk purses. His friends groan over his lack of success, in phrases which attest that the author of *this* story, at least, has a comic sense: '"The book has extraordinary beauty". "Poor duck—after trying so hard!"' In much the same way, James's own efforts to interest us in the theoretical problems of authors and artists sometimes fail; but even in the least successful parallels we may be delighted by yet another set of splendidly imagined social types who—if we really *do* share the writer's and even his ventriloquist's dummies' love for the art of fiction—interest and amuse us far in excess of the sometimes sterile debating points they were designed to make.

Another schematic parable, 'The Real Thing' (1892), which poses 'the perverse and cruel law in virtue of which the real thing could be so much less precious than the unreal', is itself saved from being an 'unreal' moral tale simply by virtue of James's own vivid portraiture of his representative types the Monarchs, who have a 'real' life far beyond that required by the parable itself. Major and Mrs Monarch, a pair of utterly authentic representatives of 'the upper class', have slipped down the financial ladder so far that in their poverty they are obliged to hire themselves out as models for a commercial artist who supplies graphic illustrations of high-society fiction written by the best-selling magazine journalists of James's day. Poor Major Monarch is a splendidly realized figure, the sort of knowing but tongue-tied man of the world whose conversation is confined to 'questions of leather and even of liquor—saddlers and breeches-makers and how to get excellent claret cheap—and matters like "good trains" and the habits of small game'. But when it comes to *imitating* people like themselves, he and his wife are of course hopeless. The sympathetic commercial artist tries hard to show them how he wants them to imitate themselves so that he in turn can imitate them in his sketches and bring them to fit graphic illustrations of the kind of fictional characters in magazine stories about the upper classes written for the delectation of lower-class readers. Alas, the Monarchs are far too authentic to pose as 'models' of themselves. They have to be supplanted, by the commercial artist, with a pair of lowly yet professionally adept *poseurs*, whose acting is far more persuasive and illustrative than 'the real thing' can ever force itself to be.

The best known of James's tales about writers is undoubtedly 'The Aspern Papers' (1888), which poses the moral problem faced by many biographers: are they justified in causing distress to the surviving friends and relations of the illustrious dead, when in the course of their researches they disinter and publish manuscript material which may bring the illustrious person into disrepute? But James himself was not (except in one instance, his more than pious life of William Wetmore Story, mentioned on p. 47) a biographer, and this story is far more objective than his other self-communing studies of writers. It is to this, no doubt, that it owes its popularity. His portraits of old Miss Bordereau, the surviving ex-mistress of the romantic poet Jeffrey Aspern (a Byron or a

Shelley character), and her now frumpish 'niece' Miss Tita as they moulder away in their dilapidated Venetian palazzo are those of a story-teller in full command of his medium. The intrusion of a would-be biographer of Aspern upon the 'mystic rites of ennui the Misses Bordereau celebrated in their darkened rooms' sets off a series of dramatic confrontations and emotional entanglements so tense that the stage success of Sir Michael Redgrave's dramatization comes as no surprise.

'The Lesson of the Master'

Here we meet a distinguished novelist named Henry St George who worries that his busy social and domestic life interferes with his literary standards ('that's the devil of the whole thing, keeping it up'); we may be excused for taking him as the author's self-portrait. That would be half correct—a half portrait! As so often, the Henry James persona is divided between two characters, Henry St George and a dedicated younger writer, Paul Overt. We meet them first as guests at a country house. For young Overt it is a memorable week-end, for he meets the great writer and also a charming young lady who has actually read one of his own novels. She admits that she herself had tried to write a novel:

> 'Well, after all, why try to be an artist?' the young man went on. 'It's so poor—so poor!'
> 'I don't know what you mean,' said Marian Fancourt, looking grave.
> 'I mean as compared with being a person of action—as living your works.'
> 'But what is art but a life—if it be real?' asked the girl, 'I think it's the only one—everything else is so clumsy!'

The Master himself (St George) is at first somewhat patronizing, but during later encounters the younger and the older writer talk quite freely about the way in which St George's standard as a novelist has steadily fallen while he pours out one book after another in order to maintain his social 'public' image. He urges the younger writer to profit by his own example as a successful public figure but a failed artist, and put his devotion to his art before everything else:

> 'Ah, my dear young man, don't talk about passing—for the likes of me! I'm passing away—nothing else than that. She [Miss Fancourt] has a better use for her young imagination (isn't it fine?) than in "representing" in any way such a weary, wasted, used-up animal!' St George spoke with a sudden sadness which produced a protest on Paul's part; but before the protest could be uttered he went on, reverting to the latter's successful novel:

113

'I had no idea you were so good—one hears of so many things. But you're surprisingly good.'

'I'm going to be surprisingly better,' said Overt.

'I see that and it's what fetches me. I don't see so much else—as one looks about—that's going to be surprisingly better. They're going to be consistently worse—most of the things. It's so much easier to be worse—heaven knows I've found it so. I'm not in a great glow, you know, about what's being attempted, what's being done. But you *must* be better—you must keep it up. I haven't, of course. It's very difficult—that's the devil of the whole thing; but I see you can. It will be a great disgrace if you don't.'

Most of all, he urges Overt not to marry:

'I'm not speaking of my dear wife, who had a small fortune, which, however, was not my bribe. I fell in love with her, as many other people have done. I refer to the mercenary muse whom I led to the altar of literature. Don't do that, my boy. She'll lead you a life!'

'Haven't you been happy?'

'Happy? It's a kind of hell.'

'There are things I should like to ask you,' Paul Overt said, hesitating.

'Ask me anything in all the world. I'd turn myself inside out to save you.'

'To save me?' Paul repeated.

'To make you stick to it—to make you see it through. As I said to you the other night at Summersoft, let my example be vivid to you.'

'Why, your books are not so bad as that,' said Paul, laughing and feeling that he breathed the air of art.

'So bad as what?'

'Your talent is so great that it is in everything you do, in what's less good as well as in what's best. You've some forty volumes to show for it—forty volumes of life, of observation, of magnificent ability.'

'I'm very clever, of course I know that,' St George replied, quietly. 'Lord, what rot they'd all be if I hadn't been! I'm a successful charlatan—I've been able to pass off my system.'

The James-who-might-have-been openly warns the James-who-was-to-be:

'I've got everything, in fact, but the great thing—'

'The great thing?'

'The sense of having done the best—the sense, which is the real life of the artist and the absence of which is his death, of having drawn from his intellectual instrument the finest music that nature had hidden in it, of having played it as it should be played. He either does that or he doesn't—and if he doesn't he isn't worth speaking of. And precisely those who really know don't speak of him. He may still hear a great chatter, but what he hears most is the incorruptible silence of Fame. I have squared her, you may say, for my little hour—but what is my little hour? Don't imagine for a moment I'm such a cad as to have brought you down here to abuse or to complain of my wife to you. She is a woman of very distinguished qualities, to whom my obligations are immense; so that, if you please, we will say nothing about her. My boys—my children are all boys—are straight and strong, thank God! and have no poverty of growth about them, no penury of needs. I receive, periodically, the most satisfactory attestation from Harrow, from Oxford, from Sandhurst (oh, we have done the best for them!) of their being living, thriving, consuming organisms.'

Paul Overt takes his old friend's advice, to the extent of going abroad for a couple of years of solitary literary work. On returning to London, he learns that St George has become a widower. Calling at the house of the young lady who had so encouraged and so attracted him, he discovers that she is on the brink of marrying St George. The old novelist—the James-who-might-have-been— himself greets him in the friendliest manner and explains his new situation:

His companion went on, as if, now that the subject had been broached, he was, as a man of imagination and tact, perfectly ready to give every satisfaction—being able to enter fully into everything another might feel. 'But it's not only that—for honestly, at my age, I never dreamed—a widower, with big boys and with so little else! It has turned out differently from any possible calculation, and I am fortunate beyond all measure. She has been so free, and yet she consents. Better than any one else perhaps—for I remember how you liked her, before you went away, and how she liked you—you can intelligently congratulate me.'

'She has been so free!' Those words made a great impression on Paul Overt, and he almost writhed under that irony in them as to which it little mattered whether it was intentional or casual.

We are left with the James-who-was-to-be:

St George's words were still in his ears, 'You're very strong— wonderfully strong.' Was he really? Certainly, he would have to be; and it would be a sort of revenge. *Is* he? the reader may ask in turn, if his interest has followed the perplexed young man so far. The best answer to that perhaps is that he is doing his best but that it is too soon to say. When the new book came out in the autumn Mr and Mrs St George found it really magnificent. The former still has published nothing, but Paul Overt does not even yet feel safe. I may say for him, however, that if this event were to befall he would really be the very first to appreciate it: which is perhaps a proof that St George was essentially right and that Nature dedicated him to intellectual, not to personal passion.

7   *The Wings of the Dove*

In *The Wings of the Dove* (1902) there is a beautiful passage of extraordinarily intense emotion, which describes the silent recognition by a rich young woman, herself beautiful alike in person and in character, that she is suffering from an incurable illness and must very soon prepare to die. The fate of this lovely girl and the influence of her fast fading life upon all those near to her, all those who love her, who admire her, who envy her riches, who strive to manipulate her or protect her—this is the theme of the most tenderly moving of all James's novels. The shifting alignments of all these attendant figures, as they seek either to entrap or release her, constitute perhaps the most successful of all the novelist's bold patterns of dramatic craftsmanship, the subtlest of all his elaborate devices for the disclosure of human passions, vile or splendid, as they struggle, now in concert and now in contradiction, beneath the deceptive decorum of social behaviour at the turn of the century. The setting—and misfiring—of a seductive trap for this innocent 'dove' is one of James's most justly admired plots. But all such mastery of 'effects' and 'presentations' would be wasted if we, the readers, had not first been led into a state of complete concern with the 'dove' herself. The passage I wish to quote for close reading is one which produces in us a wonderful feeling of kinship with the doomed heroine, and which happens at the same time to illustrate how some of the witty or ironical habits of James's conscious local commentaries on life may occasionally help, in a very strange way, to irradiate the resplendence of what *seems* to be an unlocalized display of universally shared human emotions.

The passage to which I invite closest attention is found in Book Fifth, Chapter XIII; but in order to place it in its human setting we must first take some soundings from the preceding Chapter XII which describes the two visits of the 'dove', the American heiress Milly Theale, to her London medical adviser, Sir Luke Strett. On her first visit, Milly is accompanied by her new London friend, Kate Croy. It is this 'friend' who will later set the trap for the 'dove'; for Kate, who has no money of her own, is hoping to marry a poor journalist, Merton Densher, and Milly has been quietly developing her own affection for Merton. The hidden struggle of the two young women for this not superficially very attractive prize will constitute the tensions, and ultimately harrowing solution, of all the consequent moral and personal problems. During this first brief visit, Milly instinctively trusts her doctor's judgement of her physical and emotional state, and is prepared to admit this in general terms to Kate:

The Bronzino portrait of Lucrezia Panciatichi, which her admirers considered to capture the spirit of 'the Dove'.

His large, settled face, though firm, was not, as she had thought at first, hard; he looked, in the oddest manner, to her fancy, half like a general and half like a bishop, and she was soon sure that, within some such handsome range, what it would show her would be what was good, what was best for her. She established, in other words, in this time-saving way, a relation with it; and the relation was the special trophy that, for the hour, she bore off. It was like an absolute possession, a new resource altogether, something done up in the softest silk and tucked away under the arm of memory. She hadn't had it when she went in, and she had it when she came out; she had it there under her cloak, but dissimulated, invisibly carried, when smiling, smiling, she again faced Kate Croy. That young lady had of course awaited her in another room, where, as the great man was to absent himself, no one else was in attendance; and she rose for her with such a face of sympathy as might have graced the vestibule of a dentist. 'Is it out?' she seemed to ask as if it had been a question of a tooth; and Milly indeed kept her in no suspense at all.
'He's a dear. I'm to come again.'
'But what does he say?'
Milly was almost gay. 'That I'm not to worry about anything in the world, and that if I'll be a good girl and do exactly what he tells me, he'll take care of me for ever and ever.'

She goes so far as to say: 'I feel —I can't otherwise describe it—as if I had been, on my knees, to the priest. I've confessed and I've been absolved.'

However, it is on her second visit, unaccompanied, that Milly receives the doctor's kindly advice to live as fully as possible, which she rightly interprets as a warning that her time is very short. Their dialogue is delicate but charged with meaning. Milly admits that she has no surviving family in whom she can confide:

'Only one's situation is what it is. It's *me* it concerns. The rest is delightful and useless. Nobody can really help. That's why I'm by myself to-day. I *want* to be—in spite of Miss Croy, who came with me last. If you can help, so much the better—and also of course if one can, a little, one's self. Except for that—you and me doing our best—I like you to see me just as I am. Yes, I like it—and I don't exaggerate. Shouldn't one, at the start, show the worst —so that anything after that may be better? It wouldn't make any real difference—it *won't* make any, anything that may happen won't—to any one. Therefore, I feel myself, this way, with you, just as I am; and—if you do in the least care to know— it quite positively bears me up.'

There is a quick understanding between doctor and patient that

pity would be quite misplaced: they achieve an unspoken agree-
ment that each can trust the other to be 'friends', which means that
Milly and Sir Luke recognize, on the level of conscious behaviour,
their shared 'superior' qualities:

> Then he pursued: 'I'm sure you've an excellent spirit; but don't
> try to bear more things than you need.' Which after an instant
> he further explained. 'Hard things have come to you in youth,
> but you mustn't think life will be for you all hard things. You've
> the right to be happy. You must make up your mind to it. You
> must accept any form in which happiness may come.'
> 'Oh, I'll accept any whatever!' she almost gaily returned. 'And
> it seems to me, for that matter, that I'm accepting a new one
> every day. Now *this*!' she smiled.
> 'This is very well so far as it goes. You can depend on me,' the
> great man said, 'for unlimited interest. But I'm only, after all,
> one element in fifty. We must gather in plenty of others. Don't
> mind who knows. Knows, I mean, that you and I are friends.'

This breathlessly tense yet wonderfully gallant series of hints and
comprehensions ends with their parting exchange:

> 'So you don't think I'm out of my mind?'
> 'Perhaps that *is*', he smiled, 'all that's the matter.'
> She looked at him longer. 'No, that's too good. Shall I, at any rate,
> suffer?'
> 'Not a bit.'
> 'And yet then live?'
> 'My dear young lady,' said her distinguished friend, 'isn't to
> "live" exactly what I'm trying to persuade you to take the
> trouble to do?'

The next chapter (XIII) contains, in eleven pages, so profoundly
moving a version of human loneliness in resignation to one's fate
as a social being, and so piercing an insight into the unadmitted
jealousy lying at the root of private possessive love, as to be
unmatched anywhere else in James's (or, to the best of my knowledge, any one else's) fiction. When Milly leaves Sir Luke's
consulting room,

> She was borne up for the hour, and now she knew why she had
> wanted to come by herself. No one in the world could have
> sufficiently entered into her state; no tie would have been close
> enough to enable a companion to walk beside her without some
> disparity. She literally felt, in this first flush, that her only
> company must be the human race at large, present all round her,
> but inspiringly impersonal, and that her only field must be, then
> and there, the grey immensity of London.

Her vague wanderings finally bring her to Regent's Park,

round which, on two or three occasions with Kate Croy, her public chariot had solemnly rolled. But she went into it further now; this was the real thing; the real thing was to be quite away from the pompous roads, well within the centre and on the stretches of shabby grass. Here were benches and smutty sheep; here were idle lads at games of ball, with their cries mild in the thick air; here were wanderers, anxious and tired like herself; here doubtless were hundreds of others just in the same box. Their box, their great common anxiety, what was it, in this grim breathing-space, but the practical question of life? They could live if they would; that is, like herself, they had been told so; she saw them all about her, on seats, digesting the information, feeling it altered, assimilated, recognising it again as something, in a slightly different shape, familiar enough, the blessed old truth that they would live if they could. All she thus shared with them made her wish to sit in their company; which she so far did that she looked for a bench that was empty, eschewing a still emptier chair that she saw hard by and for which she would have paid, with superiority, a fee.

No longer does Milly arrest our attention primarily as an heiress in danger of being cheated of her fortune, or as an American girl in danger of falling foul of the corrupt social *mores* of the exotic society in which she now finds herself. Her plight can be shared only by the whole of mortal humanity. The ailing 'princess', the millionairess, could indeed have paid the fee for a deck-chair—a penny or twopence! She rejects it in favour of a park bench, free to all transient mortals. And there is a very special touch of Jamesian sympathy in Milly appreciating the self-absorbed, self-deceiving yet wholly touching inflation of their lowly personalities as they read their newspapers. *Are* they reading their newspapers? No; in the nakedness of her sympathy and forgiveness the doomed princess can share their own inflated estimation of *themselves*: they are not simply 'reading the newspapers', they are important citizens choosing, in their own minds, to think of themselves as *'digesting the information'*.

Digesting the information? Readers of James's earlier novels may catch an echo here—and in so doing, may acknowledge how his irony, at times so damaging, may become subdued within a more compassionate mood to add pity, forgiveness, even love. We may remember the tone of amused inflation when in *The Bostonians* the pathetic Mrs Tarrant, mother of the heroine Verena, is left behind in her dingy home reading the newspaper: 'from this publication she derived inscrutable solace'. Her absurd husband, Selah Tarrant, preferred to read his newspapers in the public vestibules of hotels. Believing that 'if a diviner day were to come upon earth, it would be brought about by copious advertisement in the daily prints', Selah Tarrant wanders through vestibules where similar shiftless citizens are 'writing letters at a table inlaid with advertisements'—and he is described by James as making 'innumerable contemplative stations'. Looking back at that absurd figure from the standpoint of James's Milly Theale in Regent's Park, surrounded by 'wanderers anxious and tired like herself', we may suddenly recall that the phrase 'contemplative stations' borrows its imagery from the Stations of the Cross. As so often in James, a temptation to giggle at his farcical manner of stripping away man's flimsy trappings may be shamed into a resulting compassion for comic mankind's pitiful nakedness.

To match the perfection of Milly's newly won social sensitivity, we find only a few paragraphs later an almost unbearable veracity of response to a purely personal emotion. Milly, awaiting the call at her hotel from her friend Kate, happens to be on the balcony when her visitor is paying off her cabman in the street below—and suddenly she sees her not as her friend Miss Croy but rather as the eligible Merton Densher (never, now, far from her mind) must be accustomed to see her. Having, a few pages back, shared the social identify of unknown Londoners, Milly finds herself, on an instant, sharing the perception—and hence the resulting emotional state—of Kate's young lover, whom she herself mutely loves:

> What was also, however, determined for her was, again, yet irrepressibly again, that the image presented to her, the splendid young woman who looked so particularly handsome in impatience, with the fine freedom of her signal, was the peculiar property of somebody else's vision, that this fine freedom in short was the fine freedom she showed Mr Densher. Just so was how she looked to him, and just so was how Milly was held by her—held as by the strange sense of seeing through that distant person's eyes. It lasted, as usual, the strange sense, but fifty seconds; yet in so lasting it produced an effect. It produced in fact more than one, and we take them in their order. The first was that it struck our young woman as absurd to say that a girl's looking so to a man could possibly be without connections; and the second was that by the time Kate had got into the room Milly was in mental possession of the main connection it must have for herself.

This hypersensitive ability to see one person accurately through the eyes of another person rather than her own eyes tells us in brilliant economy something of the qualities of the 'dove', qualities which make her equally lovable and vulnerable. A chapter later, this psychological power of telepathy is seen even more piercingly, when Milly can tell, simply by the presence of her friend Kate Croy and with no words spoken, that after an absence their 'new' friend

Merton Densher was back in the same vast city as themselves:

> Kate had remained in the window, very handsome and upright,
> the outer dark framing in a highly favourable way her summery
> simplicities and lightnesses of dress. Milly had, given the
> relation of space, no real fear she had heard their talk; only she
> hovered there as with conscious eyes and some added advantage.
> Then indeed, with small delay, her friend sufficiently saw. The
> conscious eyes, the added advantage were but those she had now
> always at command—those proper to the person Milly knew as
> known to Merton Densher. It was for several seconds again as
> if the *total* of her identity had been that of the person known to
> him—a determination having for result another sharpness of its
> own. Kate had positively but to be there just as she was to tell
> her he had come back. It seemed to pass between them, in fine,
> without a word, that he was in London, that he was perhaps only
> round the corner; and surely therefore no dealing of Milly's with
> her would yet have been so direct.

We have seen this uncanny power operating on behalf of another
hypersensitive doomed heroine, at that tense moment in *The Portrait
of a Lady* when Isabel suddenly becomes aware of the fact that
Madame Merle, plunging gallantly on in a conversation of superficial politeness *knows* that Isabel is in possession of the secret of
Pansy Osmond's birth.

The Wings of the Dove is a long novel, graced by many subsidiary
characters who could have served to act as major figures in other
novels; but the final tension, when Milly lies dying in her Venetian
palazzo having acquired the desolating information that Merton
Densher had been for long engaged to Kate Croy, is again effected
in passages of sometimes difficult prose commentary and sometimes
quasi-telepathic dialogue, but both types of writing most successfully conveying, with subtlest economy, states of great psychological
complexity. An abbreviated account of these final scenes may serve
as samples of James's method in the three great works of his 'major
phase' (the others being *The Ambassadors* and *The Golden Bowl*,
briefly touched upon below on pp. 153–55, 156 and pp. 147–49).

In abject complicity with the callous hope of Kate Croy that he
will find a way of marrying the mortally ailing 'princess' Milly so
that as a rich widower he may very soon be enabled to marry Kate,
Merton Densher has stayed on in Venice, as it were 'on call' from
the sick-room, after Kate has returned to England. The weak but
increasingly devoted Densher suffers a sensitivity to his role so self-
accusing that he even suspects that Milly's gondolier, Eugenio, is
suspicious of him:

> Eugenio had of course reflected that a word to Miss Theale, from
> such a pair of lips, would cost him his place; but he could also

bethink himself that, so long as the word never came—and it was, on the basis he had arranged, impossible—he enjoyed the imagination of mounting guard. He had never so mounted guard, Densher could see, as during these minutes in the damp *loggia*, where the storm-gusts were strong; and there came in fact for our young man, as a result of his presence, a sudden sharp sense that everything had turned to the dismal. Something had happened—he didn't know what; and it wasn't Eugenio who would tell him. What Eugenio told him was that he thought the ladies—as if their liability had been equal—were a 'leetle' fatigued, just a 'leetle leetle,' and without any cause named for it. It was one of the signs of what Densher felt in him that, by a refinement of resource, he always met the latter's Italian with English and his English with Italian. He now, as usual, slightly smiled at him in the process—but ever so slightly, this time, his manner also being attuned, our young man made out, to the thing, whatever it was, that constituted the rupture of peace.   (Ch. XXX)

How different is the handling when Milly's friend Mrs Stringham comes to visit Densher after he, a prey to delicacy and conscience, had stayed away from Milly's palazzo:

It told Densher of the three days she on her side had spent. 'Well, anything you do for me—*is* for her too. Only, only—!'

'Only nothing now matters?'

She looked at him a minute as if he were the fact itself that he expressed. 'Then you know?'

'Is she dying?' he asked for all answer.

Mrs Stringham waited—her face seemed to sound him. Then her own reply was strange. 'She hasn't so much as named you. We haven't spoken.'

'Not for three days?'

'No more,' she simply went on, 'than if it were all over. Not even by the faintest allusion.'

'Oh,' said Densher with more light, 'you mean you haven't spoken about *me*.'

'About what else? No more than if you were dead.'

'Well,' he answered after a moment, 'I *am* dead.'

'Then *I* am,' said Susan Shepherd with a drop of her arms on her waterproof.

It was a tone that, for the minute, imposed itself in its dry despair; it represented in the bleak place, which had no life of its own, none but the life Kate had left—the sense of which, for that matter, by mystic channels, might fairly be reaching the visitor—the very impotence of their extinction. And Densher had nothing to oppose it, nothing but again: 'Is she dying?'

It made her, however, as if these were crudities, almost material pangs, only say as before: 'Then you know?'

'Yes,' he at last returned, 'I know. But the marvel to me is that *you* do. I've no right in fact to imagine, or to assume, that you do.'

'You may,' said Susan Shepherd, 'all the same. I know.'

'Everything?'

Her eyes, through her veil, kept pressing him. 'No—not everything. That's why I've come.'

(Ch. XXXI)

He saw, with the last vividness, and it was as if, in their silences, they were simply so leaving what he saw. 'She doesn't speak at all? I don't mean not of me.'

'Of nothing—of no one.' And she went on, Susan Shepherd, giving it out as she had had to take it. 'She doesn't *want* to die. Think of her age. Think of her goodness. Think of her beauty. Think of all she is. Think of all she *has*. She lies there stiffening herself and clinging to it. So I thank God—!' the poor lady wound up with a kind of wan inconsequence.

He wondered, 'You thank God—?'

'That she's so quiet.'

He continued to wonder. '*Is* she so quiet?'

'She's more than quiet. She's grim. It's what she has never been. So you see—all these days. I can't tell you—but it's better so. It would kill me if she *were* to tell me.'

'To tell you?' He was still at a loss.

'How she feels. How she clings. How she doesn't want it.'

'How she doesn't want to die? Of course she doesn't want it.'

He had a long pause, and they might have been thinking together of what they could even now do to prevent it. This, however, was not what he brought out. Milly's 'grimness,' and the great hushed palace, were present to him; present with the little woman before him as she must have been waiting there and listening. 'Only, what harm have *you* done her?'

Mrs Stringham looked about in her darkness. 'I don't know. I come and talk of her here with you.'

It made him again hesitate. 'Does she utterly hate me?'

'I don't know. How *can* I? No one ever will.'

'She'll never tell?'

'She'll never tell.'

Once more he thought. 'She must be magnificent.'

'She *is* magnificent.'

(Ch. XXXI)

It is after the tensest pages of this quality that we the readers know, before being told so, that with the ineffaceable image of Milly ever before him, Densher will refuse to accept her dying bequest, and Kate will not marry him without it.

8 Last years

When men reach their seventies, having completed the allotted span of man's life on earth, they arrive at a time when the opinions they formed and the attitudes they struck in their youth (often enough anything that would serve to prove their fathers wrong in *their* beliefs) have become a fairly settled habit of mind which they may take for granted without much further thought. Indeed as with opinions, so perhaps with life's facts: by this time they have discarded those facts which no longer interest them, and may persuade themselves that having shed much of this load, they still have left enough facts to work with. Their last admiration may be reserved for one of those rare human beings who have managed to *make* something of their experience, something that came from one individual consciousness and therefore could not have been there before. If I am right in supposing this to be a not uncommon experience among elderly consumers of the fruits of their illustrious ancestors, there may be some truth in my guess that in the case of the elderly Henry James, this rejuvenating experience, this encouragement to an enduring fortitude, sprang—most unusually—from a backward study of his *own* unflagging creative activity.

Henry James's entry upon his seventies had been marked by an act of public recognition which he greeted with feigned embarrassment and genuine delight. No fewer than 270 of his friends and admirers had conspired to present him, on his seventieth birthday on 15 April 1913, with a handsome Golden Bowl (actually a silver-gilt reproduction of some Charles II plate) plus a commission to his admired friend, John Singer Sargent, to paint the portrait opposite—much admired by the sitter, who could nevertheless wryly refer, in a letter to one of the donors, to its exposure of his own 'large and luscious rotundity'. As if to prove to himself and the world that his remaining time would indeed be used energetically, James had seen the first instalment of his autobiography, *A Small Boy and Others*, published in New York and London a couple of weeks before his birthday, and he was already within a few months of finishing the second great chunk, *Notes of a Son and Brother*, which appeared a year later, in March 1914.

This gallantly sustained effort to make something out of his own past life, just as in his fiction he had been making something out of his lifelong observation of other people, is in keeping with his oft-quoted and basically self-defensive dictum: 'The artist was what he *did*—he was nothing else.' In fact, much of his sixties had seen suffering and sorrow. His great masterpieces behind him, he had

The Sargent portrait.

been largely disillusioned when revisiting his native America in 1904–5—a disillusion reflected in *The American Scene* (1907) and such tales as 'Crapy Cornelia' (1909). The great New York Edition of his laboriously revised lifelong *oeuvre* (published 1907–9) had failed, in his own estimation, to excite the reading public or gain any proportionate financial reward. It had nevertheless represented his own effort to find in the great art of one major practitioner a sufficiently compendious summary of life's meaning—even if in his own case that great body of work had been his own.

A fresh assessment of James's astonishing effort of strenuous creative activity in tackling 'the practical workings of the literary imagination over a long literary career, the strange complexities of past and present intention in the process of revision' has been made by Dr Philip Horne. His *Henry James and Revision* will show that a sense of personal identity may shine out with an unmistakable glow even when a writer is consciously seeking to correct, to amplify, to reinterpret, almost to the point of apparent contradiction or obliteration, his own earlier interpretation of that same life he is still living. The elderly writer, having 'revised' himself so thoroughly, is still much more like his former self than either of them is like any *other* writer of, say, 1873 or forty years later in 1913. Dr Horne's study will show how 'reading through his earlier works for the Edition with an active pen, James repeatedly faced and accommodated the fact of his own (remarkable) development. His revisions register the differences made by his personal history and the continuing growth of his imagination.'

In 1910, exhausted by 'the wear and tear of discrimination', James had suffered so severe a physical and nervous breakdown that his nephew Harry thought that he was 'facing . . . the frustration of all his hopes and wishes', and he himself confessed to a friend, 'I have really been down into hell and stayed there for months . . .'. A return trip to America that same year with his beloved yet overpowering brother William, already weakened by his mortal ailment, had merely allowed Henry to stand by his brother's graveside. Not for nothing had his published work in that same black year included 'The Bench of Desolation' with its pathetic passivity and self-pitying abnegation. To have turned from all this and further bouts of illness to work on his autobiography had been a fine gesture of endurance.

One instance of the new spurt of mental health following upon James's seventieth birthday may be found in a letter of September 1913, destined for 'the delightful young man from Texas', Stark Young, in which he offers two lists of his own works, each naming five titles, intended as a guide for beginners approaching the vast Henry James *oeuvre*. Two of his great trio, *The Wings of the Dove* and *The Golden Bowl*, appear on both lists; but it seems significant that the first list also includes three of his fresher earlier works: *Roderick Hudson, The Portrait of a Lady* and *The Princess Casamassima.* Another outburst of emotional energy in the same seventieth year, 1913, may be documented in one of James's wonderful series of encouraging letters to the young novelist Hugh Walpole, with whom he had developed since their meeting in 1909 (when James was sixty-six and Walpole had just turned twenty-five) an affectionate relationship which had given much emotional satisfaction to both members of this apparently ill-matched pair of novelists. Walpole, still only twenty-nine, had published his fifth novel, *Fortitude*, in January 1913, and was well launched upon his best-selling career. It was in August of that last pre-war year that James included in one of his magisterial letters that splendid affirmation of first-hand experience as the novelist's prime source: 'We must know, as much as possible, in our beautiful art, yours and mine, what we are talking about—and the only way to know is to have lived and loved and cursed and floundered and enjoyed and suffered.—I only regret, in my chilled age, certain occasions and possibilities I *didn't* embrace.' From the thickets and tropical jungle of some of James's epistolary style at this period of his career, words like these shine out with vivid acceptance of life. They recall his recipe for story-telling when, writing for the New York Edition a Preface to *The Princess Casamassima* of as long ago as 1886, he had written: 'Give us plenty of bewilderment . . . so long as there is plenty of slashing out in the bewilderment too.'

The interaction of the private life and the public life had been a recurring theme throughout James's writing career. In a professionally limited version of this theme in his own life, one may notice how often, when his own essential loneliness as author and person had been assuaged by the willingness of some younger man to accept the novelist's abundantly affectionate friendship, these opportunities for emotional outpouring had been transferred first to his own inimitable letters and then to whatever piece of fiction he had on hand. As Leon Edel justly remarks of the exchange of letters between James and Hugh Walpole from 1909 onwards, 'the verbalization of love was important to both'. It is Leon Edel, too, who had shrewdly noted that of all the 'heroes' of the late novels, Prince Amerigo of *The Golden Bowl* is the only one who is permitted to enjoy (with both his mistress and his wife) a satisfying sexual completion, and who related this purely critical comment to the author's own release from emotional inhibitions at the time of writing. 'In adumbrating a hero who no longer rationalizes away the claims of love, of physical love, James reflected the presence in his life, at the moment that he began to write this book, of the fun-loving Jocelyn Persse, whom James adored.' It is not necessary to draw a conclusion that James's avuncular affection reached any kind of physical expression; the temporary removal from the novelist of what we lightly call a 'mental block' would have been enough to encourage his current fictional lover Prince Amerigo to follow his blood as well as his sensibilities. Of the precise nature of James's affection, Hugh Walpole—the last recipient of the 'dearest boy' epistolary treatment—gave it as his opinion that James's 'passion for his friends—Lucy Clifford, Edith Wharton, Jocelyn Persse, Mrs Prothero, among others—was the intense longing of a lonely man. It was most unselfish and noble.' It is wholly to be expected that feelings such as these would overflow into the work of a man whose pen was for ever in his hand (see also 'Illustrative passages', pp. 158–62).

To a minor extent, in James's last years, such tender personal feelings could both encourage and somewhat falsify his public efforts to keep himself up to date. It was gallant of the aging Master to accept in 1913 an invitation to write a long essay about the work of 'The Younger Generation' of novelists (which saw book form in the collection *Notes on Novelists*, published the following year). True enough, he could not resist his old hobby-horse denunciation of the lack of constructional skills in the 'fluid puddings' of Tolstoy and Dostoievsky, or to castigate a similar over-inclusiveness in Arnold Bennett's 'act of squeezing out to the utmost the plump and more or less juicy orange of a particular acquainted state and letting this affirmation of energy, however directed or undirected, constitute . . . the "treatment" of a theme . . .'. But one cannot help suspecting that his kind words for Edith Wharton and Hugh Walpole and Compton Mackenzie, so abundantly chewed over in contrast with his dismissive half-reference to D. H. Lawrence, owed more to personal friendship than rigorous grading.

What does stand out in these relationships is James's extraordinary talent for kindness. It was, for him, the one absolute in human relations. His nephew Billy, William's son, remembered Uncle Henry's admonition: 'Three things in human life are important. The first is to be kind. The second is to be kind. And the third is to be kind.' All this is in line with his elaborate efforts to praise the published work of Edith Wharton and other novelists whenever he could truthfully do so, or his outburst to a young friend that 'one must do everything to invent, to force open, the door of exit from mere immersion in one's own states'. All these and many other instances flowered from a settled habit of life which included a splendid competence in organizing, modifying and, where necessary, sternly suppressing that natural egotism which must inescapably be the motive force of most human action and expression, and especially that of creative writers.

The major, shattering, implosion of James's personal and public worlds alike came with the outbreak of the Great War of 1914. Writing of the immediate aftermath of the publication in March of *Notes of a Son and Brother*, Leon Edel speaks of 'the new-found emotional energies of his old age', and claims that 'in spite of illness and reduced activity and much suffering, all vestiges of his old depression seem to have left him. He wanted to live . . .'. He worked away at the novel *The Ivory Tower*, left unfinished at his death and posthumously published in 1917 along with his other unfinished novel *The Sense of the Past*. The remarkable vitality of *The Ivory Tower* shows James girding himself to face—and attack with the full power of his merciless antagonism—the world of the newly rich mixture of avarice and blatant ostentation he had found in his homeland. All the signs are that the rich hero of this book, wretchedly embarrassed by the behaviour of his millionaire friends, would have become the first character in modern fiction to use his wealth for the setting up of a philanthropic foundation. Henry James, of all people, seemed set to become a pioneer of the realistic political novel, radical in sympathy and perhaps a prophet, even, of the Welfare State. It was to a battered but still valiant consciousness, then, and to a collection of 'garnered wisdom' still ever watchful for new observations and new experiences, that the self-inflicted wounds of Europe at war brought full-blooded horror. His brain and sensibility were still functioning strongly enough to feel the full blast of incredulous outrage. His old heart was still warm enough to be frozen with sorrow as the young smiling hopeful friends went off to face slaughter and mutilation.

In January of that fatal year, James may have written playfully to Hugh Walpole that the young novelist's last letter had flung 'across my grey old path the cold glitter of youth and sport'—but it would be the surviving desire of the 'grey old path' to *be* so invaded by the 'cold glitter of youth' that really characterized the coming wartime months. It was that same desire that, on the onset of war, so lacerated him that he could write 'I loathed so having lived on and on into anything so hideous and horrible', yet at the same time sustained him in heroically vigorous efforts to contribute to the cause of his adopted country the extraordinary residue of intellectual power still available to him. In the eloquent words of his friend Percy Lubbock, the first editor of James's letters,

> For a while it was as though the burden of age had slipped from him; he lived in the lives of all who were acting and suffering— especially of the young, who acted and suffered most. His spiritual vigour bore a strain that was the greater by the whole weight of his towering imagination; but the time came at last when his bodily endurance failed. He died resolutely confident of the victory that was still so far off.

There are enough surviving records of James's 'war effort' between August 1914 and his death in February 1916 to support Lubbock's splendid claim. His essays posthumously collected in the volume *Within the Rim* (1918) recall his practical aid to 'Refugees in Chelsea' and 'The American Volunteer Motor-Ambulance Corps in France', and the offering of his own patient sympathetic (and, one guesses, sometimes mystifying?) conversation and willingness to listen to the talk of wounded soldiers in hospital. With another part of his mind he had been dictating to his amanuensis during the first few months of the war the opening chapters of what had been designed as his third volume of autobiography (posthumously published in 1917 as *The Middle Years*). And even when he had laid aside the unfinished *The Ivory Tower* as a commentary on the contemporary world too painful to continue when that very world was engaged in self-slaughter, there was still enough residual *habit* of energy left for him to try, well into the second half of the terrible year 1915, to add more chapters to the pseudo-historical semi-mystical fantasy *The Sense of the Past* (posthumously published in 1917). It was as if the wearied and wounded mind could still flicker a little with miasmal memories from the other extreme of the great continuum of life.

What one finally learns from the pained strenuous period of Henry James's last three years is simply that the history of human gallantry need not be restricted to the busy activities of chronic extroverts. Edel's magisterial biography may put an end, once and for all, to the popular notion that only men of violent action are fit subjects for life-stories. Although James led no armies and sat in no Cabinet, he showed throughout his life an amazingly tough stamina, physical and mental, which alone could have supported 'the wear and tear of discrimination'. He organized an increasingly complicated professional and personal life with unaided competence. When a New York reporter had met James at Hoboken on his return to his native land in 1904, at the age of sixty-one, he had been struck by 'the immensely robust figure' with a firm elastic step. Henry James may have sketched several portraits of ineffectual aesthetes: he was certainly never one of them himself. Throughout his life, James was by instinct a radical; by temperament he was a gentleman; by profession he was an artist. Yet it is surely significant that during his death-bed delirium, this disciplined artist of the sensibilities imagined himself to be—not Flaubert, but Napoleon!

It is no unusual thing in life to meet people who seem inordinately proud of some acquired skill, while remaining apparently unaware of other major assets for which we ourselves, their friends or acquaintances, value them much more highly. Such things as good health, good looks or inherited wealth tend to be taken for granted, by their lucky possessors, as their normal birthright. In the case of a professional writer, these great basic assumptions must include an intellectual energy sufficient to sustain him through a long and relentless productivity, plus a growing mastery over his medium—the language of his country—which allows comedy or tragedy, irony or deeply felt passion to appear in the greatest possible amplitude under the most intelligent possible control. It was so with Shakespeare; and it was so with James. We can all think of other writers whose brilliant secondary acquirements fail to make up for a lack of that bounteous productivity, or that seemingly automatic literary mastery over an immensely varied output. Some 'dry up' too soon; others are readable but (for lack of literary art) unmemorable. We search in them for minor, secondary, qualities.

From all the evidence collected by Leon Edel in his biography and his edition of James's letters, I think it is abundantly clear that Henry James *was* conscious of possessing those major virtues of productivity and verbal control. It was mainly during the periods of depression brought on by his disappointment at the apparent unsaleability of his cherished work he took comfort in prizing other, lesser, qualities in his formidable literary equipment.

As a man and as an artist, Henry James always saw himself as a fascinated *observer* of life. Even in his very early Civil War days, he could suffer but he did not fight. There were times when he bewailed his loneliness—again, both as a man and as an artist. But in both respects it was a positive self-induced solitude rather than the negative loneliness of neglect. There was an extraordinary robustness about him which sustained him through professional disappointments and personal unfulfilled desires. At no time does he invite (nor could he have tolerated) pity. It was by his own positive choice that he had endured the celibate life (for poor Constance Fenimore Woolson was not the only one among his many lady-friends who would gladly have shared his life); and even if this posture may be explained by some commentators as a sure sign of his personal preference for his own sex, it is equally true that his various avuncular yearnings never came anywhere near the possibility of any permanent domesticity. Henry James was for ever caught up in the twin processes 'Welcome!' and 'Farewell!' And it was one of his lady-friends, Fanny Prothero, who very perceptively remarked to Henry's secretary, Theodora Bosanquet, during one of his bouts of illness in 1909, that her employer was 'very fond of people while they are here, but I don't believe he cares a bit when they aren't'. She explained: 'friendly and charming as he is, he is really quite aloof from everyone . . . It's the artist in him.'

It *was* 'the artist in him'. To any rude questioner who, beguiled by James's verbal magic in speech or on the printed page, had ventured to ask 'But what have you actually *experienced*, what have you actually *done*?', it would have been enough for the Master to point to the shelf-loads of his lifelong professional output.

And yet . . .? And yet, recalling the observer Lambert Strether as the *central* character of that wonderful treatment, in *The Ambassadors*, of the passionate love affair between the virile young American Chad Newsome and the experienced Frenchwoman Madame de Vionnet, one does nevertheless understand why Shakespeare (another supreme observer) did not make Friar Lawrence the *central* character in *Romeo and Juliet*. Perhaps James would not have required the expository services of those gruesome Assinghams, in *The Golden Bowl*, if he himself had experienced, rather than observed, the kind of feckless infatuation of the Prince and Charlotte?

Was Henry James's noble brow maintained unraked until the end, simply by his avoidance of those awful networks of lines we may see any day, at any hotel dining-table, deeply etched on the faces of perfectly ordinary and boring couples, lines etched by the endless friction of hatred based on possessive love, lines graven by the act of living and fighting together, rather than by carefully graduated forays of hope from the castle of solitude? It is the kind of question suffering humanity may well ask. The answer, as Shakespeare (who 'never blotted a line') and Henry James knew, may well come, if at all, from the watchers who see most of the game.

'The game', as James watched it, could at times present the crudities of human greed somehow refined, in human relationships, to the urge to dominate. This in turn led, among his less aggressive fictional characters, to the urge to withdraw, to resign, to become absentees. In a story like *The Sacred Fount*, the reader is left with a choice between *voyeurs* and cannibals. For a man who always prided himself as being a realist, James could in his more despondent moods allow realism to look very much like pessimism. It is at these moments that we, his readers, have cause to greet his even more permanent qualities of sturdy endurance, a quick eye for 'beautiful' behaviour by imperfect people, and a verbal wit enhancing enough to redeem almost anything. These more positive aspects of James's life and work should enable us to accept with equally positive understanding the life work of a writer who, lonely as only an expert analyst of love could be who had never experienced a full recompense of love himself, could still work away at his writing like an heroic miner at the coalface, hacking away to find the truth about our inescapable fate in this world.

Henry James's sense of identity with his adopted country in its hour of greatest need and danger prompted him to apply for naturalization. His application indicated that 'having lived and worked in

IN MEMORY OF

HENRY JAMES. O.M

NOVELIST

BORN IN NEW YORK 1843 : DIED IN
CHELSEA 1916 : LOVER & INTER-
PRETER OF THE FINE AMENITIES
OF BRAVE DECISIONS & GENEROVS
LOYALTIES : A RESIDENT OF THIS
PARISH WHO RENOVNCED A
CHERISHED CITIZENSHIP TO GIVE
HIS ALLEGIANCE TO ENGLAND IN
THE 1st YEAR OF THE GREAT WAR

The memorial in Chelsea Old Church.

England for the best part of forty years' he wished to express 'his desire to throw his moral weight and personal allegiance, for whatever they may be worth, into the scale of the contending nation's present and future fortune'. Herbert Asquith, wartime Prime Minister, was delighted to sponsor this request from so distinguished a writer who had graced his and Margot's table and stayed with them at Walmer Castle. On 28 July 1915 James became a British subject. In the New Year's Honours of 1916 he was awarded the Order of Merit by his new sovereign, King George V. The Order was borne to his bedside. On 28 February 1916 he died, a British subject.

Part Three
Reference Section

9   Illustrative passages

The private life and the public world

THE BOSTONIANS   The introductory picture of Miss Birdseye in *The Bostonians* (see pp. 35–36) is complemented by an even more economically brilliant set-piece presenting Mrs Farrinder, with its significant contrast between the admirable public sentiments espoused by such a figure, and the actual personal qualities of the lady herself:

> Toward nine o'clock the light of her hissing burners smote the majestic person of Mrs Farrinder, who might have contributed to answer that question of Miss Chancellor's in the negative. She was a copious, handsome woman, in whom angularity had been corrected by the air of success; she had a rustling dress (it was evident what *she* thought about taste), abundant hair of a glossy blackness, a pair of folded arms, the expression of which seemed to say that rest, in such a career as hers, was as sweet as it was brief, and a terrible regularity of feature. I apply that adjective to her fine placid mask because she seemed to face you with a question of which the answer was preordained, to ask you how a countenance could fail to be noble of which the measurements were so correct. You would contest neither the measurements nor the nobleness, and had to feel that Mrs Farrinder imposed herself. There was a lithographic smoothness about her, and a mixture of the American matron and the public character. There was something public in her eye, which was large, cold, and quiet; it had acquired a sort of exposed reticence from the habit of looking down from a lecture desk, over a sea of heads, while its distinguished owner was eulogized by a leading citizen. Mrs Farrinder, at almost any time, had the air of being introduced by a few remarks. She talked with great slowness and distinctness, and evidently a high sense of responsibility; she pronounced every syllable of every word and insisted on being explicit. If, in conversation with her, you attempted to take anything for granted, or to jump two or three steps at a time, she paused, looking at you with a cold patience, as if she knew that trick, and then went on at her own measured pace. She lectured on temperance and the rights of women; the ends she laboured for were to give the ballot to every woman in the country and to take the flowing bowl from every man. She was held to have a very fine manner, and to embody the domestic virtues and the graces

of the drawing room; to be a shining proof, in short, that the forum, for ladies, is not necessarily hostile to the fireside. She had a husband, and his name was Amariah.

(Ch. IV)

THE PRINCESS CASAMASSIMA   This was published in the same year (1886) as *The Bostonians*, and attacked a considerably more ambitious political subject: the scene is London, but the characters include international anarchists, and the young hero, an illegitimate bookbinder named Hyacinth Robinson, is played upon by a group of contrasting characters, Cockney and Continental, who illustrate different personal responses to the political problems of the day. As in *The Bostonians*, it is more by the personal impressions made by these individuals than by their very different acquired political creeds or inherited political habits that the young hypersensitive 'revolutionary' is influenced and confused.

Young Hyacinth is brought up by a foster-parent, the genteel Miss Pynsent, a penniless dressmaker living in barren decorum in a decayed neighbourhood. The neighbouring family, the Hennings, have a healthy rumbustious warm-hearted vulgar girl who had played with the boy as a child and would gladly, the reader feels, prolong their games beyond adolescence:

An inner sense told him that her mingled beauty and grossness, her vulgar vitality, the spirit of contradiction yet at the same time of attachment that was in her, had ended by making her indispensable to him. She bored him as much as she irritated him; but if she was full of execrable taste she was also full of life, and her rustlings and chatterings, her wonderful stories, her bad grammar and good health, her insatiable thirst, her shrewd perceptions and grotesque opinions, her mistakes and her felicities, were now all part of the familiar human sound of his little world.

(Ch. XXV)

How different from Miss Pynsent, who had 'a certain stiff, quaint, polished politeness, of which she possessed the secret and which made her resemble a pair of old-fashioned sugar-tongs'. The contrast between these two female neighbours of Pentonville is made neatly in a passage which opens with young Millicent's reaction to Miss Pynsent's room:

the whole place seemed to that prosperous young lady to smell of poverty and failure. Her childish images of its mistress had shown her as neat, fine, superior, with round loops of hair fastened on the temples by combs and associations of brilliancy arising from the constant manipulation of precious stuffs—tissues at least that Millicent regarded with envy. But the little woman before her was bald and white and pinched; she looked shrunken and sickly and insufficiently nourished; her small eyes were sharp and suspicious and her hideous cap didn't disguise the way everything had gone. Miss Henning thanked her stars, as she had often done before, that she hadn't been obliged to get *her* living by drudging over needlework year after year in that undiscoverable street, in a dismal little room where nothing had been changed for ages; the absence of change had such an exasperating effect upon her vigorous young nature. She reflected with complacency on her good fortune in being attached to a more exciting, a more dramatic department of the great drapery interest, and noticed that though it was already November there was no fire in the neatly-kept grate beneath the chimney-piece, on which a design, partly architectural, partly botanical, executed in the hair of Miss Pynsent's parents, was flanked by a pair of vases, under glass, containing muslin flowers.

If she thought that lady's eyes suspicious it must be confessed that her hostess felt much on her guard in presence of so unexpected and undesired a reminder of one of the least honourable episodes in the annals of Lomax Place. Miss Pynsent esteemed people in proportion to their success in constituting a family circle—in cases, that is, when the materials were under their hand. This success, among the various members of the house of Henning, had been of the scantiest, and the domestic broils in the establishment adjacent to her own, the vicissitudes of which she was able to follow, as she sat near her window at work, by simply inclining an ear to the thin partition behind her—these scenes, rendering the crash of crockery and the imprecations of the wounded frequently and peculiarly audible, had long been the scandal of a humble but harmonious neighbourhood.

(New York Edition, Ch. IV)

With precisely the same social setting and economic plight, the different reactions of Miss Pynsent and Millicent throw a good deal of silent scepticism on the large generalizations of some Hyacinth's more overtly political friends.

One of these is another neighbour, old Mr Vetch, who is the kind of English radical who can say 'The way certain classes arrogate to themselves the title of the people has never pleased me.' His friend, the retired exile Monsieur Poupin, supplies the Continental theorizing with which Mr Vetch is not at home:

M. Poupin was an aggressive socialist, which Anastasius Vetch was not, and a constructive democrat (instead of being a mere scoffer at effete things), and a theorist and an optimist and a visionary; he believed that the day was to come when all the nations of the earth would abolish their frontiers and armies and customs-houses, and embrace on both cheeks, and cover the globe with boulevards, radiating from Paris, where the human family would sit, in groups, at little tables, according to affinities, drinking coffee (not tea, *par exemple!*) and listening to the music of the spheres. Mr Vetch neither prefigured nor desired this organized felicity; he was fond of his cup of tea, and only wanted to see the British constitution a good deal simplified ...

(New York Edition, Ch. VI)

The plot of the novel, which cannot be followed here, requires that young Hyacinth should meet far more professional members of the revolutionary movement than the harmless old Vetches and Poupins of this world. One of them, an attractive activist named Paul Muniment,

> moved in a dry statistical and scientific air in which it cost Hyacinth an effort of respiration to accompany him ... he sometimes emitted a short satiric gleam which showed that his esteem for the poor was small and that if he had no illusions about the people who had got everything into their hands he had as few about those who had egregiously failed to do so.

Of these practical conspirators, Hyacinth

> wondered at their zeal, their continuity, their vivacity, their incorruptibility; at the abundant supply of conviction and prophecy which they always had on hand. He believed that at bottom he was sorer than they, yet he had deviations and lapses, moments when the social question bored him and he forgot not only his own wrongs, which would have been pardonable, but those of the people at large, of his brothers and sisters in misery.

These few sketches are of the kind which greatly enliven this long serious attempt by James to tackle a political theme. They help, perhaps, to explain how to the very end of his days James always shrank from joining political parties or ideological movements. Even an invitation to accept honorary office in the purely literary and academic English Association brought forth from him a wry self-caricature as

> a mere stony, ugly monster of *Dis*sociation and Detachment ... the rough sense of it is that I believe only in absolutely independent, individual and lonely virtue, and in the serenely unsociable ... practice of the same ... the associational process for bringing it on is but a bright and hollow artifice, all vain and delusive.

As Sir Arthur Quiller-Couch once remarked in another context,

141

'Whoso would recruit him from one category to another is mixing up things that differ . . .'. If James had a political ideology (as these passages may hint) it was that in a civilized society personal behaviour *was* political.

External and internal domestic landscapes

Henry James, civilized and celibate American, was not only a celebrated diner-out in London, but also a welcome guest at many great English country houses. Very many of the characters of his novels and tales are for dramatic convenience gathered together at house-parties, where the observant James-like narrator may watch the comings and goings, the polite preliminaries to adultery, the shifting alliances and antagonisms, all the pirouettes and prancings of discretion and immorality played out against the background of well-tended lawns and carefully studied relaxation. Although he became more critical, he never lost his pleasure in the changing human and natural scenery of country week-ends. Indeed, after becoming the owner of Lamb House, Rye, in 1897, he could in modest fashion play the country host himself.

A telling sidelight on the novelist's development may be offered by three samples of country-house settings, ranging from the 'passionate pilgrim' admiration, through a satirical knowingness when wealthy ownership can be merely the occasion for the demonstration of appallingly bad taste, to the last phase when the novelist's attention is so intensely concentrated on his characters' spoken and unspoken states of mind and feeling. By this time, the external setting, though mostly quite acceptably present as contributing an appropriate atmosphere, loses sharpness of focus as the reader prepares himself no longer for a vivid entertaining landscape or domestic setting, but rather for one brief remark, or one significant silence.

THE PORTRAIT OF A LADY In the opening paragraphs of *The Portrait of a Lady* (1881), the 'tea in the garden' setting of Gardencourt, the American Mr Touchett's Thames-side house, is all of a piece with the elegant, amusing, relaxed conversation between Lord Warburton and Isabel Archer's aesthetic cousin, Ralph Touchett, which will in turn introduce Isabel herself.

> Under certain circumstances there are few hours in life more agreeable than the hour dedicated to the ceremony known as afternoon tea. There are circumstances in which, whether you partake of the tea or not—some people of course never do—the

Lamb House, Rye.

situation is in itself delightful. Those that I have in mind in beginning to unfold this simple history offered an admirable setting to an innocent pastime. The implements of the little feast had been disposed upon the lawn of an old English country-house, in what I should call the perfect middle of a splendid summer afternoon. Part of the afternoon had waned, but much of it was left, and what was left was of the finest and rarest quality. Real dusk would not arrive for many hours; but the flood of summer light had begun to ebb, the air had grown mellow, the shadows were long upon the smooth, dense turf. They lengthened slowly, however, and the scene expressed that sense of leisure still to come which is perhaps the chief source of one's enjoyment of such a scene at such an hour. From five o'clock to eight is on certain occasions a little eternity; but on such an occasion as this the interval could be only an eternity of pleasure. The persons concerned in it were taking their pleasure quietly, and they were not of the sex which is supposed to furnish the regular votaries of the ceremony I have mentioned. The shadows on the perfect lawn were straight and angular; they were the shadows of an old man sitting in a deep wicker-chair near the low table on which the tea had been served, and of two younger men strolling to and fro, in desultory talk, in front of him. The old man had his cup in his hand; it was an unusually large cup, of a different pattern from the rest of the set, and painted in brilliant colours. He disposed of its contents with much circumspection, holding it for a long time close to his chin, with his face turned to the house. His companions had either finished their tea or were indifferent to their privilege; they smoked cigarettes as they continued to stroll. One of them, from time to time, as he passed, looked with a certain attention at the elder man, who, unconscious of observation, rested his eyes upon the rich red front of his dwelling. The house that rose beyond the lawn was a structure to repay such consideration, and was the most characteristic object in the peculiarly English picture I have attempted to sketch.

It stood upon a low hill, above the river—the river being the Thames, at some forty miles from London. A long gabled front of red brick, with the complexion of which time and the weather had played all sorts of picturesque tricks, only, however, to improve and refine it, presented itself to the lawn, with its patches of ivy, its clustered chimneys, its windows smothered in creepers. The house had a name and a history; the old gentleman taking his tea would have been delighted to tell you these things: how it had been built under Edward the Sixth, had offered a night's hospitality to the great Elizabeth (whose august person had extended itself upon a huge, magnificent, and terribly angular bed which still formed the principal honour of the sleeping apartments), had been a good deal bruised and defaced in Cromwell's wars, and then, under the Restoration, repaired and much enlarged; and how, finally, after having been remodelled and disfigured in the eighteenth century, it had passed into the careful keeping of a shrewd American banker, who had bought it originally because (owing to circumstances too complicated to set forth) it was offered at a great bargain; bought it with much grumbling at its ugliness, its antiquity, its incommodity, and who now, at the end of twenty years, had become conscious of a real aesthetic passion for it, so that he knew all its points, and would tell you just where to stand to see them in combination, and just the hour when the shadows of its various protuberances—which fell so softly upon the warm, weary brickwork—were of the right measure.

(Ch. I)

THE SPOILS OF POYNTON   The opening paragraphs of *The Spoils of Poynton* (1897) are entirely different, indicating that for every occasion for positive admiration there must be the possibility of contrary opportunities for critical disdain. Mrs Gereth, recently widowed, has had to surrender her keeping of the great house Poynton, withdrawing to her dower house while her son inherits the main estate. We meet her, in the opening sentences of the novel, as a very unwilling guest at Waterbath, the vulgar home of a wealthy vulgar family, the Brigstocks, whose daughter is becoming over-friendly with her son:

Mrs Gereth had said she would go with the rest to church, but suddenly it seemed to her that she should not be able to wait even till church-time for relief: breakfast, at Waterbath, was a punctual meal, and she had still nearly an hour on her hands. Knowing the church to be near, she prepared in her room for the little rural walk, and on her way down again, passing through corridors and observing imbecilities of decoration, the aesthetic misery of the big commodious house, she felt a return of the tide of last night's irritation, a renewal of everything she could secretly suffer from ugliness and stupidity. Why did she consent to such contacts? Why did she so rashly expose herself? She had had, heaven knew, her reasons, but the whole experience was to be sharper than she had feared. To get away from it and out into the air, into the presence of sky and trees, flowers and birds, was a necessity of every nerve. The flowers at Waterbath would probably go wrong in colour and the nightingales sing out of tune; but she remembered to have heard the place described as possessing those advantages that are usually spoken of as natural. There were advantages enough it clearly didn't possess. It was hard for her to believe that a woman could look presentable who had been kept awake for hours by the wall-paper in her room; yet none the less, as in her fresh widow's weeds she rustled across the hall, she was sustained by the consciousness, which always added to the unction of her social Sundays, that she was, as usual, the only person in the house incapable of wearing in her preparation the horrible stamp of the same exceptional smartness that would be conspicuous in a grocer's wife. She would rather have perished than have looked *endimanchée*.

(Ch. I)

A younger house-guest, Miss Fleda Vetch, is equally affronted by the vulgarity of Waterbath, and blurts out:

'Isn't it too dreadful?'

'Horrible—horrible!' cried Mrs Gereth with a laugh; 'and it's really a comfort to be able to say it.' She had an idea, for it was her ambition, that she successfully made a secret of that awkward oddity her proneness to be rendered unhappy by the presence of the dreadful. Her passion for the exquisite was the cause of this, but it was a passion she considered that she never advertised nor gloried in, contenting herself with letting it regulate her steps and show quietly in her life, remembering at all times that there are few things more soundless than a deep devotion. She was therefore struck with the acuteness of the little girl who had already put a finger on her hidden spring. What was dreadful now, what was horrible, was the intimate ugliness of Waterbath, and it was of that phenomenon these ladies talked while they sat in the shade and drew refreshment from the great tranquil sky, from which no blue saucers were suspended. It was an ugliness fundamental and systematic, the result of the abnormal nature of the Brigstocks, from whose composition the principle of taste had been extravagantly omitted. In the arrangement of their home some other principle, remarkably active, but uncanny and obscure, had operated instead, with consequences depressing to behold, consequences that took the form of a universal futility. The house was bad in all conscience, but it might have passed if they had only let it alone. This saving mercy was beyond them; they had smothered it with trumpery ornament and scrapbook art, with strange excrescences and bunchy draperies, with gimcracks that might have been keepsakes for maid-servants and nondescript conveniences that might have been prizes for the blind. They had gone wildly astray over carpets and curtains; they had an infallible instinct for disaster, and were so cruelly doom-ridden that it rendered them almost tragic. Their drawing-room, Mrs Gereth lowered her voice to mention, caused her face to burn, and each of the new friends confided to the other that in her own apartment she had given way to tears. There was in the elder lady's a set of comic water-colours, a family joke by a family genius, and in the younger's a souvenir from some centennial or other Exhibition, that they shudderingly alluded to. The house was perversely full of souvenirs of places even more ugly than itself and of things it would have been a pious duty to forget. The worst horror was the acres of varnish, something advertised and smelly, with which everything was smeared: it was Fleda Vetch's conviction that the application of it, by their own hands and hilariously shoving each other, was the amusement of the Brigstocks on rainy days.

(Ch. I)

The high-spirited glee of this cruel pyrotechnic display may remind us of James's equally brilliant portrait of Mrs Farrinder. But in addition, we are instantly introduced to a pair of discriminating ladies whose self-conscious superiority will, before the end of the novel, lose our sympathy as it helps to thwart, in different ways, their own possibilities for contentment.

THE GOLDEN BOWL   The third passage, from Chapter XXXVI of the long forty-two-chapter *The Golden Bowl* (1904), produces Maggie the beloved daughter of the American millionaire Adam Verver, as she momentarily leaves a small party at his country-house, Fawns, to face her psychological problems. She is pacing on the terrace while her father and his young wife Charlotte are indoors with Maggie's husband the Italian Prince Amerigo. By this time, Maggie shares the reader's own knowledge that Amerigo and Charlotte had once been lovers, and have on one recent occasion betrayed both her father (Charlotte's husband) and herself (Amerigo's wife). The two women, outwardly close friends as well as mother- and daughter-in-law, are about to confront one another in a polite exchange of dreadful truths or heroic lies. Fawns is indeed another Gardencourt, but we are no longer charmed by it. It could be as ugly as Waterbath, and neither Maggie nor the reader could spare time to notice the difference. All our moral–aesthetic discrimination is by this time engaged not on land-scape gardening or interior decoration, but simply by the question: how will Maggie and Charlotte *behave*? Maggie is on the terrace:

Several of the long windows of the occupied rooms stood open to it, and the light came out in vague shafts and fell upon the old smooth stones. The hour was moonless and starless and the air heavy and still—which was why, in her evening dress, she need fear no chill and could get away, in the outer darkness, from that provocation of opportunity which had assaulted her, within,

147

on her sofa, as a beast might have leaped at her throat.

Nothing in fact was stranger than the way in which, when she had remained there a little, her companions, watched by her through one of the windows, actually struck her as almost consciously and gratefully safer. They might have been—really charming as they showed in the beautiful room, and Charlotte certainly, as always, magnificently handsome and supremely distinguished—they might have been figures rehearsing some play of which she herself was the author; they might even, for the happy appearance they continued to present, have been such figures as would, by the strong note of character in each, fill any author with the certitude of success, especially of their own histrionic. They might in short have represented any mystery they would; the point being predominantly that the key to the mystery, the key that could wind and unwind it without a snap of the spring, was there in her pocket—or rather, no doubt, clasped at this crisis in her hand and pressed, as she walked back and forth, to her breast. She walked to the end and far out of the light; she returned and saw the others still where she had left them; she passed round the house and looked into the drawing-room, lighted also, but empty now, and seeming to speak the more, in its own voice, of all the possibilities she controlled. Spacious and splendid, like a stage again awaiting a drama, it was a scene she might people, by the press of her spring, either with serenities and dignities and decencies, or with terrors and shames and ruins, things as ugly as those formless fragments of her golden bowl she was trying so hard to pick up.

She continued to walk and continued to pause; she stopped afresh for the look into the smoking-room, and by this time—it was as if the recognition had of itself arrested her—she saw as in a picture, with the temptation she had fled from quite extinct, why it was she had been able to give herself so little, from the first, to the vulgar heat of her wrong. She might fairly, as she watched them, have missed it as a lost thing; have yearned for it, for the straight vindictive view, the rights of resentment, the rages of jealousy, the protests of passion, as for something she had been cheated of not least: a range of feelings which for many women would have meant so much, but which for *her* husband's wife, for *her* father's daughter, figured nothing nearer to experience than a wild eastern caravan, looming into view with crude colours in the sun, fierce pipes in the air, high spears against the sky, all a thrill, a natural joy to mingle with, but turning off short before it reached her and plunging into other defiles. She saw at all events why horror itself had almost failed her; the horror that, foreshadowed in advance, would, by her thought, have made everything that was unaccustomed in her cry out with pain; the horror of finding evil seated, all at its ease, where she had only dreamed of good; the horror of the thing hideously *behind* so much trusted, so much pretended, nobleness, cleverness, tenderness.

(Ch. XXXVI)

Conversation, dialogue, telepathy

The Complete Plays of Henry James edited by Leon Edel (Rupert Hart-Davis, 1949) runs to more than 800 pages. The editor's fifty-page introductory essay traces James's interest in the theatre from his childhood visits to the New York stage; through the mainly disappointing years in the 1890s when he tried to increase his public and his income by turning from the novel to the drama, a long effort which even survived the dreadful occasion when on the first night of his play *Guy Domville* (1893) the author was summoned to the stage to receive the polite applause of the stalls and boos from the gallery, to the private notebooks in which, as late as 1910, he was still goading himself 'all throbbingly and yearningly and passionately' back to 'the dramatic way'. This being so, it may be expected that his changing use of dialogue in his novels will provide a more than usually accurate clue to his development as a creative artist whose permament subject matter was always the interplay of human beings. Space has prohibited more than a mere reference to Henry James the dramatist. In notebooks, prefaces and letters, Henry James the novelist is for ever urging himself to 'dramatize, dramatize!' In commenting on his fiction, it is easy to drop into the habit of referring to 'acts' and 'scenes'. Sometimes the major actors are most effective when they are either silent or hesitative.

THE EUROPEANS   The first passage, from the early novel *The Europeans* (1878), gives us a revealing and wholly natural conversation between the old New England patriarch Mr Wentworth, his Europeanized kinsfolk Felix and the Baroness Münster, and his daughter Gertrude: as in a play, their individual contributions to a family chat manage to edge on the plot by revealing, in every phrase, yet another aspect of the nature of the individual players:

'I should like to do your head, sir,' said Felix to his uncle one evening, before them all—Mr Brand and Robert Acton being also present. 'I think I should make a very fine thing of it. It's an interesting head; it's very mediaeval.'

Mr Wentworth looked grave; he felt awkwardly, as if all the company had come in and found him standing before the looking-glass. 'The Lord made it,' he said. 'I don't think it is for man to make it over again.'

'Certainly the Lord made it,' replied Felix, laughing, 'and He made it very well. But life has been touching up the work. It is a very interesting type of head. It's delightfully wasted and emaciated. The complexion is wonderfully bleached.' And Felix looked round at the circle, as if to call their attention to these interesting points. Mr Wentworth grew visibly paler. 'I should like to do you as an old prelate, an old cardinal, or the prior of an order.'

'A prelate, a cardinal?' murmured Mr Wentworth. 'Do you refer to the Roman Catholic priesthood?'

'I mean an old ecclesiastic who should have led a very pure, abstinent life. Now I take it that has been the case with you, sir; one sees it in your face,' Felix proceeded. 'You have been very—a—very moderate. Don't you think one always sees that in a man's face?'

'You see more in a man's face that I should think of looking for,' said Mr Wentworth coldly.

The Baroness rattled her fan and gave her brilliant laugh. 'It is a risk to look so close!' she exclaimed. 'My uncle has some peccadilloes on his conscience.' Mr Wentworth looked at her, painfully at a loss; and in so far as the signs of a pure and abstinent life were visible in his face they were then probably peculiarly manifest. 'You are a *beau vieillard*, dear uncle,' said Madame Münster, smiling with her foreign eyes.

'I think you are paying me a compliment,' said the old man.

'Surely, I am not the first woman that ever did so!' cried the Baroness.

'I think you are,' said Mr Wentworth gravely. And turning to Felix he added, in the same tone, 'Please don't take my likeness. My children have my daguerreotype. That is quite satisfactory.'

'I won't promise,' said Felix, 'not to work your head into something!'

Mr Wentworth looked at him and then at all the others; and then he got up and slowly walked away.

'Felix,' said Gertrude, in the silence that followed, 'I wish you would paint my portrait.'

(Ch. V)

THE AWKWARD AGE Written after the years of theatrical experiments and disappointments, *The Awkward Age* (1899) is almost wholly dramatic in structure. The background of the adolescent heroine's story is that of her mother's *fin-de-siècle* attempt at a London *salon*, wherein Nanda's mother Mrs Brookenham ('Mrs Brook' to her intimates) rules and sets the tone, which is briefly that of a society in which the now lowered standards of Victorian hypocrisy and Victorian intellectual efforts have created the possibility of an 'emancipated' circle within which partners may be switched and hitherto 'unmentionable' subjects discussed with a self-consciously feckless wit which reminds the reader that the Bloomsbury group will soon be claiming its ascendance over London's literary life. Such a group, at any rate, supplies a ready-made list of minor characters and 'extras'. It is against this background that the plight of young Nanda may be discussed between her mother's favourite courtier Vanderbank, whom Nanda herself secretly loves, and her grandmother's old friend Mr Longdon who from his country retreat has visited the Mrs Brook *clique* and set himself the chivalrous task of rescuing Nanda from it. The following dialogue between old Mr Longdon and his chosen substitute knight-errant Vanderbank takes place after he has offered the younger man a marriage settlement to make the rescue possible:

Vanderbank gave a head-shake that was both restrictive and indulgent. 'I must live into it a little. Your offer has been before me only these few minutes, and it's too soon for me to commit myself to anything whatever. Except,' he added gallantly, 'my gratitude.'

Mr Longdon, at this, on the divan, got up, as Vanderbank had previously done, under the spring of emotion; only, unlike Vanderbank, he still stood there, his hands in his pockets and his face, a little paler, directed straight. There was disappointment in him even before he spoke. 'You've no strong enough impulse—?'

His friend met him with admirable candour. 'Wouldn't it seem that if I had I would by this time have taken the jump?'

'Without waiting, you mean, for anybody's money?' Mr Longdon cultivated for a little a doubt. 'Of course she has seemed—till now—tremendously young.'

Vanderbank looked about once more for matches and occupied a time with relighting. 'Till now—yes. But it's not,' he pursued, 'only because she's so young that—for each of us, and for dear old Mitchy too—she's so interesting.' Mr Longdon had now stepped down, and Vanderbank's eyes followed him till he stopped again. 'I make out that, in spite of what you said to begin with, you're conscious of a certain pressure.'

'In the matter of time? Oh yes, I do want it *done*. That,' the old man simply explained, 'is why I myself put on the screw.' He spoke with the ring of impatience. 'I want her got out.'

'"Out"?'

'Out of her mother's house.'

Vanderbank laughed, though, more immediately, he had coloured. 'Why her mother's house is just where I see her!'

'Precisely; and if it only were not we might get on faster.'

Vanderbank, for all his kindness, looked still more amused.

'But if it only were not, as you say, I seem to see that you wouldn't have your particular vision of urgency.'

Mr Longdon, through adjusted glasses, took him in with a look that was sad as well as sharp, then jerked the glasses off. 'Oh, you understand me.'

'Ah,' said Vanderbank, 'I'm a mass of corruption!'

'You may perfectly be, but you shall not,' Mr Longdon returned with decision, 'get off on any such plea. If you're good enough for me you're good enough, as you thoroughly know, on whatever head, for any one.'

'Thank you.' But Vanderbank, for all his happy appreciation, thought again. 'We ought at any rate to remember, oughtn't we? that we should have Mrs Brook against us.'

His companion faltered but an instant. 'Ah, that's another thing I know. But it's also exactly why. Why I want Nanda away.'

'I see, I see.'

The response had been prompt, yet Mr Longdon seemed suddenly to show that he suspected the superficial. 'Unless it's with Mrs Brook you're in love.' Then on his friend's taking the idea with a mere head-shake of negation, a repudiation that might even have astonished by its own lack of surprise, 'Or unless Mrs Brook's in love with you,' he amended.

Vanderbank had for this any decent gaiety. 'Ah, that of course may perfectly be!'

'But *is* it? That's the question.'

He continued light. 'If she had declared her passion shouldn't I rather compromise her—?'

'By letting me know?' Mr Longdon reflected. 'I'm sure I can't say—it's a sort of thing for which I haven't a measure or a precedent. In my time women didn't declare their passion. I'm thinking of what the meaning is of Mrs Brookenham's wanting you—as I've heard it called—herself.'

Vanderbank, still with his smile, smoked a minute. 'That's what you've heard it called?'

'Yes, but you must excuse me from telling you by whom.'

He was amused at his friend's discretion. 'It's unimaginable. But it doesn't matter. We all call everything—anything. The meaning of it, if you and I put it so, is—well, a modern shade.'

'You must deal then yourself,' said Mr Longdon, 'with your modern shades.' He spoke now as if the case simply awaited such dealing.

But at this his young friend was more grave. '*You* could do nothing?—to bring, I mean, Mrs Brook round.'

Mr Longdon fairly started. 'Propose, on your behalf, for her daughter? With your authority—to-morrow. Authorise me, and

I instantly act.'

Vanderbank's colour again rose—his flush was complete.
'How awfully you want it!'

Mr Longdon, after a look at him, turned away. 'How awfully
you don't!'

(Ch. XX)

THE AMBASSADORS   Both the conversation in *The Europeans* and the
dialogue in *The Awkward Age* help forward the stories, the first
sample by revealing individual characters which will later react
upon one another, and the second sample by presenting in
dramatic form just such a reaction. The closing pages of *The
Ambassadors* offers an example of James's late practice in *tête-à-tête*
exchanges, where two people have become so wincingly aware of
their own and their partner's likely responses to any given situation, any given word, that a reader who happens to come upon
the passages without having read earlier chapters of the novel
would find great difficulty in understanding the words spoken or
even the unstated assumptions behind them. It is an attempt to set
down 'in action', from the fully shared viewpoint of the partici-
pants, precisely that quality which the novelist had already
described, then as it were from outside observation only, a full
quarter of a century earlier when sketching in an off-hand manner
the amicable chat between Lord Lambeth and his travelling
companion Percy Beaumont in 'An International Episode':

> The young Englishmen . . . talked together as they usually
> talked, with many odd silences, lapses of logic, and learned to
> supply each other's missing phrases; or, more especially like
> people thoroughly conscious of a common point of view, so that
> a style of conversation superficially lacking in finish might suffice
> for reference to a fund of associations in the light of which every-
> thing was all right.

The occasion of the brief exchanges between Lambert Strether
and Maria Gostrey as *The Ambassadors* draws to its final curtain is
in broad terms much like a variation on the theme of *The Awkward
Age* above. There, Mr Longdon is trying to bribe Vanderbank to
rescue Nanda. Here, Strether had already officially failed in his
attempt to persuade the American Chad Newsome to abandon his
Parisian mistress Madame de Vionnet and return to America; but
in the course of doing so, he had come to believe that Chad's sense
of priorities was a better one than that of his shocked American
kinsfolk, and was now distressed to know that the young man, on
the promise of high success in the commercial world, *had* decided
to jilt his lady and return to New England. This changed situation
is assumed in the first excerpt from the final Strether–Gostrey

dialogue. The assumption behind the second excerpt is that Maria Gostrey, in the course of watching his own development as a character during his Paris embassy, has herself fallen in love with Strether and offers herself as *his* reward for his new-found maturity of judgement.

There was nothing clearly for Maria Gostrey that signified now—save one sharp point, that is, to which she came in time. 'I don't know whether it's before you as a possibility that, left to himself, Mr Chad may after all go back. I judge that it *is* more or less so before you, from what you just now said of him.'

Her guest had his eyes on her, kindly but attentively, as if fore-seeing what was to follow this. 'I don't think it will be for the money.' And then as she seemed uncertain: 'I mean I don't believe it will be for that he'll give her up.'

'Then he *will* give her up?'

Strether waited a moment, rather slow and deliberate now, drawing out a little this last soft stage, pleading with her in various suggestive and unspoken ways for patience and under-standing. 'What were you just about to ask me?'

'Is there anything he can do that would make you patch it up?'

'With Mrs Newsome?'

Her assent, as if she had had a delicacy about sounding the name, was only in her face; but she added with it: 'Or is there anything he can do that would make *her* try it?'

'To patch it up with me?' His answer came at last in a conclusive headshake. 'There's nothing any one can do. It's over. Over for both of us.'

Maria wondered, seemed a little to doubt. 'Are you so sure for her?'

'Oh yes—sure now. Too much has happened. I'm different for her.'

She took it in then, drawing a deeper breath. 'I see. So that as she's different for *you*—'

'Ah but,' he interrupted, 'she's not.' And as Miss Gostrey wondered again: 'She's the same. She's more than ever the same. But I do what I didn't before—I *see* her.'

He spoke gravely and as if responsibly—since he had to pro-nounce; and the effect of it was slightly solemn, so that she simply exclaimed 'Oh!' Satisfied and grateful, however, she showed in her own next words an acceptance of his statement. 'What then do you go home to?'

'There's nothing, you know, I wouldn't do for you.'

'Oh yes—I know.'

'There's nothing,' she repeated, 'in all the world.'

'I know. I know. But all the same I must go.' He had got it at last. 'To be right.'

'To be right?'

She had echoed it in vague depreciation, but he felt it already clear for her. 'That, you see, is my only logic. Not, out of the whole affair, to have got anything for myself.'

She thought. 'But with your wonderful impressions you'll have got a great deal.'

'A great deal'—he agreed. 'But nothing like *you*. It's you who would make me wrong!'

Honest and fine, she couldn't greatly pretend she didn't see it. Still, she could pretend just a little. 'But why should you be so dreadfully right?'

'That's the way that—if I must go—you yourself would be the first to want me. And I can't do anything else.'

So then she had to take it, though still with her defeated protest. 'It isn't so much your *being* "right"—it's your horrible sharp eye for what makes you so.'

'Oh but you're just as bad yourself. You can't resist me when I point that out.'

She sighed it at last all comically, all tragically away. 'I can't indeed resist you.'

'Then there we are!' said Strether.

(Book Twelfth, Ch. V)

Verbal exchanges of this subtlety have more in common with telepathy than with conversation or dialogue. It is a development to a point which some of James's readers may with luck instantly recognize as an accurate transcription of much actual 'talk' between human beings who have come to take one another's responses for granted. But it is likely that most readers are best advised to become acquainted first with James's earlier, simpler, more traditional use of conversation and dialogue, before they can fully appreciate these late exchanges where less depends on what is said than on what is left unexpressed in words.

Expressions of love

In the freer language of today, readers of Henry James may come to the conclusion that he was a great expert on love, but a duffer on sex. However much we may be persuaded (via his Prefaces) to admire the structural felicities of novels and stories where off-stage passion between absentee principals is claimed to be best communicated in terms of its effect on curious observers, the almost complete absence from his work of even the simplest reference to actual love-making is nowadays remarkable. But while the combined effect of his nineteenth-century upbringing and his own personal habits make any overt reference to sex rare indeed in his works, when it *does* occur its effect is proportionately great.

THE GOLDEN BOWL   In this novel, for example, Maggie Verver is prepared to go on indefinitely pretending injured innocence (or injured ignorance) whenever the existence of a love affair between her husband Prince Amerigo and her father's wife Charlotte threatens to break surface. One strange effect of this attitude is that she and the Prince become linked in a new deception, pretending to believe that Charlotte does not know that Maggie knows . . . There has been but one clear reference to Maggie's own satisfied physical love for her husband (apart, of course, from the existence of their little Principino) in a marriage to which we have already been told that she 'surrendered herself to her husband without the shadow of a reserve or a condition'; and that reference, strangely enough, came immediately after his return from his one-night truancy with Charlotte. Returning to their London home in Portland Place in time for dinner, the Prince 'was already holding out his arms', and after their *tête-à-tête* meal we are told that 'It was, for hours and hours, later on, as if she had somehow been lifted aloft, were floated and carried on some warm high tide beneath which stumbling-blocks had sunk out of sight.' His own wife, we are given vaguely to understand, had become the residuary legatee of the Prince's freshly aroused passion.

THE PORTRAIT OF A LADY   In *The Portrait of a Lady*, we were given a very brief taste of the devoted physical love Isabel finally rejected in the person of Caspar Goodwood:

> He glared at her a moment through the dusk, and the next instant she felt his arms about her and his lips on her own lips. His kiss was like white lightning, a flash that spread, and spread again, and stayed; and it was extraordinarily as if, while she took it, she felt each thing in his hard manhood that had least pleased her, each aggressive fact of his face, his figure, his presence, justified of its intense identity and made one with this act of possession. So had she heard of those wrecked and under water following a train of images before they sink. But when darkness returned she was free. She never looked about her; she only darted from the spot.
>
> (Ch. LV, New York Edition)

By this time, the effect of this scene is not so much to make us feel the sadness of her renunciation of Goodwood as to underline, physically as well as morally, the awfulness of her return to Gilbert Osmond.

Isabel's loss of the love of her cousin Ralph is a far more affecting scene, not only because his deep affection was something she could wholeheartedly accept, but also because it was something the novelist himself could wholeheartedly describe:

'You've been like an angel beside my bed. You know they talk about the angel of death. It's the most beautiful of all. You've been like that; as if you were waiting for me.'

'I was not waiting for your death, I was waiting for—for this. This is not death, dear Ralph.'

'Not for you—no. There's nothing makes us feel so much alive as to see others die. That's the sensation of life—the sense that we remain. I've had it—even I. But now I'm of no use but to give it to others. With me it's all over.' And then he paused. Isabel bowed her head further, till it rested on the two hands that were clasped upon his own. She couldn't see him now; but his far-away voice was close to her ear. 'Isabel,' he went on suddenly, 'I wish it were over for you.' She answered nothing; she had burst into sobs; she remained so, with her buried face. He lay silent, listening to her sobs; at last he gave a long groan. 'Ah, what is it you have done for me?'

'What is it you did for me?' she cried, her now extreme agitation half smothered by her attitude. She had lost all her shame, all wish to hide things. Now he must know; she wished him to know, for it brought them supremely together, and he was beyond the reach of pain. 'You did something once—you know it. O Ralph, you've been everything! What have I done for you— what can I do to-day? I would die if you could live. But I don't wish you to live; I would die myself, not to lose you.' Her voice was as broken as his own and full of tears and anguish . . .

'For me you'll always be here,' she softly interrupted. It was easy to interrupt him.

But he went on, after a moment: 'It passes, after all; it's passing now. But love remains. I don't know why we should suffer so much. Perhaps I shall find out. There are many things in life. You're very young.'

'I feel very old,' said Isabel.

'You'll grow young again. That's how I see you. I don't believe—I don't believe—' But he stopped again; his strength failed him.

She begged him to be quiet now. 'We needn't speak to understand each other,' she said.

'I don't believe that such a generous mistake as yours can hurt you for more than a little.'

'Oh Ralph, I'm very happy now,' she cried through her tears. 'And remember this,' he continued, 'that if you've been hated you've also been loved. Ah but, Isabel—*adored*!' he just audibly and lingeringly breathed.

'Oh my brother!' she cried with a movement of still deeper prostration.

(New York Edition, Ch. LIV)

There could hardly be a more convincing demonstration than the difference in quality between these two farewells by Isabel to Caspar Goodwood and Ralph Touchett. The first is awkward, hurried, makes its point with embarrassed crudity. The second (much shortened in the excerpts above) allows Henry James to indulge to the full his lifelong willingness to verbalize strong affection. However murky the plots of some of his more saturnine explorations of possessive sexual love (ranging from child murder in *The Other House* to emotional cannibalism in *The Sacred Fount*), his own immense personal correspondence overflows with the most generous outpourings of loving tenderness, from the earliest youthful letters to his family to those late elaborate protestations from a man deeply dependent on the matching resonant affection of his friends. During spells of infatuation he had been capable of wasting much epistolary flirtatiousness over such uncomprehending recipients as the young sculptor Hendrik Andersen; but far more characteristic are the letters written to friends of both sexes who understood and gratefully returned his outspoken regard for them. From the now extensive range of Henry James's available correspondence it is indeed difficult to select examples, but three samples may serve to indicate something of the unbridled warmth of feeling he could express, most especially when close friends of his were passing through periods of sorrow, danger or depression.

LETTER OF 1883   Grace Norton, a New England spinster confidante ten years older than Henry James, kept up a long and steady pen-friend correspondence. When writing to her, James could recount foreign adventures or passing thoughts with equal freedom, often with a gay mock-gallantry: 'Let us be flexible, dear Grace'; he wrote in July 1887, 'let us be flexible! and even if we don't reach the sun we shall at least have been up in a balloon.' In July 1883 she had been in a depressed state. Here are some extracts from James's letter to her:

My dear Grace,
    Before the sufferings of others I am always utterly powerless, and your letter reveals such depths of suffering that I hardly

know what to say to you. This indeed is not my last word—but it must be my first. You are not isolated, verily, in such states of feeling as this—that is, in the sense that you appear to make all the misery of all mankind your own; only I have a terrible sense that you give all and receive nothing—that there is no reciprocity in your sympathy—that you have all the affliction of it and none of the returns. However—I am determined not to speak to you except with the voice of stoicism. I don't know *why* we live—the gift of life comes to us from I don't know what source or for what purpose; but I believe we can go on living for the reason that (always of course up to a certain point) life is the most valuable thing we know anything about, and it is therefore presumptively a great mistake to surrender it while there is any yet left in the cup. In other words consciousness is an illimitable power, and though at times it may seem to be all consciousness of misery, yet in the way it propagates itself from wave to wave, so that we never cease to feel, and though at moments we appear to, try to, pray to, there is something that holds one in one's place, makes it a standpoint in the universe which it is probably good not to forsake. You are right in your consciousness that we are all echoes and reverberations of the *same*, and you are noble when your interest and pity as to everything that surrounds you, appears to have a sustaining and harmonizing power. Only don't, I beseech you, *generalize* too much in these sympathies and tendernesses—remember that every life is a special problem which is not yours but another's, and content yourself with the terrible algebra of your own. Don't melt too much into the universe, but be as solid and dense and fixed as you can. We all live together, and those of us who love and know, live so most.

You will do all sorts of things yet, and I will help you. The only thing is not to *melt* in the meanwhile. I insist upon the necessity of a sort of mechanical condensation—so that however fast the horse may run away there will, when he pulls up, be a somewhat agitated but perfectly identical G. N. left in the saddle. Try not to be ill—that is all; for in that there is a failure. You are marked out for success, and you must not fail. You have my tenderest affection and all my confidence.
Ever your faithful friend—

Henry James.

LETTER OF 1894 James's happy personal and professional relations with Robert Louis Stevenson were close enough to have become the subject of an attractive book (*Henry James and Robert Louis Stevenson: A Record of Friendship and Criticism*, ed. Janet Adam Smith (Rupert Hart-Davis, 1948)). When the mortally sick Stevenson had settled in Samoa, James wrote to assure him that 'the mere thought of you is better company than any that is tangible to me here, and London is more peopled to me by your living in Samoa than by the residence of almost anybody else in Kensington or Chelsea'—a fine flourish in which literal truth, amused self-parody and his inextinguishable verbal enjoyment are equally evident. He claims to be following his distant correspondent in Samoa with 'an aching wing, an inadequate geography and an ineradicable hope'. But the full measure of James's goodwill may best be measured by the wonderful letter of condolence he sent to Stevenson's widow on receiving news of the death of his friend and colleague in December, 1894:

> For myself, how shall I tell you how much poorer and shabbier the whole world seems, and how one of the closest and strongest reasons for going on, for trying and doing, for planning and dreaming of the future, has dropped in an instant out of life. I was haunted indeed with a sense that I should never again see him—but it was one of the best things in life that he was *there*, or that one had him—at any rate one heard him, and felt him and awaited him and counted him into everything one most loved and lived for. He lighted up one whole side of the globe, and was in himself a whole province of one's imagination. We are smaller fry and meaner people without him. I feel as if there were a certain indelicacy in saying it to you, save that I know that there is nothing narrow or selfish in your sense of loss—for himself, however, for his happy name and his great visible good fortune, it strikes one as another matter. I mean that I feel him to have been as happy in his death (struck down that way, as by the gods, in a clear, glorious hour) as he had been in his fame. And, with all the sad allowances in his rich full life, he had the best of it—the thick of the fray, the loudest of the music, the freshest and finest of himself. It isn't as if there had been no full achievement and no supreme thing. It was all intense, all gallant, all exquisite from the first, and the experience, the fruition, had something dramatically complete in them. He has gone in time not to be old, early enough to be so generously young and late enough to have drunk deep of the cup. There have been—I think—for men of letters few deaths more romantically right. Forgive me, I beg you, what may sound cold-blooded in such words—or as if I imagined there could be anything for you 'right' in the rupture of such an affection and the loss of such a presence. I have in my mind in that view only the rounded career and the consecrated work. When I think of your own situation I fall into a mere confusion of pity and wonder, with the sole sense of your being as brave a spirit as he was (all of whose bravery you shared) to hold on by. Of what solutions or decisions

you see before you we shall hear in time; meanwhile please believe that I am most affectionately with you ... More than I can say, I hope your first prostration and bewilderment are over, and that you are feeling your way in feeling all sorts of encompassing arms—all sorts of outstretched hands of friendship. Don't, my dear Fanny Stevenson, be unconscious of *mine*, and believe me more than ever faithfully yours,

Henry James.

The wild extravagances of James's verbal affection, so prevalent in his letters and so very rare in his published novels and stories, was a lifelong habit. The frequent touches of self-parody (as in the instructions to his 'dearest Mother' to 'Osculate my sister most passionately. Likewise my aunt.'—phrases from a letter from London in his twenty-fifth year) do not disqualify the genuine warmth of heart which caused him, over and over again, to write about his longing to hug, embrace, enfold and in general quite overwhelm his friends and kinsfolk with violent physical manifestations. These protestations reached a climax of palpability with the outbreak of the 1914 war, in his seventy-first year, when his young friends went off to various types of war service, leaving him ashamed of his own safety, his own impotent sorrow as his world crumbled about him.

LETTER OF 1914   One such friend was the young novelist Hugh Walpole, who received this *bon voyage* message before setting out for Russia in the autumn of 1914—the terms of which would sound strange indeed to a reader who had not grown accustomed to these lavish demonstrations from a weary old celibate:

Dearest, dearest Hugh,

I am deeply moved by your news, and only a bit heartbroken at the thought you will have left London, I gather, by the time this gets there—though I write it but an hour after receipt of your note; so that the best I can do is to sent it to the Garrick to be 'forwarded.' You will probably be so much forwarder than my poor pursuing missive always, that I feel the dark void shutting me out from you for a long time to come—save as I shall see your far-off light play so bravely over the public page. Your adventure is of the last magnificence of pluck, the finest strain of resolution, and I bless and cheer and honour it for all I am worth. It will be of the intensest interest and of every sort of profit and glory to you—which doesn't prevent however my as intensely yearning over you, my thinking of you with all the ache of privation. But of such yearnings and such aches, such privations and such prides, is all our present consciousness made up; and I wait for you again with a confidence and courage which

161

I try to make not too basely unworthy of your own. Feel yourself at any rate, dearest boy, wrapped round in all the affection and imagination of your devotedest old

Henry James.

Tensions of unreciprocated 'genius'

Even in the small proportion of Henry James's great outpouring of fiction we have had space to consider, there has recurred time and time again the figure (sometimes male, sometimes female) of an observer, or semi-passive participant, whose role it is to throw into relief, comment upon, add sidelong views of, some main character who is marked out from the rest by the unexplainable constituents of a kind of self-sustaining vitality to which nowadays the useful word 'charisma' is often attached, but which in James's day could be termed 'genius'. Most of these subsidiary figures play their part and fade tactfully away, like Winterbourne of 'Daisy Miller' or Lord Warburton of *The Portrait of a Lady*. Some of them, however, achieve a stature equal to that of their more gifted friends, or even end by surpassing them as central figures in the fictional structure. In *The Ambassadors*, the recording agent Lambert Strether becomes a more rounded and substantial figure than the lovers Chad Newsome and Madame de Vionnet whose love affair reaches the reader almost wholly through Strether's consciousness of it.

Two very striking instances of the tension and human suffering caused by strongly 'charismatic' characters on their close friends and supporters occur in *Roderick Hudson* between the young sculptor hero and Rowland Mallet, and in *The Bostonians* between the inspired girl elocutionist Verena Tarrant and Olive Chancellor. These two novels have been considered within the contexts, respectively, of Americans discovering Europe and the claims of public political life. The passages now to be quoted focus rather on the pain caused to their devoted friends by the two young possessors of 'charisma' or 'genius.'

RODERICK HUDSON   By the time the reader reaches the last third of *Roderick Hudson*, the 'genius' in Roderick which responded so whole-heartedly to the stimulus of Rome has also responded, destructively, to the beauty of the brilliant young woman Christina Light. An Italian art expert has now openly accepted the 'genius' ascribed to Roderick. At the same time, the young sculptor is downcast because Christina Light is engaged to the highly eligible Prince Casamassima. Roderick's mother and his forgotten New England fiancée Mary Garland join them in Rome. Christina breaks off her engagement to the Prince, and confesses to Rowland that she so envied the good 'character' of Mary that she knew that Mary, in her place, would never have been tempted to throw over Roderick for a prince. Roderick himself, ecstatic at the news, spurns Mary and wallows for a time in self-absorbed triumph, neglecting his work. Suddenly all is changed once more: Christina marries the Prince in a swift private ceremony. We know that she has been told that she is the illegitimate daughter of her social-climbing American mother and her devoted Italian Cavaliere—this revelation leads their daughter to become the Prince's bride as an act of obliterating respectability. The effect on Roderick is dramatic indeed:

> 'I mean that I am an angry, savage, disappointed, miserable man!' Roderick went on. 'I mean that I can't do a stroke of work nor think a profitable thought! I mean that I am in a state of helpless rage and grief and shame! Helpless, helpless—that's what it is. You can't help me, poor mother—not with kisses nor tears nor prayers! Mary can't help me—not for all the honour she does me nor all the big books on art that she pores over. Mallet can't help me—not with all his money nor all his good example nor all his friendship, which I am immensely well aware of: not with all of it multiplied a thousand times and repeated to all eternity! I thought you would help me, you and Mary; that's why I sent for you. But you can't, don't think it! The sooner you give up the idea the better for you. Give up being proud of me too; there's nothing left of me to be proud of! A year ago I was a mighty fine fellow; but do you know what has become of me now? I have gone to the devil!'
>
> (Ch. XXI)

In his collapse, the selfishness behind the charisma appears:

> Since he was hurt he must cry out; since he was in pain he must scatter his pain abroad. Of his never thinking of others save as they figured in his own game, this extraordinary insensibility to the injurious effects of his eloquence was a capital example; the more so as the motive of his eloquence was never an appeal for sympathy or compassion—things to which he seemed perfectly indifferent and of which he could make no use. The great and characteristic point with him was the perfect exclusiveness of his emotions. He never saw himself as part of a whole; only as the clear-cut, sharp-edged, isolated individual, rejoicing or raging, as the case might be, but needing in any case absolutely to affirm himself.

The artistic 'passionate pilgrim' even blames his earlier good fortune: 'If I had not come to Rome I shouldn't have risen, and if I had not risen I shouldn't have fallen.'

For the sake of Roderick's 'genius' they all move away to Florence, where Rowland learns to love the gentle Mary. But her own infatuation for the 'genius' of Roderick is as complete as his own for the 'genius' of Princess Christina. As he recalls to Rowland, 'A great man was what she was looking for, and we agreed to find our happiness for life in each other.' Roderick himself sinks deeper into idleness, while 'his dead ambitions were a cruel burden to the heart of a girl who believed that he possessed "genius"' . . . the other girl, Mary, herself devoid of Christina's charisma. A further move to Switzerland brings a climax, where Rowland runs across the Casamassima pair and Roderick himself sees Christina again. He gazes enraptured at her beauty, and she at his: the two charismatic destroyers of the peace of their mundane friends exchange a fleeting glance, and she departs with her prince. And all this time the yearning of Rowland for Mary is stifled, for all he can see is her yearning for Roderick.

It is underneath all these endlessly changing convolutions of the Rowland/Mary/Roderick/Christina chain of unappeased love situation that we finally have revealed for us the hitherto unspoken unreciprocated emotion which has silently sustained the whole tragi-comic structure, namely Rowland's own unselfish devotion to Roderick. Roderick, like everybody else, had for long taken for granted Rowland's 'constitutional tendency to magnanimous interpretations'. It came as a shock to him, as it does to the reader, when his long-suffering friend is finally goaded to a wholly justified outburst.

That revelation is reserved for the penultimate chapter. Still talking about Christina, Roderick had said to his benefactor: 'Women for you, by what I can make out, mean nothing. You have no imagination—no sensibility, nothing to be touched!' Rowland's first riposte is to recall his own services to Christina:

'You are incredibly ungrateful,' he said. 'You are talking arrogant nonsense. What do you know about my senses and my imagination? How do you know whether I have loved or suffered? If I have held my tongue and not troubled you with my complaints, you find it the most natural thing in the world to put an ignoble construction on my silence! I loved quite as well as you; indeed I think I may say rather better. I have been constant. I have been willing to give more than I received. I have not forsaken one mistress because I thought another more beautiful, nor given up the other and believed all manner of evil about her because I had not my way with her. I have been a good friend to Christina Light, and it seems to me my friendship does her quite as much honour as your love!'

'Your love—your suffering—your silence—your friendship!' cried Roderick. 'I declare I don't understand!'

'I dare say not. You are not used to understanding such things—you are not used to hearing me talk of my feelings. You are altogether too much taken up with your own. Be as much so as you please; I have always respected your right. Only when I have kept myself in durance on purpose to leave you an open field, don't, by way of thanking me, come and call me an idiot.'

(Ch. XXV)

It is with the rejected Mary as well in mind that he makes his so unexpected puncturing of the failed young artist's egotism:

Rowland frowned; if Roderick would not take generosity he should have full justice. 'It's a perpetual sacrifice to live with a transcendant egotist!'

'I am an egotist?' cried Roderick.

'Did it never occur to you?'

'An egotist to whom you have made perpetual sacrifices?' He repeated the words in a singular tone; a tone that denoted neither exactly indignation nor incredulity, but (strange as it may seem) a sudden violent curiosity for news about himself.

'You are selfish,' said Rowland; 'you think only of yourself and believe only in yourself. You regard other people only as they play into your own hands. You have always been very frank about it, and the thing seemed so mixed up with the temper of your genius and the very structure of your mind that often one was willing to take the evil with the good and to be thankful that considering your great talent you were no worse. But if one believed in you as I have done one paid a tax on one's faith!'

(Ch. XXV)

There is a touch of quite penetrating psychological acumen in the narrator's comment that the main effect of this on Roderick was to stir in him 'a sudden violent curiosity for news about himself'. So, too, in Rowland's admission, even in the spate of this uncharacteristic outpouring, that all the problems in Roderick were 'so mixed up with the temper of your genius'. And it will be over the broken body of that same genius, a few hours later, that Rowland will bend, after the headstrong young man had crashed to his death in an Alpine thunderstorm. 'Now that all was over Rowland understood how exclusively, for two years, Roderick had filled his life. His occupation was gone.' Echoing *Othello*, he is added as chief mourner and chief victim to those other mere mortals who—just like Roderick himself at the hands of Christina—had poured out their vital force in unreciprocated love for genius.

In *The Bostonians*, Olive Chancellor as protectress of Verena Tarrant plays a role very similar to that of Rowland as mentor to Roderick. But there is one important difference which renders her final defeat less fully complete than that of Rowland. Rowland

Mallet was doubly in thrall to his younger friend: he loved him as a person and he always deferred to his 'genius' as an artist. In Olive's case, she may have become increasingly involved emotionally with her gifted young *protégée*, but in the great cause of Women's Rights in which they were both embroiled, it was Olive herself who was always the leader, the planner. Verena was her inspired young speaker who could command the attention of audiences by her fiery eloquence and disarming appearance, but even when Olive lost her Verena she was still herself a militant leader of the cause. Rowland, when he lost Roderick, had no 'cause' either to save or lose, for he himself had never been an artist. He was well aware that he 'wholly lacked the prime requisite of a graceful *flâneur*—the simple, sensuous, confident relish of pleasure . . .'. He also knew that Roderick's genius was 'priceless, inspired, divine; but it was also at its hours capricious, sinister, cruel; and men of genius accordingly were alternatively very enviable and very helpless'. At the end of *Roderick Hudson*, Rowland has lost his whole investment in Roderick as man and 'genius'. His occupation has gone. His plight, back home in New England, will be pathetic.

THE BOSTONIANS   At the end of *The Bostonians*, the plight of Olive Chancellor is not pathetic but heroic. The tension of her relationship with 'charisma' was more complex than Rowland's. When she had adopted Verena from her absurd Tarrant parents, she saw her as a junior partner:

> 'We will work at it together—we will study everything,' Olive almost panted; and while she spoke the peaceful picture hung before her of still winter evenings under the lamp, with falling snow outside, and tea on a little table, and successful renderings, with a chosen companion, of Goethe; almost the only foreign writer she cared about; for she hated the writing of the French, in spite of the importance they had given to women.

Verena herself (granddaughter of Abraham Greenstreet the Abolitionist) was genuinely devoted to Olive's public cause. She was still devoted to it even after she found herself returning the personal affections of Olive's cousin, the unreconstructed Southerner, Basil Ransom: her public mind (such as it was) was still in Olive's keeping while her emotions veered away to a perfectly natural personal love for Basil. Some kind of compromise might have been effected, but for Olive's own fatal flaw: she, usually so impervious to personal attachments for which her public self had neither time nor inclination, had come to love Verena as a person as well as a prize recruit to the cause. Verena's public self could love her protectress on Olive's public terms, but when a bitter contest arose between Olive and Basil for Verena's personal self, then Basil—

whose magnetism was wholly and undividedly personal—was bound to win. If Basil had lost Verena to Olive, he would have lost an attractive wife for whose public opinions he cared not a straw. When Olive lost her to Basil, she lost her collaborator first chosen for her genius in the cause; and also, unexpectedly and with the addition of insult to injury, someone she had miserably come to love as a person.

The illustrative passages chosen to exhibit James's further treatment of this bondage-to-genius theme are selected from the last short chapter of the novel. A tense dramatic situation has been built up in the previous chapters. A very large enthusiastic audience is awaiting the appearance of the 'star turn' of the evening, the now famous young Verena whose charisma inspires them to greater efforts for the cause of Women's Rights. Basil has forced an entry to the wings of the stage and is determined to 'rescue' Verena before she can make her speech. A distraught Olive, also in the wings, is desperate to propel her prize public exponent onto the stage and away from Basil's piratical raid upon her personal love as well:

Verena spoke to the others, but she looked at her lover, and the expression of her eyes was ineffably touching and beseeching. She trembled with nervous passion, there were sobs and supplications in her voice, and Ransom felt himself flushing with pure pity for her pain—her inevitable agony. But at the same moment he had another perception, which brushed aside remorse; he saw that he could do what he wanted, that she begged him, with all her being, to spare her, but that so long as he should protest she was submissive, helpless. What he wanted, in this light, flamed before him and challenged all his manhood, tossing his determination to a height from which not only Doctor Tarrant, and Mr Filer, and Olive, over there, in her sightless, soundless shame, but the great expectant hall as well, and the mighty multitude, in suspense, keeping quiet from minute to minute and holding the breath of its anger—from which all these things looked small, surmountable, and of the moment only. He didn't quite understand, as yet, however; he saw that Verena had not refused, but temporized, that the spell upon her—thanks to which he should still be able to rescue her—had been the knowledge that he was near.

'Come away, come away', he murmured, quickly, putting out his two hands to her.

She took one of them, as if to plead, not to consent. 'Oh, let me off, let me off—for *her*, for the others! It's too terrible, it's impossible!'

'Good God! that I should make her suffer like this!' said Ransom to himself; and to put an end to the odious scene he would have seized Verena in his arms and broken away into the outer world, if Olive, who at Mrs Tarrant's last loud challenge had sprung to her feet, had not at the same time thrown herself between them with a force which made the girl relinquish her grasp of Ransom's hand. To his astonishment, the eyes that looked at him out of her scared, haggard face were, like Verena's, eyes of tremendous entreaty. There was a moment during which she would have been ready to go down on her knees to him, in order that the lecture should go on.

(Ch. XLII)

Up to the last moment, Verena tries to preserve both the public charisma she has for Olive and the great expectant audience, and the personal charisma she has for Ransom, who is there to sweep her off to marriage:

'I didn't know—it was terrible—it's awful! I saw you in your place, in the house, when you came. As soon as we got here I went out to those steps that go up the stage and I looked out, with my father—from behind him—and saw you in a minute. Then I felt too nervous to speak! I could never, never, if you were there! My father didn't know you, and I said nothing, but Olive guessed as soon as I came back. She rushed at me, and she looked at me—oh, how she looked! and she guessed. She didn't need to go out to see for herself, and when she saw how I was trembling she began to tremble herself, to believe, as I believed, we were lost. Listen to them, listen to them, in the house! Now I want you to go away—I will see you tomorrow, as long as you wish. That's all I want now; if you will only go away it's not too late, and everything will be all right!'

(Ch. XLII)

Alas, she cannot keep her public 'genius' and at the same time concede to Ransom's ultimatum. His own personal power is greater than Olive's, and the decision Verena now has to make is a personal and not a public one. Olive's defeat at the hands of her public enemy Basil is now complete; her extra tragic plight is that in the same irrevocable betrayal Verena's personal 'genius', her personal love, is also lost to her for ever:

Olive was close at hand, on the threshold of the room, and as soon as Ransom looked at her he became aware that the weakness she had just shown had passed away. She had straightened herself again, and she was upright in her desolation. The expression of her face was a thing to remain with him for ever; it was impossible to imagine a more vivid presentment of blighted hope and wounded pride. Dry, desperate, rigid, she yet wavered and seemed uncertain; her pale, glittering eyes straining forward, as if they were looking for death. Ransom had a vision, even at that crowded moment, that if she could have met it there and then, bristling with steel or lurid with fire, she would have rushed on it without a tremor, like the heroine that she was.

(Ch. XLII)

10   Brief biographies

Family

JAMES, HENRY SENIOR (1811–82), Henry's father. The published works of Henry James Senior (mostly, one presumes, at his own expense) included such daunting titles as *Moralism and Christianity, or Man's Experience and Destiny; The Secret of Swedenborg* (which one friendly reader considered he had very well kept); *Socialism and Civilization in Relation to the Development of the Individual Life*; or *Christianity the Logic of Creation*. It is a fair guess that this outpouring of lectures, discourses, personal philosophies and composite theology would all have sunk without trace, but for the careers of his two eldest sons, William the psychologist and Henry the novelist, which stir some sort of curiosity about their father's forgotten works. But the impression summoned up by these titles would not be complete unless we bracket with it, to complete the relaxed domestic scene behind such heavy labours, the story of young William getting hold of the frontispiece of one of these abstruse publications entitled *Substance and Shadow, or Morality and Religion in their Relation to Life*, and sketching for it a comic picture of a man flogging a dead horse. This combination of 'flagrant morality' (a term which, according to his son, his father amusingly used of himself) with an easy-going freedom of thought, all social conscience and magnanimity for himself and humane toleration for the views of others, represents the atmosphere of liberal enquiry in which the young Jameses grew up (see also pp. 20–23).

Henry Senior had been born in Albany, state capital of New York State, the fourth son of his father's third wife. A severely Presbyterian upbringing, including membership of Union College, Schenectady, from which he graduated in 1830, caused him to espouse religious unorthodoxy at the earliest opportunity. He thought for himself, and as his brain teemed with changing ideas his mostly genial views were as varied as the changing houses (and countries) in which his own children patched together their kaleidoscopic but always highly literate education. His strange spiritual 'vastation', mentioned in Chapter 2, must have come back alarmingly to the minds of his sons William and Henry when they in their turn, at different times and for different reasons, stumbled into pits of depression.

To the intellectual world of Boston or Concord or Albany or New York, or London, the eccentric Henry Senior was an accepted and respected figure, numbering among his familiar friends such unimpeachable figures as Emerson, Carlyle and Thackeray (who played with young Henry and admired the brass buttons on his little jacket). One of his friends credited him with 'the look of a broker, and the brains and heart of a Pascal'. To his son Henry he had stood for unworldliness and the life of the spirit. Just before his death in the last days of 1882 ('I am going with great joy!') it is recorded that he had asked to be remembered as one who believed that 'the only true life is the spiritual one and that this is only interfered with by those foolish words and doings that man has invented'. His own words were always noteworthy; his son poured out some of his own best words in loving letters to his father. Having hurried over to Boston from London only to arrive on the very day of his father's funeral, Henry was assured by Aunt Kate that the dying old gentleman had murmured: 'Oh, I have such good boys—*such* good boys!'

JAMES, MARY, née WALSH (1810–82), Henry's mother. As became a nineteenth-century wife, Henry's mother Mary figures very largely to her children as the appropriate complement and counterpart to her husband, the paterfamilias. We have noted (see p. 22) that because of her husband's attractive but distracting tendency to avoid all authoritarian attitudes while devoting himself more to a varying sequence of Utopian thoughts than to the practical affairs of day-to-day living, it fell to Mary Walsh James to make the daily family decisions and arrangements. There is no doubt that young Henry and the other children were extremely devoted to both of their parents: surviving letters of the family themselves and of many family friends make this abundantly clear. If mother Mary should have been remembered by Mrs Cabot Perry, recalling her childhood friends, as 'the very incarnation of banality' within 'the poky banality of the James house', it may be remarked that in a house guided by the ever-changing general principles of Henry James Senior, a little banality must have been welcome enough. One way or another, young Henry's parents seem quite often to have exchanged the normal paternal and maternal roles. So long as both roles were somehow filled, perhaps no great harm was done—but it comes as no surprise that throughout Henry's fiction we often meet men who dither and withdraw, and women who are obliged, even when officially and discreetly remaining in the background, to pull all the important strings. Leon Edel has suggested that Henry had his own parents in mind when in *The Portrait of a Lady*, Ralph Touchett thought that his father 'was the more motherly; his mother, on the other hand, was paternal, and even, according to the slang of the day, gubernatorial'.

The banal mother Mary, like most banal mothers of her day, was a great writer and receiver of letters, well able to keep up with the correspondence of her literate brood; she was far more fluent with her pen than many mothers of today who would claim a larger share of intellectual gifts. A week or so after her death, Henry confided to his private notebooks a long and moving tribute, ending with these words:

> She passed her nights and her days in that dry, flat, hot, stale and odious Cambridge, and had never a thought while she did so but for father and Alice. It was a perfect mother's life—the life of a perfect wife. To bring her children into the world—to expend herself, for years, for their happiness and welfare—then, when they had reached a full maturity and were absorbed in the world and in their own interests—to lay herself down in her ebbing strength and yield up her pure soul to the celestial power that had given her this divine commission. Thank God one knows this loss but once; and thank God that certain supreme impressions remain!

JAMES, WILLIAM (1842–1910), Henry's elder brother. In the English-speaking world there must be many who think not of William James as 'Henry's elder brother' but of Henry James as 'William's younger brother'. The author of *The Varieties of Religious Experience* (1902) and a dozen or more important works such as *The Principles of Psychology* (2 volumes, 1890), *Pragmatism* (1907), *The Meaning of Truth* (1909) has an honoured place in the history of both philosophy and psychology which needs to borrow no lustre from his novelist brother. True, the titles of some of his major works sound alarmingly like those of his father—but although Henry James Senior may have provided the appropriate intellectual background, nobody is likely to think of William as 'the son of the elder Henry James'. What is common to all the Jameses is their unremitting literacy, which was certainly handed on to William's eldest son Henry who edited his father's letters in a two-volume edition (1920) which included his own admirable memoir, scattered through the volumes in many introductory paragraphs to the different sections. This was the same 'young Harry' who had delighted and invigorated his Uncle Henry when staying as his guest at Lamb House, Rye.

William James the distinguished psychologist would no doubt have been intrigued to know how much he and brother Henry have figured, in recent commentaries on both of the James sons, as prime examples of 'sibling rivalry'. It may well be that the 'split personality' characters who so often appear in Henry's novels represent his attempt to create a workable combination of William the elder and Henry the younger, William the active and Henry the observant, William the successful husband and father as against Henry

Henry and William in 1901.

the celibate. Leon Edel, in particular, finds traces of William throughout the whole corpus of Henry's work. There seems little doubt that William was an object of brotherly jealousy as well as of brotherly love—but if this is true, it worked both ways. Henry had been elected a member of the new American Academy of Arts and Letters in 1905, and when William in turn was invited to become a member a few months later, he refused the honour partly on the grounds that 'my younger and shallower and vainer brother is already in the Academy . . .'. This may perhaps be yet another example of the exaggerated expressions which both brothers had used from early youth; one feels like giving the professional psychologist the benefit of the doubt. It may well be that Henry went on being overawed by his older brother, always one step ahead of himself on life's escalator, and also a most successful Harvard professor who had become a recognized authority before Henry's own emergence as 'the Master'. It can only be hoped that the affectionate endearments with which the brothers addressed one another in their lifelong correspondence were signals of their permanent attachment. Each was wary of the other, and William could be a severe critic of Henry's later style; but neither could ever ignore the other, and deep down the two elder James brothers had far more in common than the accidents of temperament and individuality which kept them different.

From the innumerable 'pairs' in Henry's stories (sometimes brothers, very often cousins, sometimes even twin souls inhabiting one carcase), who are now knowingly offered as 'William/Henry' figures, I select one possible sample from Henry's very first novel, the little known *Watch and Ward*, written in his twenty-seventh year and later effectively disowned:

> They had between them a kind of boyish levity which kept them from lingering long on delicate ground; but they felt at times that they belonged by temperament to irreconcilable camps, and that the more each of them came to live his own life, the more their lives would diverge. Roger was of a loving turn of mind, and it cost him many a sigh that a certain glassy hardness of soul on his cousin's part was for ever blunting the edge of his affection. He nevertheless had a deep regard for Hubert; he admired his talents, he enjoyed his society, he wrapped him about with his good-will.

My own reading of the surviving evidence is that Henry wrapped his brother about with his goodwill to the end of his life.

JAMES, GARTH WILKINSON (1845–82), Henry's younger brother, known in the family as 'Wilky'. Beloved by Henry for his 'native gaiety and sociability', he joined the Northern Army immediately on the outbreak of the Civil War, and was badly wounded off Charleston during the siege of Fort Wagner. His return to Newport, gaunt and ill on a stretcher, was undoubtedly in Henry's mind when he described the ailing young warrior in his first signed story, 'The Story of a Year' (1865). After the war he joined his younger brother Bob in an unsuccessful plantation enterprise in Florida, and later drifted to various unremarkable jobs in the Western states, dying young in self-imposed exile from his family still in New England.

JAMES, ROBERTSON (1846–1910), Henry's youngest brother, known in the family as 'Bob'. Like his brother Wilky he fought in the Civil War, attaining Captain's rank, and after the failure of their joint investment in a Florida plantation he wandered from job to job in erratic sequence. Henry praised the 'vivacity of his intelligence' but he seemed to suffer from a melancholy rootlessness, with bouts of absorption in different branches of religion. There is no lasting testimony to his generally accepted brilliance in debate. His son's name was withdrawn from Uncle Henry's list of bequests in his will, because the young man had published a scandalous pamphlet about King George V.

JAMES, ALICE (1848–92), Henry's sister. The youngest of the five James children and the only girl, Alice shared with her brothers the peripatetic nature of their childhood and schooling, and accompanied Henry and their aunt on a European tour in 1872. She had inherited much of the family stoicism and the family scepticism, plus an overdose of the family tendency to neurasthenia. After the death of both their parents in 1882, she and Henry stayed on together in the current family home in Boston in what her brother termed 'an harmonious little *ménage*'. She herself had devotedly nursed their parents, and Henry would soon find occasion to act for various stages in her declining years as a devoted and understanding nurse for Alice. For she became a permanent, almost a professional, invalid. Even in her youth, her father had written in a letter to one of her brothers that she was 'half the time, indeed much more than half, on the verge of insanity and suicide', and although this smacks of familiar family exaggeration, she had certainly been subject to hysteria, neuralgia and other distressing ailments.

In 1884, Alice came on a trip to England with her close friend and companion Katherine Peabody Loring, and the inseparable pair remained in England, in London or Leamington with brief spells at other resorts, until Alice's long awaited death occurred. Cancer had finally supplanted nervous prostration as the accepted plight of this highly intelligent yet mainly recumbent figure, who spoke of herself, after the utterances of various physicians, as 'neither dead nor recovered'. While she lived, she was an ever present illustration of Henry's strong sense of the harm done to women by their exclusion from any form of professional activity, or any practical outlet, other than marriage, for their talents. Alice certainly contributed much to many of her brother's fictional characters, such as the ever recumbent invalid Rosie in *The Princess Casamassima*; but her presence is also felt in any number of other Jamesian portraits of unemancipated unfulfilled young women.

For Alice, like all the Jameses, was highly literate; her letters have vivid and often ironic passages, and she was sympathetically involved with her beloved brother's writing career. He, for his part, could write eloquently of the diary she kept in the last few years of her tormented life. When the faithful Miss Loring arranged for the printing of four copies of this diary, which records among other things some penetrating criticisms of English society and politics which bear tribute to her Irish ancestry, Henry himself was aghast at the risk of the exposure of family privacy, and destroyed his own copy. The other three copies were for brothers William and Robertson and the editress herself. *The Diary of Alice James*, edited by Leon Edel, with a sympathetic memoir, was published in 1964. From it we may now fully appreciate to what an extent this strangely valorous yet self-repressive lady had inherited her share of the intelligent creativy which distinguished her brothers William and Henry, as well as the weaknesses which they, as nineteenth-century males, were better able to overcome or conceal.

TEMPLE, MINNY (1845–1870), Henry's cousin. Of the all too short life of Mary Temple, known in the family as 'Minny', there is pathetically little to be said. She was one of the orphaned daughters of Mary Walsh James's sister Catherine, born in Albany, New York. During the post-war summer of 1865, Henry and his brother William were among a group of eligible young gentlemen who fell under her young spell while living at or visiting Newport, Rhode Island. Those who, like Henry, had not returned as heroes from the Civil War felt at a distinct disadvantage in the highly competitive if light-hearted courtship games and rituals. But the memory of her 'young and shining apparition' stayed with him all his life. When she died of tuberculosis in March 1870, in her twenty-fifth year, Henry was staying at Malvern during the course of his exploration of England. He had tried to nerve himself in advance against the 'possible extinction of that immense little spirit', but when the news reached him he poured out his heart in letters home to his mother, brother William, and his friend Grace Norton (all reprinted in the first volume of Leon Edel's edition of the *Letters*),

176

in which with extraordinary beauty of phrasing he pays reiterated tributes to her 'divinely restless spirit'. They are pages of unmatched tenderness which after well over a hundred years can still move a reader to tearful resignation. One sentence from the letter to William may alert us to the probability that many of his most attractive fictional heroines are but later contributions to his tribute to the lost girl: 'Among all my thoughts and conceptions I am sure I shall never have one of greater sereneness, and purity; her image will preside in my intellect, in fact, as a sort of measure and standard of brightness and repose.'

Daisy Miller, Isabel Archer, Maisie of *What Maisie Knew*, Nanda of *The Awkward Age*, the dying heroine Milly Theale in *The Wings of the Dove*—in all these and many others a reader may suspect that he can discern some traces of Minny. For James it was so personal and lifelong an emotion that one may only fully understand it if one happens in one's own life to have been conscious of both mourning and being inspired by the snuffing out of a young 'immense little spirit'.

Some mentors and friends

When literary critics direct our attention to the 'influence' of one writer on the works of another writer, they are in effect inviting us to note how the second writer has exercised his own right to choose his own model. There is nothing passive in the process, when we stop to consider how many *other* different kinds of literary models our author could have preferred. And the more sensitively studious a young writer may be, the more deliberate will be his choice. With whole libraries of authors surrounding him, he selects *this* one to be, for the moment, his guide. It was with this positive act of choice in mind (and excluding, of course, those sheer copy-cats whose work is not worth study) that John Dryden said of Ben Jonson that 'he invades authors like a monarch; and what would be theft in other poets, is victory in him'. It was during young Henry's hard-working year in Paris, 1875–6, that he was received as a literary colleague by several of the writers whose works he had read, and would himself make the subject of some of his best critical essays. In the words of Philip Grover's *Henry James and the French Novel*: 'If James's novels are important as works of art and through their so being have importance for their humanity and morality, this is in no small part owing to the manner in which throughout his career he was able to assimilate and transmute the lessons of the French novelists of his time.' James wrote and spoke French with easy fluency and was mildly surprised that his new friends were imperfectly acquainted with the English language. The one French novelist for whom he had unreserved admiration was Balzac, who had died in mid-century but whose enormous output of fiction, realistic and analytical, was the dominating 'influence' on the young American writer.

Before coming to the names of the three Continental writers with whom James felt most in sympathy (Balzac, model from the past; Flaubert, the living French novelist; Turgenev, James's favourite living novelist who was an émigré in Paris), mention must be made of one American predecessor whose novels and stories had an influence on his earliest work, and of whom he wrote a critical biography—Nathaniel Hawthorne.

HAWTHORNE, NATHANIEL (1804–64). Born in Salem, Massachusetts, the son of a sea captain, Hawthorne lived an unadventurous life mainly in his native New England, though after the publication of most of his best-known works he was rewarded for his loyal services to the Democratic Party by being made U.S. Consul at Liverpool for the four years 1853–7. He had previously lived almost as a recluse, a state tactfully described by Henry James in his study of Hawthorne for the English Men of Letters series (1879): 'Hawthorne's career had few vicissitudes or variations; it was passed for the most part in a small and homogeneous society, in a provincial, rural community; it had few perceptible points of contact with what is called the world, with public events, with the manners of his time, even with the life of his neighbours.'

Two series of *Twice-Told Tales* (1837 and 1842) and some journalistic work were varied by a brief sojourn at the pastoral retreat of the Transcendentalists at Brook Farm and some work at the Boston Customs House. Then followed in rapid succession his three American romances: *The Scarlet Letter* (1850), *The House of the Seven Gables* (1851) and *The Blithedale Romance* (1852). During his years at the Liverpool consulate he performed his duties conscientiously, but it was not until he left that post for a two-year stay in Italy with his family that he collected material for his fourth major romance, *The Marble Faun* (1860) which in its English edition was entitled *Transformation*. Unlike the New England trio, which tend to a mixture of stern Puritan living plus the hauntings and uncanny happenings which remind us that these same Puritans had also indulged in witch-hunting, *The Marble Faun* has an Italian setting and an Italian artist (by no means made of marble) named Donatello.

James's first printed story was published in the year of Hawthorne's death. Some of his early tales (such as 'The Romance of Certain Old Clothes'), have the eeriness made popular by Hawthorne, and critics have seen in Selah Tarrant of *The Bostonians* a likeness to a character from *The Blithedale Romance*. But James's account of his predecessor, apart from the references to his provincial background which annoyed many American readers of this slight but very readable critique, shows no sign of being a pupil's tribute to his master. It is a charmingly sympathetic memoir which tells us rather more about the biographer than about his subject, and leaves one with the general impression that in the opinion of his young countryman Hawthorne was amiable, old fashioned, 'a beautiful, natural, original genius' whose 'life had been singularly exempt from worldly preoccupations and vulgar efforts'. It is not thus that one writes of a literary hero, and the moralizing allegorical fantast of Salem emerges from the pages of the London-based New Yorker as something of a bore.

BALZAC, HONORÉ DE (1799–1850). His great collection of novels, some forty in number, had been gathered together under the comprehensive umbrella-title *La Comédie Humaine*, covering approximately the two decades 1829–47, stuffed with every possible revelation of Parisian and French provincial life, with particular studies of various types of monomania. Titles most often mentioned by James included *Eugénie Grandet* (1833) and *Le Père Goriot* (1835). If James may be said to have had a 'model' as a writer, that model was certainly Balzac; but his own distinctive contribution to the style and structure of the novel would make that distant magisterial influence seem more and more remote. His first essay on Balzac, written in 1875, appeared in his *French Poets and Novelists* of 1878; the *Notes on Novelists* of 1914 reprints two more essays on Balzac, and the article 'The Lesson of Balzac' had been published together with another lecture in *The Question of our Speech*, 1905. His debt to 'the father of us all' was generously acknowledged. It is, after all, rather like an English-speaking dramatist remembering to mention his obligations to Shakespeare. James expressed this overall homage most eloquently in an essay of 1902, reprinted in *Notes on Novelists*:

> The authors and the books that have, as we say, done something for us, become part of the answer to our curiosity when our curiosity had the freshness of youth, these particular agents exist for us, with the lapse of time, as the substance itself of knowledge: they have been intellectually so swallowed, digested and assimilated that we take their general use and suggestion for granted, cease to be aware of them because they have passed out of sight. But they have passed out of sight simply by having passed into our lives. They have become a part of our personal history, a part of ourselves, very often, so far as we may have succeeded in best expressing ourselves.

TURGENEV, IVAN (1818–83). As practitioner and theorist of the art of the novel, Henry James is often remembered for his description of the more comprehensive efforts of Tolstoy and Dostoevsky as 'fluid puddings'. His own favourite Russian novelist was Ivan Turgenev, whom he termed 'the first novelist of the day'. In 1875–6, during his year in Paris, James met and greatly admired the émigré Russian for whose works he had a close sympathy—they had included the play *A Month in the Country* (1855) as well as the novels *Fathers and Sons* (1862), *The Torrents of Spring* (1872), and the shorter fictions *Rudin* (1856) and *On the Eve* (1860). It was Turgenev who first introduced James to the literary 'at homes' of Gustave Flaubert, an honour much appreciated by the 32-year-old young American visitor. James's 1884 essay on Turgenev was reprinted in *Partial Portraits* (1888).

FLAUBERT, GUSTAVE (1821–80). Best remembered for the novel *Madame Bovary* (1857) which James admired for its realistic presentation of bourgeois life, though the young American shrank with distaste from the explicit acknowledgement of sexual passions which were at the time considered no decent subject for literature. Flaubert welcomed the American visitor to his regular parties in the Faubourg St Honoré, where he met on terms of equality such figures as Edmond de Goncourt, Emile Zola (whom he disliked), Alphonse Daudet and the young Guy de Maupassant. Reporting on the great Flaubert in a letter to brother William, Henry speaks of 'so much talent, so much naiveté and honesty, yet so much dryness and coldness'—a judgement which included *L'Education sentimentale* (1870). Philip Grover's study, mentioned on p. 64, traces the influence of Flaubert on James's technique in such matters as the way in which descriptions of settings march in step with revelations of characters, as in *The Tragic Muse* in the introduction of Nick Dormer and his family against the background of the Parisian *salon*, or in *The Wings of the Dove* in the significance of our meeting Kate Croy in the squalid surroundings of her immediate family, her revulsion of which explains much of her later action in the novel. Flaubert had tried to fashion 'a style that allows him to combine the reflections and feelings of his characters with the descriptions and narration of external events in one linguistic medium'. James, pursuing the same quest rather than simply imitating its results, stakes so much on a unifying style that he is able at times to make his dialogue 'particularly pointed and suggestive. The weight of the whole book seems to be behind it.' So, Kate's 'remarks are presented as *remembered* by Densher. They are part of *his* thoughts and feelings'—which is one result of so unifying a style that it not only embodies, as in Flaubert, a particular way of viewing the world, but also has the effect of creating 'a fictional humanity far more conscious, inquiring and percipient than we normally are'.

CHARLES DICKENS, WILLIAM MAKEPEACE THACKERAY AND GEORGE ELIOT (pen-name of Mary Ann Evans). The three famous English novelists to whom James was most indebted are too well known to need 'biographical notes' and it would have been more remarkable if any writer of fiction in James's lifetime had *not* known their works well. Dickens (*d*.1870) had been the subject of one of Henry's apprentice reviews (1865), significantly entitled 'The Limitations of Dickens', and although he contributed a book on Hawthorne to the English Men of Letters series, James turned down an invitation to write on Dickens in the same series; it was his view that Dickens 'entered so early into the blood and bone of our inheritance that it always remained better than the taste of overhauling him'. Thackeray (*d*.1863) had admired little Henry's schoolboy jacket, and in 1875 James repaid the compliment by reviewing a collection of Thackerayana. George Eliot (*d*.1880) inspired him with an admiration tinged with awe. He wrote a few essays on her work, the best known being 'Daniel Deronda: A Conversation', and he reviewed *Middlemarch* on its appearance in 1873. On calling upon her in 1869 the young Henry had found her 'magnificently ugly— deliciously hideous', but the twenty-six-year-old writer was so entranced by the meeting that he wrote home to his father: 'behold me literally in love with this great horse-faced blue-stocking'.

Of the English novelists of his own generation and those younger than himself, the sociable and ultra-literate James naturally knew more than most. But although he met and respected George Meredith and Thomas Hardy, it has never been thought that because these three men happened to be writing at the same time they ever acknowledged, or felt, any cross-fertilizing influence. Apart from his much younger friend Hugh Walpole whom James met in his later years (see pp. 129–31 and 'Illustrative passages', pp. 161–62) the three novelists whom James knew well, both as reader and friend, were Conrad, Stevenson and Wells; to which trio one must add James's closest and most sympathetic fellow novelist, the American Edith Wharton.

CONRAD, JOSEPH (1857–1924), novelist. It was Conrad who described James as 'the historian of fine consciences'. He was a frequent visitor at Lamb House. Leon Edel's sentence—'The Pole and the American exchanged compliments and books'— suggest that though each respected the other as a craftsman in the art of fiction, and praised one another's writing in person and in public, they were both too strongly developed as personalities to become close friends. James's paragraphs on Conrad in the essay on 'The New Novel' (1914), attached to his recently published novel *Chance*, exemplify this magisterial but unsympathetic approval.

STEVENSON, ROBERT LOUIS (1850–94), novelist. Entirely different as they were, both as men and as artists, James and Stevenson became friends from their first meeting at Bournemouth in 1885. This affectionate relationship between two such unlikely contemporaries could last in person but for two years, as the Stevensons left England in 1887 for America and the Pacific in the vain hope of restoring Louis to health; but until his friend's death in Samoa in 1894 the two writers kept up their delightful correspondence (see also James's letter to Louis's widow, in 'Illustrative Passages', pp. 159–61). These letters, plus their printed views of the other's work, were gathered together in *Henry James and Robert Louis Stevenson: A Record of Friendship and Criticism*, edited by Janet Adam Smith (1948).

WELLS, H. G. (1886–1946), novelist. In 1905, James wrote a long letter to Wells in which he praised the latter's novel *Kipps*, just published, as 'not so much a masterpiece as a born gem,' with 'such a brilliancy of *true* truth', adding: 'You have for the very first time treated the English "lower middle" class, etc., without the picturesque, the grotesque, the fantastic and romantic interference of which Dickens, e.g., is so misleadingly, of which even George Eliot is so deviatingly, full.' These were indeed generous words from the man who had done precisely that himself, twenty years earlier, in *The Princess Casamassima* (see 'Illustrative passages', pp. 139–42). Ten years later, Wells published a satirical collection entitled *Boon*, which included a cruel lampoon of James's later style. James, in a pained letter of response to the presentation copy sent by Wells, acknowledged that 'it is difficult of course for a writer to put himself *fully* in the place of another writer who finds him extraordinarily futile and void, and who is moved to publish that to the world'. These are the extremes of a strange relationship, best surveyed in the book *Henry James and H. G. Wells: A Record of their Friendship, their Debate on the Art of Fiction, and their Quarrel*, edited by Leon Edel and Gordon Ray (1959). They had met at the turn of the century, exchanging visits between Lamb House, Rye, and Wells's country retreat at nearby Sandgate, across Romney Marsh.

WHARTON, EDITH, née JONES (1862–1937), novelist. After one or two false starts and an exchange of correspondence in which James rightly advised the younger writer to concentrate her efforts on recreating the New York social scene she knew at first hand ('All the same *do NEW YORK*! The 1st-hand account is precious'), Henry James and Edith Wharton did not significantly meet until 1903, when he was sixty and she, forty. They immediately became fast friends, each pretending at times to be in awe of the other (she of his genius, he of her wealth), but each ever happy to endure the stresses and strains in order to enjoy their very obvious sense of shared superiority over her, his, or friends common to them both. In 1904 she visited him at Lamb House, Rye, arriving with her rather pathetic husband in a splendid motor-car—and it would become their elaborate joke that she was his 'Angel of Devastation' who descended upon him in her 'Chariot of Fire' and dragged him, protesting, off for strange mechanical flights—in England, in New England, in France—all of which he enjoyed enormously. In the following year, during his return to his homeland after a twenty-year absence, he stayed with the Whartons at their splendid new home The Mount, at Lenox in Massachusetts. During the return visits to Lamb House, with husband and chauffeur in attendance, they would spend their mornings writing and their afternoons motoring. After one such visit by the 'Angel of Devastation' he wrote in a jocular letter to a friend: 'Devoted as I am to her, I feel even as one of those infants of literary allusion whom their mothers hush to terror by pronouncing the name of the great historic ravagers of *their* country, Bonaparte, or Attila, or Tamerlane.'

In the words of her biographer R. W. B. Lewis,

> Both James and Edith Wharton later agreed that their friend-ship had formed so rapidly, their social and intellectual rapprochement had begun with such immediacy, that neither of them could recall the exact times and places of these first meet-ings. Literature, the craft of fiction, fellow artists in several coun-tries, mutual friends in two hemispheres, the varying fascinations of Europe and the finest niceties of the English language, a love of laughter: these and other things the two could enjoy together and discourse about endlessly.

Her own memoirs, *A Backward Glance* (1934) contain many oft-quoted stories about her friend James. She had flung herself into heroic wartime activities in France, where she later restored and lived in two beautiful homes, one near Paris and one at Hyères on the Riviera. Of her own large output of fiction, the best-known novels are still in print and enjoying a vogue: *The Age of Innocence, The Custom of the Country, Ethan Frome, The House of Mirth.*

Throughout his entire writing life, Henry James enjoyed the friend-ship of very many ladies who figured as hostesses, correspondents, confidantes and sometimes critics of his work. They help to populate the Leon Edel biography and collection of James's wonderful letters; they were American, British, Continental in their cultural backgrounds. The one lady out of all this group who came closest to seeing herself as his novel-writing soul-mate was unfor-tunately unable to generate an equal response in Henry's breast. It was she, Miss Woolson, who had hoped in vain to occupy in his

The Angel of Devastation in her Chariot of Fire. Edith Wharton and Henry James in state. In front, her husband and chauffeur (1904).

life the close 'friend-and-colleague' relationship he later enjoyed with Edith Wharton.

WOOLSON, CONSTANCE FENIMORE (1840–94), novelist. Three years older than Henry, her ancestral home was Cooperstown, New York, but, like Henry, she had devoted herself to a writing career and like him she spent much of her life comfortably enough in various lodgings in London or Florence or Venice or wherever she might plod away, in solitude, with her work. When she settled in London in 1883 for a year or so, Henry reported that 'the *Littératrice* is here and is really an angel of quiet virtue'. They also coincided now and then in Venice and Florence, she always in Henry's estimation a 'friend and *confrère*' whom he enjoyed seeing at 'discreet intervals'. If one traces her through the Leon Edel volumes of biography, one gains the conviction that 'my excellent friend' would very gladly have shared his life and extended their intimacy as writers to a more personal intimacy. She was prolific and apparently commanded an American reading public, though I have never met anyone who had read, or could name, one of her novels. James wrote a brief essay on her work, but quite clearly considered her 'local colour' boring and her love romances verbose. In 1893 this deaf lonely lady settled once more in Venice (her Continental peregrinations remind one of Mrs Church of 'The Pension Beurepas') and continued to plod away, also continuing to send Henry very long letters in which she pretends to share his literary problems. In January 1894 she fell to her death from her Venetian balcony—whether accidentally or voluntarily can now not be decided. Nor, if it was suicide, can we be more completely certain than a reader of *Roderick Hudson* can be certain about the motive for self-slaughter—if it was so. A lonely middle-aged undistinguished novelist, she was valued by her overpowering *confrère* for her quiet faithful understanding. It seems that in this one case, at least, he who so often loved and hoped not for reciprocity, suffered the not less galling experience of coping with an affection stronger than any he could return. To a friend he wrote: 'her liability to suffering was like the *doom* of mental disease'.

One final representative of the elder James's younger friends may claim notice here as the man who kept 'the Master's' fame alive in the troubled years immediately after his death—Percy Lubbock.

LUBBOCK, PERCY (1879–1965). Lubbock deserves mention as the editor who saw through the press in 1917 James's two unfinished novels, *The Ivory Tower* and *The Sense of the Past*, and who in 1920 published two substantial volumes of James's *Letters*, with sensitive biographical commentaries. His continuing interest in James's profession and his friends was exemplified by his books *The Craft of Fiction* (1921) and *Portrait of Edith Wharton* (1947). The opening chapters of Lubbock's own novel *The Region Cloud* (1925), when a 'stray young man' finds himself addressed in friendly fashion by a famous painter who suddenly looms in front of him as a man of 'distinction and splendour', gives one some impression of how 'the Master' in his later years must have struck any young acolyte; though it is difficult to imagine James himself blurting out on first acquaintance, as does Lubbock's egotistic mandarin:

> 'I am alone in the world, and yet, you see, I lead a life of endless adventure at any time, in any place; and it isn't lost, it is saved and perpetuated—some day I will show you what is saved. I make my life in secret, I bring it to light when it is made; you may see it then, you and the world, if you care for the sight of a life that has been given form and substance.'

They are, nonetheless, the sort of claims made by the author of the story 'The Middle Years' which treats of a distinguished stylist who opens his soul (with distinguished self-pity) to a young stranger whom he meets reading one of his books, or, in a negative way, by the lapsed genius of 'The Lesson of the Master' (see pp. 113–16).

11 Domestic and social geography

United States

The plaque indicating Henry James's birthplace at No. 21 Washington Square is now affixed to a block of building forming a part of New York University. Within months the house was sold and the James family were off on one of their European jaunts. A two-year spell at the ancestral base at Albany, state capital of New York, when Henry was in his infancy, was followed by yet another trans-Atlantic excursion. A later Manhattan address was a house in 14th Street near Fifth Avenue. The New York City of James's youth, wonderfully recaptured in sight and sound and smell in *A Small Boy and Others*, has disappeared as completely as the London of Charles Dickens.

In Henry's fifteenth year the family moved to Newport, Rhode Island. It was not yet the seaside haunt of millionaires which would affront him when he revisited it in 1905 as recorded in *The American Scene* and recreated with aversion in *The Ivory Tower*; it had not yet become the Newport of *nouveaux riches* described with loving hatred in the pages of his friend Edith Wharton. When the James family returned from yet another European trip in 1860 they resumed residence in Newport; but *being* the family of Henry Senior they naturally occupied two houses in three years, both substantial but not over-elaborate. This earlier Newport would be figured in the charming tale 'An International Episode' (see p. 71).

In 1864 Henry Senior moved his family to Boston, and two years later they were established in the quasi-suburban Cambridge, seat of Harvard University, where they lived at 20 Quincy Street, the address to which Henry returned in 1870 after his first solo trip to Europe. How the New England domestic and social geography of those years came to form a lively background for his fiction has already been documented in Chapter 2. From 1875 onwards, James's geography is mainly that of Europe. His rare return visits were prompted by mortal illnesses in the family, and brought him back to familiar New York and New England scenes. Not until his planned American tour of 1904–5 did he venture in the steps of his younger brothers to such exotic states as Florida and California which had previously figured as the mysterious background for some of his more flamboyant American characters. He himself, during that wide-eyed tour which bore fruit in the exquisitely literate sociology of *The American Scene*, was more at home when staying at Edith Wharton's country seat at Lenox, Massachusetts.

England

Before turning to a list of James's main London bases after he had finally decided to make England his country of habitation, it is well to recall his very first impressions of the city before he took up residence in the comfortable areas of Mayfair, Kensington and Chelsea. It is often suggested that James 'borrowed' much of his London scene from the pages of Dickens. What really happened was that the Dickensian London he had heard recited aloud as a child was at a very early age confirmed by his own observation. The London of the deprived and downtrodden, as he recreated it in *The Princess Casamassima*, he had first glimpsed as a boy of twelve (as he recalled in *A Small Boy and Others*):

> . . . on the occasion of a flying return from the Continent with my father, by a long, an interminable drive westward from the London Bridge railway-station. It was a soft June evening, with a lingering light and swarming crowds, as they then seemed to me, of figures reminding me of George Cruikshank's Artful Dodger and his Bill Sikes and his Nancy, only with the bigger brutality of life, which pressed upon the cab, the early-Victorian fourwheeler, as we jogged over the Bridge, and cropped up in more and more gas-lit patches for all our course, culminating, somewhere far to the west, in the vivid picture, framed by the cab-window, of a woman reeling backward as a man felled her to the ground with a blow in the face.

And when he came to describe in *The Princess Casamassima* the scene when his young hero Hyacinth Robinson is taken to his dying mother in gaol, he made a special visit to Millbank Prison, 'a worse act of violence than any it was erected to punish'.

Late in 1876, having finally decided to exchange Paris for London, he took bachelor's rooms just off Piccadilly, at No. 3 Bolton Street, a writing-base partly relieved by temporary guest-membership of the Athenaeum, of which he later became a full member. Ten years later, in 1886, he promoted himself to a large flat in Kensington, in De Vere Mansions at 34 De Vere Gardens, off Kensington Road and not far from Kensington Gardens. This was his base for another decade or so, to which he returned from the innumerable Continental visits, mostly to Italy. Then in 1878 he became the owner of Lamb House, Rye, a Sussex home on which he had his eye for some time past, his 'russet Arcadia'. In 1900 he secured a private living-room at the Reform Club which provided an admirable bachelor's perch in London for the burgeoning squire of Rye. After yet another decade, on the brink of his seventies, when he needed more spacious London quarters in which his amanuensis Theodora Bosanquet could cope with his dictation, he moved into a flat at 21 Carlyle Mansions, Cheyne Walk, Chelsea. It was here that he died on 28 February 1916. His ashes were taken to the family plot in the cemetery at Cambridge, Massachusetts. A memorial tablet in Chelsea Old Church commemorates 'A resident of this parish who renounced a cherished citizenship to give his allegiance to England in the 1st year of the Great War.' A memorial plaque was unveiled in Westminster Abbey in 1976.

The contributions of these various residences (and of his subsidiary resting-places such as the Osborne Hotel, Torquay) to James's social and literary life may be most conveniently studied in the readable account of *Henry James At Home* (1969) by H. Montgomery Hyde, who was himself one of the tenants of Lamb House, now the property of the National Trust, to which body James's nephew Henry presented it. It was from these comfortable if hardly luxurious bases that he made his highly successful forays into the social life of his adopted country in its late Victorian and Edwardian heyday. He was not only a popular diner-out in London; he was also privileged to enjoy the lavish entertainment of country house parties. His social life in London allowed him to observe the contrasts between older standards of propriety and the *fin-de-siècle* loose-living circles in which divorce had become habitual rather than exceptional. A whole cluster of tales treat of the cruelties and deceptions of the marriage market, and two major novels make this their main subject—*What Maisie Knew*, where the pathetic neglected little girl Maisie is confronted, after her parents' divorce and remarriages, with two fathers and two mothers, plus the extra claimants to consanguinity picked up via the new parents' various partners; and *The Awkward Age* in which the plight of a charming young girl amidst a somewhat similar set of 'modern' emancipated men and women is placed for contrast against the higher standards of an elderly benefactor (see the dialogue on pp. 151–53 of 'Illustrative passages'). The social life of great country houses may have been enjoyed by the American writer whose conversation won him an honoured place at the most distinguished tables; but his judgement of intellectual and artistic standards could be as acute as that of his friend Edith Wharton who at the turn of the century was analysing New York society with a similar, if more pithy, relentless analysis, as in *The House of Mirth* (1905) which castigated social vulgarity made explicit 'in the stupid costliness of the food and the showy dullness of the talk, in the freedom of speech which never arrived at wit and the freedom of act which never made for romance'.

The sheer accuracy with which James was able to depict the life of the rich and socially exalted as exemplified in *The Golden Bowl* has been documented in an article by Adeline R. Tinter (in *Apollo*,

August 1976) which describes his intimate familiarity with the house and contents of Waddesdon Manor, seat of Baron Ferdinand de Rothschild, and after his death in 1898, of Miss Alice de Rothschild. James stayed there at least a half dozen times during the Baron's tenure; in a letter to an American friend he confesses that 'the gilded bondage of that gorgeous palace will last me for a long time'. It lasted long enough, we now know, for many of the actual works of art he admired there to be precisely described when he came to recreate the splendours of the house and grounds of Fawns, where the American millionaire Adam Verver and his daughter the Princess hold court with their spouses. A further piece of detective work by Bernard Richards (in *Country Life*, 21 April 1983) has suggested that the fictional country house Matcham where Charlotte Verver and Prince Amerigo resumed their adulterous relationship was probably based on James's memories of a visit, twenty-five years earlier, to Kentchurch Court, Herefordshire.

James's power to discriminate between the cared-for treasures of inherited family seats and the more boisterous piling-up of bought knick-knacks in modern pseudo-mansions is most clearly demonstrated in the contrast between the ancient Poynton and the modern Waterbath in *The Spoils of Poynton* (see 'Illustrative passages', pp. 146–47). Another writer possessing James's gift for satirical irony might have managed to describe Mrs Gereth and her young *protégée* Fleda Vetch making fun of Waterbath, but only a novelist of his psychological acuteness could have gone on to display how much the gracious dowager Gereth, deprived of her palace, was as much subject to the sin of greed as the *nouveau-riche* Brigstocks of Waterbath she so much despised.

The Continent

James himself claimed (in *A Small Boy and Others*) to have reacted favourably to Paris at the age of one year and a few months when, 'as a baby in long clothes . . . I had been impressed with the view, framed by the clear window of the vehicle as we passed, of a great stately square surrounded with high-roofed houses and having in its centre a tall and glorious column'—the Place Vendôme. On a later visit he had been fascinated to watch 'the incomparable passage, as we judged it, of the Prince Imperial borne forth for his airing or his progress to Saint-Cloud in the splendid coach . . . beside which the *cent-gardes*, all light-blue and silver and intensely quick jolt, rattled with pistols raised and cocked'. As for the rest of the country, his surrender to its history and charm may best be sampled by reference to the attractive selection of travel sketches *A Little Tour & France* (1884, reprinted in 1900, with illustrations by Joseph Pennell). Readers of Italian may pursue the theme even further in *Henry James e la Francia* by Alberta Fabris (Rome, 1969). It was not until his solo year in Paris, 1875–6, when he had been made a freeman of the literary group frequented by Turgenev and Flaubert (see 'Brief biographies' above) that James began to taste the daily life of the city to which all good Americans go when they die. He enjoyed an apartment at 29 rue de Luxembourg, now renamed rue Cambon, from which he made discoveries not only of the literary profession and its current masters but also of the social scene (in both the capital city and its surrounding countryside) into which his hero Christopher Newman first fought an entry and from which he later made his honourable retreat, in *The American* (see Chapter 4). By Christmas of 1876 he had transferred to London. Henceforth, his visits to Paris would be those of a knowing French-speaking, experienced Anglo-American.

Even the author of the monograph *Switzerland in the Life and Work of Henry James* (1966), Jorg Hasler, is obliged to confess 'the relative unimportance of Switzerland for James'. As a schoolboy of twelve he had experienced at Geneva 'the fond New York theory of Swiss education', and in 1859 there was a longer visit to Geneva, described in the first chapter of *Notes of a Son and Brother*, where he remembered himself as an earnest student who 'sat out lecture after lecture' much like 'alternate tragedy and comedy, beautifully performed'. His impressions of a certain type of Swiss boarding-house are released in 'The Pension Beaurepas', and it was in Geneva that we first meet Daisy Miller and her family, though it is in Rome that she meets her fate.

The diligently earthbound James who could refer to the Pope as a 'dusky Hindoo idol' was the same James who could go 'reeling and moaning' for sheer rapture through the streets of Rome. We may recall that it was after his own enjoyment of Roman pleasures, partly based on the *salon* kept by the American artist Story at the Barberini Palace, that he could allow even the staid New Englander Mary Garland of *Roderick Hudson* to exclaim: 'This place has undermined my stoicism . . . I love it!' From the Hôtel de Rome in the Corso, or from a nearby apartment, he joined in the round of parties given by American expatriates including Francis Boott of whom he would see more in Florence, and Luther Terry at the Odescalchi Palace, or go riding in the Campagna with an ample selection of American ladies. Later in 1873, brother William joined him first in Florence and then in Rome, at the Hôtel de Russie on the Via del Babuino near the Piazza del Popolo, where some twenty-six years later at the turn of the century he would first meet the sculptor Hendrik Andersen whose nearby studio at the Villa Helena was crammed with monstrous statues. In the spring of 1874 he was busily writing at an apartment in Piazza Santa Maria Novella, Florence: the outcome was *Roderick Hudson*. During this

same fruitful visit he toured many of the Tuscan and Umbrian towns.

In 1880 the London-based James set out again for Italy, and in Florence he started writing *The Portrait of a Lady*, while staying at the Hôtel de l'Arno. Here he first met Constance Woolson (see 'Brief biographies' above), whom he encountered again in Venice the following year, where he was ensconced in 'dirty apartments with a lovely view' on the Riva degli Schiavoni, opposite the church of San Giorgio Maggiore. Like all right-minded Anglo-Saxons he fell in love with Venice. From the balcony of the house at the opening of the Grand Canal belonging to his Bostonian friend Mrs Katherine De Kay Bronson, named Casa Alvisi, he could survey that other Venetian landmark church, Santa Maria della Salute. A few years later he was lucky enough to occupy a guest apartment at the same Casa Avisi. He also stayed with other American friends, Daniel and Ariana Curtis, at the Palazzo Barbaro on the Grand Canal, a splendid Venetian mansion whose interior is shown on our cover and which must certainly have become the fictional home and last resting-place of the stricken 'princess' Milly Theale of *The Wings of the Dove*. On later visits to Florence, James was often drawn to visit the Europeanized American Francis Boott who owned the Villa Castellani up in the surrounding hills at Bellosguardo. Boott and his daughter Lizzie are thought to have lent their physical appearance to Gilbert Osmond and Pansy of *The Portrait of a Lady*—but there, fortunately, the likenesses ended. At times when Constance Woolson lodged with the Bootts, James would stay in the neighbouring Villa Brichieri-Colombi. Of all his much loved Italian resting places, he probably found the Bellosguardo ambience most conducive to good fellowship and the steady exercise of his creative energy.

Italy figures so largely in James's novels, tales, letters and travel sketches that his abiding love for the country is always happily apparent. A handsome volume, made up mainly of selections from earlier travel essays, and with colour plates by Joseph Pennell, was issued in 1909 under the title *Italian Hours*. It remains the most evocative reminder of the Italy which captivated the young James, and which by the time he wrote the 1909 Preface could already claim 'the fond appeal of the observer . . . to the interesting face of things as it mainly *used* to be'.

Casa Alvisi: an illustration by Joseph Pennell for James's Italian Hours.

12 Notes on further reading

Bibliography

The standard guide to all James's published writing is *A Bibliography of Henry James* by Leon Edel and Dan H. Laurence (Hart-Davis, 1957; second edition, revised, 1961). Professor Edel describes himself as 'the literary historian in this otherwise technical book'.

Biography

Leon Edel's five-volume life of Henry James was published by Hart-Davis over the twenty-year span 1953–72. The titles of the individual volumes are: *The Untried Years: 1843–1870*, *The Conquest of London: 1870–1883*, *The Middle Years: 1884–1894*, *The Treacherous Years: 1895–1901*, *The Master: 1901–1916*. A revised two-volume edition has been published by Penguin Books. James's own autobiographical volumes (*A Small Boy and Others, Notes of a Son and Brother* and the unfinished *The Middle Years*) were gathered into one volume by F. W. Dupee (W. H. Allen, 1956).

Letters

Percy Lubbock's two-volume selection *The Letters of Henry James* (Macmillan, 1920) swiftly established James as a superb letter-writer and several collections of letters to individual correspondents followed. These are supplanted, for most purposes, by Leon Edel's four-volume selection from all known James letters which was published over the period 1974–84; the first three volumes by Macmillan, and all four by Belknap Press of the Harvard University Press.

Novels and tales

The story of James's own minutely revised New York Edition of the main bulk of his fiction has already been told in the 'Introduction' (pp. 14–18). It was from this revised set of volumes that most pre-war reprints were made, including the very useful Macmillan Pocket Edition in thirty-five volumes which may still be found by lucky combers of second-hand bookshelves. In my own view, the one hundred and twelve 'short stories', some almost as long as a short modern novel, are best read in the twelve-volume *Complete Tales of Henry James* (Hart-Davis, 1962–4), edited by Leon Edel, in which they are reprinted as they first appeared in the many collections of stories prepared by James during his lifetime.

In recent years there has been a welcome outpouring of James titles in very many forms of paperback, which come and go from booksellers' shelves too rapidly for any complete list at any one moment. As I write (spring, 1985), Penguin Books have in print the following fifteen titles: *The Ambassadors, The Awkward Age, The Bostonians, Daisy Miller* (singly), *Daisy Miller and Other Stories, The Golden Bowl, In the Cage and Other Stories, The Princess Casamassima, Roderick Hudson, Selected Short Stories, The Spoils of Poynton, The Tragic Muse, Washington Square, What Maisie Knew, The Wings of the Dove.* (My own brief introductions to the Penguin editions of *Roderick Hudson, The Aspern Papers and Other Stories* and *An International Episode and Other Stories* have been quoted or adapted in the present Preface book.) The Oxford University Press paperback version of the World's Classics series currently offer eleven titles, many of which overlap with Penguin: *The Aspern Papers and Other Stories, The Awkward Age, The Bostonians, The Europeans, The Golden Bowl, The Portrait of a Lady, Roderick Hudson, The Spoils of Poynton, Washington Square, What Maisie Knew, The Wings of the Dove.* In both these enterprises (and other paperback ventures), certain titles may be out of print for certain periods and then re-emerge.

Other works

Henry James's sustained siege of the theatre, omitted in this Preface for lack of space, is fully documented by Leon Edel in his substantial introduction to *The Complete Plays of Henry James* (Hart-Davis, 1949). Leon Edel, with Mark Wilson, has also gathered the whole body of James's criticism in the two-volume *Henry James: Literary Criticism*, a vast compendium stretching from a review of Charles Dickens in 1865 to a review of the posthumous letters of Rupert Brooke in 1916. These volumes have appeared in 1985, published in New York by The Library of America and in England by Macmillan. Samples of James's views may be plucked from *Selected Literary Criticism* edited by Morris Shapira (Heinemann, 1963). As for James's travel essays, they were collected in several volumes listed here in the 'Chronological table'. Perhaps the most revealing, to modern readers, would be the Leon Edel reprint of *The American Scene* (Hart-Davis, 1968) which documents his impressions of his native land after a European absence of twenty years.

Critical commentaries

My own chapter on James in *The English Novel; Select Bibliographical Guides* (O.U.P., 1974) was an attempt to squeeze into twenty pages a small sample only of the great outpouring of Jamesiana of recent years. James has at least one quality in common with Shakespeare: neither writer was narrow enough to found a 'school' or formulate a creed. Because both the poet–dramatist and the novelist chose to expose to life's full range of experiences an immensely generous circumference of sensibility without any discernible bias from any centrally directed 'belief' or 'theory', it has followed that both writers have been recruited, by many and various commentators, into a host of different political, religious, sociological and stage-army camps. In addition to this magnetic quality of central neutrality (a vacuum into which we all rush with our kit of ready-made responses), there is the extra phenomenon that James himself, via his Prefaces to the New York Edition and elsewhere, has begotten a quite different progeny of critics who echo his own professional concern with 'form'—with patterns, shapes, antitheses, contrasts and so forth. Some such technical analysts remain apparently unmoved by his quite evident concern for the national and international politics (but not *party*-politics) of both his native and adopted worlds. In short, the student of James, like the student of Shakespeare, may nowadays find plentiful documentation for every conceivable view of his author.

It is fortunate, therefore, that at least four volumes exist which offer a wide range of Jamesian criticism. The first, Roger Gard's volume in the *Critical Heritage* series (Routledge and Kegan Paul, 1968) covers the whole of James's own lifetime, up to 1916. The second, *The Question of Henry James* (Allan Wingate, 1947), collects F. W. Dupee's selection of critical commentaries up to the 1940s. The third is Tony Tanner's edited volume (1968) in Macmillan's *Modern Judgements* series. The fourth, a collection of critical essays by nine contemporary scholars, edited by John Goode under the title *The Air of Reality* (Methuen, 1972), will appeal mainly to advanced students who enjoy a very close reading of the Jamesian text. Any Preface reader who ventures on these four critical selections, with their own multifarious bibliographies and cross-references, will require no further lengthy catalogues at this stage of his journey.

By way of footnote, I would confess that two topics seem to be understressed, for reasons of space, in the present volume. My own personal view of James as a profound critic of English society is developed more fully in two chapters on 'Marriage and Society' in *A Reader's Guide to Henry James* (Thames and Hudson, 1966), reprinted by Penguin Books as *The Fiction of Henry James* (1968). The second important topic has been briefly but perceptively dealt with by Seymour Chatman in his study of *The Later Style of Henry James* (Basil Blackwell, 1972), and will be further illuminated when Philip Horne's *Henry James and Revision* is published.

General Index

A selection of commentaries on James is to be found in the 'Notes on further reading' (pp. 194–96). Only critics mentioned in the text are listed here.

Index to James's Works

All the 22 novels and 112 tales are listed in the Chronological table (pp. 1–10) plus a selection of other works. Only titles discussed in the text are listed here.

Novels

Ambassadors, The: 51, 134, 153–5, 162
American, The: 51–60, 100
Awkward Age, The: 103, 106, 150–3
Bostonians, The: 25, 33–40, 106, 121–2, 138–9, 165–9
Europeans, The: 24, 51, 60–4, 149–50
Golden Bowl, The: 51, 129, 134, 147–9, 156
Ivory Tower, The: 16, 131–2, 187
Other House, The: 103, 158
Portrait of a Lady, The: 13, 56, 81, 87–100, 123, 142–5, 156–8, 171
Princess Casamassima, The: 33, 139–41, 176, 182, 188
Reverberator, The: 39
Roderick Hudson: 16–18, 24, 44, 46–50, 162–6
Sacred Fount, The: 103–4, 109, 134, 158
Sense of the Past, The: 16, 45, 131–2
Spoils of Poynton, The: 106, 145–7
Tragic Muse, The: 104, 180
Washington Square: 24–33
Watch and Ward: 24, 174
What Maisie Knew: 103, 106, 108
Wings of the Dove, The: 51, 117–25, 180

Tales

'Aspern Papers, The': 112–13
'Bench of Desolation, The': 128
'Brooksmith': 108
'Covering End': 105
'Crapy Cornelia': 65, 128
'Daisy Miller': 66–9
'Eugene Pickering': 43
Georgina's Reasons': 108
'Glasses': 108

'International Episode, An': 67–73, 153
'In the Cage': 104, 108–10
'Jolly Corner, The': 45
'Lady Barberina': 80
'Last of the Valerii, The': 43
'Lesson of the Master, The': 113–16, 186
'London Life, A': 64
'Madame de Mauves': 43
'Madonna of the Future, The': 43
'Middle Years, The': 186
'Next Time, The': 111
'Passionate Pilgrim, A': 24, 41–6, 65
'Pension Beaurepas, The': 73–7, 191
'Private Life, The': 104
'Real Thing, The': 112
'Romance of Certain Old Clothes, The': 43, 178
'Siege of London, The': 77–80, 85
'Story of the Year, The': 175
'Turn of the Screw, The': 45

Other works

American Scene, The: 42, 128, 187
French Poets and Novelists: 110, 179
Guy Domville: 149
Hawthorne: 65
Italian Hours: 193
Little Tour of France, A: 190
Middle Years, The: 132
Notes of a Son and Brother: 24, 33–4, 126, 191
Notes on Novelists: 110, 130, 179
Partial Portraits: 180
Small Boy and Others, A: 25, 126, 187–8, 190
Transatlantic Sketches: 24
Within the Rim: 132